KIERKEGAARD

KIERKEGAARD AS A YOUTH

By CHR. KIERKEGAARD

VOLUME I

Kierkegaard

WALTER LOWRIE, D.D.

Thus conscience doeth make cowards of us all;
And thus the native hue of resolution
Is sicklied o'er with the pale cast of thought.

HAMLET.

HARPER TORCHBOOKS / The Cloister Library
HARPER & BROTHERS, NEW YORK

KIERKEGAARD

Printed in the United States of America

This book was originally published in 1938 by Oxford University Press, New York and London, and is reprinted by arrangement with the Estate of Walter Lowrie.

First HARPER TORCHBOOK edition published 1962

TO

DAVID F. SWENSON

PROFESSOR OF PHILOSOPHY IN
THE UNIVERSITY OF MINNESOTA AND
THE NESTOR OF KIERKEGAARDIAN STUDIES
IN AMERICA
THIS BOOK IS DEDICATED
WITH ADMIRATION
AND ESTEEM

THE POET

WHAT is a poet? An unhappy man who conceals deep torments in his heart, but whose lips are so formed that when a groan or a shriek streams out over them it sounds like beautiful music. His fate is like that of those unfortunates who in Philaris' ox were slowly tortured by a slow fire, whose shriek could not reach the tyrant's ears to affright him, it sounded to him like sweet music. And men are gathered in a crowd around the poet and say to him, 'Sing again at once'—which is as much as to say, May new sufferings afflict thy soul, and may thy lips continue to be fashioned as before; for the shriek would only distress us, but the music, that is delicious. And reviewers come forward and say, 'That is just right, just as it should be according to the rules of aesthetics.' Well, of course: a reviewer in fact resembles a poet to a hair—except that he has no torments in his heart, no music upon his lips. I tell you I had rather be a swineherd upon the flats of Amager and be understood of the swine, than be a poet and be misunderstood of men.

The first of the *Diapsalmata* which stand at the beginning of *Either/Or*.

PREFACE

Like many others, I owe it to Karl Barth that my attention was first directed to Søren Kierkegaard about ten years ago. But as I was living then on the continent of Europe, it could not long escape my notice that S. K. had become one of the major intellectual interests in Germany, among theologians the prime interest, and that through the influence of Unamuno this interest had spread throughout the Spanish-speaking world. In Italy and France the name of S. K. was beginning to be well known. However, it was not his popular fame which fixed my attention upon this author—it was rather the presentiment that what he had to offer me was what I personally was in need of. Hence I would spare no effort to learn what he had to teach.

S. K. exacts of his reader a very great effort. He declines to make things easy for him by presenting a 'result', and he obliges him, therefore, to approach the goal by the same difficult path he himself has trod.

At first it seemed as if one might become acquainted with S. K. by reading the German translations of his works, which are almost complete and include even two small volumes of selections from the Journals. And when it became evident that help was needed to understand the deeper intention of these works, it seemed as if the prodigious output of German books about S. K. must supply all the aid that was wanted. They have been pouring from the press during the last twenty years.

This hope proved to be a delusion, and I look back upon several years of wrestling with erudite German works as a complete loss of time. The two exceptions I must expressly make are the recent *Studies* of Professor Emanuel Hirsch and occasional publications by Theodor Haecker. Even the translations which Schrempf has produced with prodigious labour are not faithful enough (as he himself admits) to serve as a basis for study, and his own comments upon them are entirely perverse.

I recognize now that it was absurd to expect to know S. K. without becoming acquainted with the eighteen volumes of his Journals and Papers which can be read only in Danish. And when I had taken the pains to learn Danish I discovered that several of the studies made by S. K.'s compatriots are so important that they deserve to be ranked with the primary sources. It is a matter of minor importance that I learnt to pronounce the name of Kierkegaard correctly—as Kĕrkĕgōr.

At the time when I began to write this book there existed in English no translation of any work of S. K.'s and no work about him that was generally known and available. The various articles by Professor Swenson were hidden away in the back numbers of specialist reviews. Dr. Hollander's *Selections* was published in 1923 as a bulletin of the University of Texas. It was only at the end of the year last past that there began to appear concrete expressions of a growing interest in S. K. both in England and in America. In the autumn of 1935 two books about S. K. appeared in England. In the spring of this present year Eduard Geismar, Professor of Theology in the University of Copenhagen, and the chief authority on S. K., came to America to deliver a course of lectures in Princeton Theological Seminary and subsequently lectured on the same subject from coast to coast. In anticipation of the demand which would be prompted by these lectures Professor Swenson's translation of the *Philosophical Fragments* has been published through the Princeton University Press by the American-Scandinavian Foundation, which proposes to proceed, with the aid of Professor Swenson, to publish the *Unscientific Postscript*, and later *Either/Or*. In England Mr. Alexander Dru has persuaded the Oxford University Press to take this matter very seriously. It has just published his translation of Haecker's sketch of S. K., and expects to follow this with his *Selections from the Journal*. It is expected that *Fear and Trembling*, *Repetition*, and *Stages on Life's Road* will be published in England before long. Harper will publish this year Douglas Steere's translation of the discourse entitled *Purity of Heart*. Before my book is out Geismar's lectures will have been published in America by the Augsburg Press, with an important introduction by Prof. Swenson. I have already translated *The Point of View*, but I shall hold it back until several of the works to which it refers shall have been published in English.

The material for a biography of S. K. is prodigious, overwhelming. It is to be found not only in his journals, the most voluminous that ever were written, but also in his pseudonymous works, so that almost the whole story can be told in his own words—

and much of it is told more than once. And because his works are so largely autobiographical, or reflect his own life in its successive stages, no interpretation of them can be intelligible which is not essentially biographical.

A kind friend and counsellor has chidden me for telling the story in S. K.'s own words, preferring that I should tell it in my own way, more coherently, more succinctly perhaps, and perhaps with a view to shining with my own light. He asserts that a book must be either a biography *or* an autobiography. But I am not impressed by this either/or. It does not seem to me to express a necessary alternative. Inasmuch as S. K. was impeded by a constitutional reticence from telling his own story in a straightforward way, by the 'method of direct communication', and did not gather into one book the fragments of self-revelation which he casually and indirectly furnished, some one else must compose them into an autobiography and supply the connecting links. It is indifferent to me whether this book of mine be regarded as my biography of S. K. or as his autobiography accompanied by my commentary. I am very sure that I could not tell the story as well as he does, and I doubt if even a very able writer could do that. For my part, I have preferred not only to cite S. K.'s own words but to cite them *in extenso*, quoting many and very long passages to illustrate either the story of his life or the character of his thinking. In this respect my method is different from that of Geismar, who quotes as much as I do, but in smaller doses. I am convinced that S. K. will be more clearly revealed and the reader more agreeably entertained by the longer passages. However that may be, a difference of method is prescribed by *our* situation. When one is writing for a public (either in Scandinavia or Germany) which has all of S. K.'s works at its disposal and presumably is acquainted with them, it would be superfluous to quote long passages. When I began to write this book it seemed a matter of course that a great abundance of quotations from S. K. must be furnished to readers who might never be in a position to learn more about his works. If at that time I had been able to foresee that my agitation for the publication of these works would have so great an effect in so short a time, I might have hesitated to make the quotations abound so greatly that they now constitute two-fifths of this book, notwithstanding that many have already been discarded. Yet now I am not willing to discard more of them. For they are of such a sort that they must serve to whet the appetite for reading more of S. K. when a greater number of his books are translated; and at the present time S. K. cannot be adequately known or justly appreciated except as he is allowed to introduce himself, autobiographically, by means of such a method as I have followed. And although the many passages I have quoted from the *Works* are none of them complete enough to give a fair notion of the character of a whole book, yet many are complete as the treatment of a single theme; and introduced as they are in the course of a commentary which explains them and in the course of a narrative which they serve to illustrate, I am confident that they will not produce the tedious and exasperating effect of a volume of 'selections'. Looking back upon my early efforts to acquaint myself with S. K., I reflect that my rejoicing would have been great had I found such an introduction as this. Indeed I did rejoice at finding something like it in the modest brochures of Bärthold.

My translations from Danish are more literal than literary. I am inclined to boast of this rather than to apologize. For I have too great a reverence for the author to presume that I could improve upon his style; and I am mindful of a remark of Nietzsche's to the effect that a translation is not faithful if it alters the *tempo* of the original. The style is the man. The Danish idiom is for the most part not so remote from English that a translator is compelled to paraphrase S. K.; and in so far as the reader is limited to my quotations as the basis for his own independent study, I feel bound to provide a translation as faithful as Haecker and Hirsch have made in the German tongue.

Presuming that many of the readers of this book will be prompted to study S. K.'s works in the German translation, in case they are not able to use the Danish original, and would not wait until the English edition approaches completion, I am obliged to provide here the necessary helps for the understanding of books which the author has perversely made so difficult of comprehension. For though on the surface they are clear enough to be delightful, yet the thought which the author principally desired to convey lies commonly far beneath the surface. I speak of his method as 'perverse', in spite of my appreciation of the fact that S. K. was actuated by a purpose as noble as it was modest. He would proffer no definite results because he preferred to regard his works as a way rather than as a goal, and himself as a stimulus to thought rather than as an authoritative teacher. In his day he would have no disciples, and now one may claim to follow S. K. more faithfully by thinking *as* he thought, than by adopting thoughtlessly *what* he thought. In his last days S. K. himself was ready to admit that his 'indirect communication' was, as I have called it, perverse; for he recognized that a *daemon* (and not a good one) had compelled him to employ it. To a less studious reader the 'helps' I have thus provided may seem a hindrance, and I would counsel him to leap over them as lightly as possible.

Although it cannot be presumed that many readers of this book are acquainted with Danish, yet for the sake of my own repute I cannot refrain from indicating the source of all my quotations and references in the latest Danish edition of the *Works* and *Papers*. Inconspicuous numerals in the text refer to these notes in Appendix I, whereas Appendix II gives a survey of all the quotations I present here. The short list of dates in Appendix III gives a *résumé* of the principal events in S. K.'s life. After what has been said above it will not seem strange that the '*Select* Bibliography' in Appendix V ignores the greater number of works I have read and mentions only those from which I have profited. A complete bibliography of works about S. K. in all languages would occupy a volume. The Rev. Edward Underwood has undertaken this stupendous task. He has it now complete in a card catalogue and may perhaps some day publish it to amaze the world. Appendix VI contains a discussion of the portraits of S. K. with particular reference to the six which are published in this volume. Appendix VII is a glossary of characteristic Kierkegaardian words, which the reader would do well to study before reading the book. There is finally a short but '*Discriminating* Index' to this book. It would have been longer but less useful had I delegated this responsibility to a scribe. It remains for me to speak almost apologetically of Appendix IV, which devotes an immense amount of space to a synopsis of S. K.'s complete works. Until the *Works* are all of them translated such a synopsis is needed. Moreover it may serve the purpose of ensuring some measure of conformity in the translation of S. K.'s characteristic and significant titles, which contain most of the terms that are difficult to translate. This synopsis, so far from being my own invention, represents the result of a long and laborious correspondence with every one in America, England, and Denmark from whom I could expect assistance in formulating locutions which might be accounted worthy of general adoption.

I venture to call attention to the Table of Contents. I have used striking titles to designate the different phases of S. K.'s life and literary production. Of that I have no reason to boast—and still less to apologize—for they are to be found in S. K.'s own writings. But I confess to some complacency in view of the arrangement of the matter as a whole, which is calculated to give the reader a perspicuous survey of S. K.'s character and 'productivity', with a just emphasis upon the salient features. I hope that some one in time to come may succeed in writing a more spirited life of S. K. in a freer and more literary form, unencumbered by so many quotations. But no one has yet done such a thing in any language with faithfulness and accuracy; and I am inclined to believe that ultimately when it is done, as I trust it will be done, the general arrangement of the vast material, as it is reflected here in brief by the Table of Contents, will not be radically altered or substantially improved. I can say this with the more confidence—and without arrogance—because I have not been left at this point to my own devices, but have been able to profit by the example of earlier works (even if they were exemplary only as a warning), and especially by the *Studies* of Professor Hirsch.

This is the place to say (if such a thing needs to be affirmed) that even a book so imperfect as this of mine could not have come into existence, or could not, at least, have handled securely the immense material, if it had not the advantage of utilizing the minute and ingenious studies of P. A. Heiberg, V. Ammundsen, Frithiof Brandt, Eduard Geismar, and Emanuel Hirsch. No writer of the nineteenth century has been the subject of such careful study. Standing on the shoulders of giants one is not tempted to be boastful that he can stretch higher than they.

S. K.'s life was tragic, and the fate of his works has been hardly less so. Prophetically he predicted that his works would fall into the hands of the 'Professor'. Three years before his death he wrote in his journal:[1]

A Sad Reflection

In one place in a Psalm it is said of the rich man that he heaps up treasures with great toil 'and knoweth not who shall inherit them'. So shall I leave behind me, in an intellectual sense, a capital by no means insignificant—and, alas, I know also who will be my heir. It is he, that figure so exceedingly distasteful to me, he that till now has inherited all that is best and will continue to do so: the Docent, the Professor.

Yet this also belongs to my suffering as a necessary part of it—to know this and then go calmly on with my endeavour, which will bring me toil and trouble, and the profit of which, in one sense, the Professor will inherit. 'In one sense'—for in another sense I take it with me.

Note. And even if the 'Professor' should chance to read this, it will not give him pause, will not cause his conscience to smite him; no, this too will be made the subject of a lecture. And again this observation, if the Professor should chance to read it, will not give him pause; no, this too will be made the subject of a lecture. For longer even than the tape-worm which was extracted from a woman (according to a recent advertisement in which the husband expresses his gratitude and gives the length as 100 yards)—even longer is the Professor, and the man in whom the Professor is lodged cannot be rid of this by any human power, only God can do it, if the man himself is willing.

This prophecy has been only too literally fulfilled. S. K. has fallen almost exclusively into the hands of the Professor and the Docent. He has even become a favourite subject for the doctor's thesis. This of course is true especially of Germany, but already the thesis is threatening us here. The Professor is prone to treat as a topic of objective interest the matters which S. K. with passionate 'inwardness' proposed as questions of subjective concern to 'the single individual' whom he called his reader. To use another expression of his, the professors are 'eating' him. Of all the professors who are dealing with S. K. I can think of only two from whom the 'Professor' has been completely extracted: Professor Unamuno and Professor Swenson.

I might plume myself upon the fact that I am not a professor, were I not painfully conscious of another disability which would perhaps seem even more serious in S. K.'s eyes. For I am a parson. For a parson—and especially for one who has enjoyed rather ornamental positions in the Church—it is embarrassing to report with obvious approval, or without obvious disapproval, S. K.'s 'God-fearing satire' upon the parsons and conventional Christianity. Although I am a repentant parson, I felt this embarrassment so keenly that I proposed to publish my book pseudonymously. In fact it was originally ascribed to two pseudonyms, the subordinate part being taken by a rather pedantic fellow, a Scotchman, who accordingly was made responsible for all the passages which display unusual erudition. In spite of that he was a droll character—both of them indeed were humorous in their several ways—and both of them so copious that the book grew to prodigious size, and finally, when I saw clearly what it was coming to, I was not disposed to restrain them, thinking that I could lop off a great deal at the beginning of the book which is not nearly so important. As a matter of fact I had to suppress the pedant altogether, making a clear sweep of all the learning the book displayed; and since I found it no fun, and hardly Kierkegaardian, to have only one pseudonym at my service, I assumed responsibility for the whole and eliminated as far as possible every element of humour in order to make the text prosaic enough for my signature.

I recite this sad story as an apology for the defects of this book. The reader will perhaps be generous enough to assume that the serious omissions he may notice are due to the necessary exclusion of 80,000 words. On the whole it may be an advantage that this book has been so mutilated that no one will suspect it of presuming to be a complete exposition of S. K.'s thought or an adequate explanation of his life. If it were a bigger and a better book, or even the best that was ever written, it could not be more than an incentive and a guide for the individual who would study S. K. for himself. In the original draft of this book my pseudonyms had definite opinions, but they were so perfectly balanced against one another that the reader was left free to make his choice. Perhaps all expressions of personal opinion have not been eliminated with the suppression of the pseudonyms, but the undersigned author is so far from being intent upon making his own opinions prevail that he has furnished the reader with abundant material for forming an independent judgement.

If in the text (because of the peculiar way in which this book was originally composed) I have not duly acknowledged my many obligations to Professor Eduard Geismar of Copenhagen and to Professor Emanuel Hirsch of Göttingen, I would say here once for all that my debt is very great. But this might go without saying, since no other scholars have understood so profoundly the thought of Søren Kierkegaard.

I owe also an expression of gratitude to Professor Geismar for reading the greater part of my manuscript when he was my guest in America, and for suggesting many improvements. Professor David F. Swenson of the University of Minnesota did me the favour of criticizing the philosophical part of this book. Professor Douglas V. Steere of Haverford College has recently read with me a great part of it very much to my advantage. And in England Alexander Dru has studied the whole manuscript with care and favoured me with many suggestions which I was glad to accept. That is to say, I have sought and obtained help for the revision of this manuscript from every scholar in America and in Europe from whom I could expect it. And when I mention the names of these scholars I am not ungrateful enough to forget that my wife, with more continuous and painstaking labour, has helped me more than any one else in the making and the revision of this book.

And did not Dr. Johannes Prip-Møller, author of a stupendous work in folio on *Chinese Buddhist Monasteries*, which is just now being published by the Oxford University Press—did not he and his wife meet us graciously as we crossed the German border in our car, to guide us for a fortnight throughout all Denmark, on a visit to every spot which had an interest for Kierkegaard, and to many of the people who now are more especially interested in him. *Tak, kære Ven, mange, mange Tak!*

Last but not least, I am indebted to the Oxford University Press, and to Mr. Charles Williams in particular, for the knowledge and skill with which the imperfections of the copy were corrected, and for the gentle firmness with which the peculiarities of American speech (Shakespearian in good part) were eliminated—with the result that the author, who is in fact a stranger to the British Isles and cannot boast a drop of English blood, will commonly be recognized as an Englishman,

Not by his individual whiskers,
But by his dialect and discourse.

In *The Point of View* S. K. looked forward to the coming of a poet whom he referred to affectionately as 'my poet', who would celebrate his memory. Such a poet has not yet come. I am not deluded by the notion that I might faintly resemble such a figure. But S. K. also spoke of the time when 'my lover' will come—and the reader will easily discern that this book is written by a lover.

WALTER LOWRIE.

PRINCETON. *June 10th*, 1937.

TABLE OF CONTENTS

VOLUME I

VOLUME II

LIST OF ILLUSTRATIONS

See APPENDIX VI *for a discussion of S. K.'s portraits*

Volume I

Volume II

What I require is a voice as piercing as a lynx's eye, as terrible as the sigh of a giant, as persistent as a note of nature, with a range extending from the deepest bass to the highest and most melting chest-tone, with a modulation capable of the lightest sacred whisper and the fire-spouting violence of madness. That is what I need in order to get my breath, to deliver myself of what lies in my mind, to thrill the bowels both of anger and of sympathy.

From a letter to Emil Boesen, July 17, 1838.[1]
Repeated (with alterations) as one of the *Diapsalmata*.[2]

KIERKEGAARD

INTRODUCTION

KIERKEGAARD was first made known to the European world outside Scandinavia by the publication of Brandes' *Literary Character-Sketch* in German in 1879. It had been published two years earlier in Danish and originally (as the Swedes like us to remember) it was a course of lectures delivered at Stockholm. Georg Moses Cohen Brandes, as a freethinking Jew, was attracted to S. K. especially by his aesthetic writings, yet he was so strongly attracted that he could say: 'The sauce with which the theologico-philosophical discussions are served is so highly flavoured that one could enjoy a less nourishing dish if it were so piquantly served.' He quotes Judge William in *Either/Or* as saying, 'I have an idiosyncracy against edifying discourses and printed sermons'; yet he himself goes on to say, 'Even if in general one shares that feeling, one reads Kierkegaard's edifying discourses with respect.' And of *Training in Christianity*, one of S. K.'s most uncompromising Christian works, he says, 'I account this book one of his most admirable writings; and it is a work highly distinguished by clearness of thought and love of the truth.' He is even more extravagant in his praise of the aesthetic works. About *The Diary of the Seducer* and *In Vino Veritas* he says, 'From a literary point of view they are undoubtedly the most admirable of Kierkegaard's productions. . . . And when one compares *In Vino Veritas* with Plato's *Symposium*, which was confessedly the model he had in view, one must recognize with amazement that it holds its own in this comparison as well as any modern composition could.' Yet according to Brandes it was deplorable that S. K. had no appreciation of the great and fruitful thought of his day, such as the progress of human culture, the intellectual conquests of science, the proof of God from nature, the doctrine of political liberalism. He hazards the guess that if S. K. had lived till Darwin's time he would have ridiculed his doctrine. Very likely—but this suspicion does not seem so dreadful now, when everybody has abandoned that doctrine. 'Kierkegaard neither can nor will understand', says Brandes, 'that the history of modern literature is identical with its deliverance from the moral and religious conceptions of tradition.' In fact, it was in the twilight of all these gods which Brandes worshipped that S. K.'s position began to be appreciated.

Although Brandes undoubtedly directed to S. K. the attention of a wide class of readers, it must not be supposed that he was previously unknown in Germany. In fact a number of his books had already been translated, and in 1873 Pastor A. Bärthold began to publish a series of booklets and translations which, unassuming as they are, evince a just and profound knowledge of S. K. which hardly any of the later German publications can be said to equal. It must have been as early as 1870 that Prof. Beck at Tübingen began to interest his theological students in S. K. At all events, one of them, Dr. Hermann Gottsched, was by 1879 so deeply interested in this cause that he abandoned his post as a school-teacher in order to go to Copenhagen and assist Barfod, the first editor of S. K.'s papers, to complete the work which his failing health made difficult. He arrived in the nick of time, for Barfod died before the end of that year, and Gottsched laboured alone, a stranger in Denmark, to bring the five last volumes to completion. Later he published in German a small book of selections from the Journals, entitling it, as S. K. had proposed: *The Book of the Judge*. One of Bärthold's books[1] was written to offset the impression made by Brandes. He says:

> 'Brandes' final opinion is, that "By Kierkegaard the intellectual life of Denmark was pushed to the brink where a leap must be made into the black abyss of Catholicism, or over to the headland of freedom."—One can readily guess that Brandes himself has already vaulted over to that headland. For we learn that where he finds himself freedom of the will has come to look "as a werewolf does in zoology". On the headland of freedom, therefore, freedom is regarded as nonsense. An alluring prospect indeed for souls thirsting after freedom! Connected with this is Brandes' judgement that Kierkegaard's undeniable greatness lies in the fact that he discovered the "America" of splendid independence, and his "incurable madness" in the fact that he persistently confused this new continent with the old India of tradition. As viewed from that headland these things perhaps are not to be seen very clearly.'

Apart from the little misunderstanding about the supposed liberalism of America, Brandes was correct in his perception that S. K., by his inexorable logic, had pushed men (not only in Denmark) to a brink where a leap has to be made. Some have leapt 'into the black abyss of Catholicism'; perhaps more have vaulted 'over to the headland of freedom'. Evidently S. K. is a dangerous author, and those who wish to stand pat had better not meddle with him. With respect to Christianity especially he has posited sharply the either/or. His exposition of what Christianity essentially is he has made so clear, so uncompromising, and so convincing that every attempt to evade the dilemma is frustrated, every mediating solution, every 'this as well as that', rigorously excluded. S. K. is hardly responsible for the fact that the theological liberalism of a generation ago is now antiquated, but he is an accomplice, and Harnack's once celebrated essay on *The Essence of Christianity* seems incredibly trivial when one has read S. K.

S. K. is quite capable of convincing you that you are not a Christian, and perhaps of making it clear to you that you do not wish to become such. He may even persuade you not to pretend any longer to be a Christian. Such was the effect he had upon so distinguished a friend and admirer as Hans Brøchner, and later upon Harold Höffding, Professor of Philosophy at Copenhagen and one of S. K.'s best-known interpreters. But the most striking instance of such a conversion was that of Christoph Schrempf, a Lutheran pastor in Germany, who ascribes to the influence of S. K. the extreme theological liberalism which subjected him to exclusion from the ministry of the Lutheran Church, upon which he and his family were dependent for their daily bread, and drove him eventually to a position of bitter hostility. Incongruously he has spent his life translating S. K. and combating Christianity. His is the only German edition of S. K.'s works which can lay any claim to be 'complete'. And he has used this opportunity to revenge himself. Every book that he edits contains a postscript of his own in which he strives to show how perverse and foolish S. K. was in sticking to Christianity, and how unkind it is of him not to furnish any proof of the existence of God. I wonder if any author has ever been so shabbily treated! For a long while I was enraged by Schrempf's Postscripts; but in the end I began to realize that such treatment is just what S. K. would have desired, as a protection against readers who might accept, without criticism or reflection, what they found written in his works, and above all as a protection against disciples who do not understand how dialectical everything is.

Höffding, inasmuch as he suffered no hardship in heeding S. K.'s exhortation to 'honesty' by separating himself from the Church, is not passionate in his opposition. Far from it! He has neither passion nor humour. With the dispassionateness appropriate to a professor he interprets S. K. 'as a Philosopher',[1] and corrects him by the infallible rule of—'see my book on *Humour*'! 'my *Psychology*', 'my *Ethics*', 'my *Philosophy of Religion*', 'my *Introduction to English Philosophy*', &c. That is the only amusing trait in the book. His chief fault is that he makes even S. K. dull. It is recognized now that he was not a great thinker, yet his books were translated into English while S. K. was ignored.

Perhaps nothing so strikingly reveals the greatness of S. K. as the fact that his interpreters commonly feel compelled to fight with him for permission to retain their own positions. He had a singular power of arousing 'sympathetic antipathy'. Przywara says justly, 'But there is almost no movement which comes quietly and soberly to terms with him in a debate eye to eye. They flee from him with averted eyes; yes, many repudiate him so far as they can, though they can accomplish this only by fleeing from one side of Kierkegaard to the other, from the "seducer" to the "married man", from Climacus to Anti-Climacus.' It seems almost as if Przywara repudiates him in the end; for he says,[2] 'And so Kierkegaard becomes for his disciple a passage-way, which he must leave behind him, with a sense of gratitude, but decisively.'

Eric Przywara, one of the most talented of the younger Jesuit theologians, has written a prodigiously clever book about S. K.[3] —so clever that I do not pretend to understand it. Professor R. Guardini is another Catholic who writes in German about S. K. Theodor Haecker is an example of a man who found S. K. a passage-way from Lutheranism to Catholicism; and it may be said that in a certain sense he left him behind when he 'took his way over Pascal and Newman to Catholicism' (to quote the phrase communicated to me by a friend of his). In another sense he did not leave him behind, for he still continues to perform a very great service by making known and accessible in excellent translations parts of S. K.'s Journals, Discourses, and other writings of importance which had been neglected in Germany.

Martin Heidegger[1] and Karl Jaspers[2] are the philosophers whose names are most intimately associated with S. K. It is a matter, perhaps, of only curious interest that they were born Catholics; for though they both show acquaintance with the traditional theology of the Church, they claim only to be philosophers. They may be pagan philosophers for anything that appears to the contrary. It is evident that it is not a religious interest which attracts them to S. K. They attach themselves to him as philosophers, as exponents of the Existential Philosophy which now has so great a vogue in Germany as an alternative to Idealism. The philosophical family tree, as I construct it, suggests that S. K. was not grandfather of the Existential Philosophy but only a great-uncle. For this philosophy is rooted in a tradition common to both. In his conflict with the Hegelian philosophy, S. K. valued most highly the support he found in Trendelenburg's *Logische Untersuchungen*,[3] and the master of Heidegger and Jaspers is Edmund Husserl, who calls his great work by that same name to indicate that he is a continuator of Trendelenburg. Yet both of these new philosophers attach themselves so closely to S. K. that they seem to regard him as a father and may be inclined to reject the genealogy I have provided for them. Jaspers' recent book, a little volume entitled *The Spiritual Situation of the Time*,[4] is a reproduction of S. K.'s ethical reflections in the Second Part of *Either/Or*, although this fact is obscured by the strange medium in which it is presented, the technical nomenclature invented by the 'Existential Philosophy'. As expressed in S. K.'s language these same thoughts are very much more luminous. And yet this difficult little book has already had such a success as rarely attends the work of a philosopher. Sixty thousand copies of it have been printed. S. K., it seems to me, has a better claim to popularity.

The mention of Trendelenburg suggests a sad story. He was lecturing in Berlin at the very time when S. K. went there to hear Schelling's lectures and was so bitterly disillusioned by them. He never heard Trendelenburg because he too readily trusted the report of a Danish compatriot that he was not worth listening to. It is like ships that pass in the night. But it seems to me even sadder that he came near knowing Gustav Theodor Fechner, the greatest thinker that lived in his day, and one who, like him, has been ignored by the English-speaking world, in spite of the effort of William James to make him known. There would have been much in Fechner's philosophy distasteful to S. K.—and yet there was so much he might have learnt from him, and he came so near it! In 1849 an entry in his journal refers to a review of *Nanna*—'yes, and it's called also *The Soul Life of Plants*, by a certain Fechner'—in which he finds 'several pretty things'.[1] It went no farther; but I remark that Fechner's *Little Book of Life after Death* concludes with a sentence which exactly matches a remark of Johannes Climacus.[2] And certainly Fechner was dealing with reality.

It is important to note that S. K.'s influence has been felt in philosophy[3] as well as in aesthetics, morals, and religion. But it is in the religious realm that his influence is greatest.

Don Miguel de Unamuno was a Catholic deeply affected by S. K. who has done much to spread his influence throughout the Spanish world. *The Tragic Sense of Life*[4] is not expressly an interpretation of S. K. but a very free rendering of his thought through the medium of a liberal but austere Catholic thinker. S. K., who wanted no disciples, would surely have been pleased with such independent discipleship as this. And it cannot be said that S. K.'s thoughts suffer more distortion in this Catholic and distinctively Spanish Catholic medium than in the Swiss Calvinistic medium through which they have been made more broadly known to the world.

But Karl Barth is also a legitimate interpreter of S. K.—I mean the earlier Barth of *The Epistle to the Romans*—and wherever his influence is felt the importance of S. K. is beginning to be recognized. Through him even the Danes have acquired a new appreciation of their own most celebrated author. Few readers of Barth are aware how many of his most striking phrases are borrowed from S. K. This influence was very far-reaching. It was by the example of S. K. that he was prompted to be a 'corrective', and through him he found his way back to Calvinism. This is very ironical, for no serious Christian was ever farther than S. K. from being a Calvinist. He repudiated the doctrine of predestination and contended passionately for the freedom of the will. In his latest period Barth has clearly discriminated his fundamental position from that of S. K. He did this dramatically in the same document, *Nein!*, in which he renounced his partnership with Brunner.[1] In this he admits Przywara's contention that S. K., so far as concerns the Catholic doctrine of the *analogia entis* (which Barth accounts the dividing line between Protestantism and Catholicism), is definitely on the Catholic side. The passage is the more dramatic for the fact that it was written in Rome, at a *pension* alongside of the Trinità dei Monti which enjoys a view of the Vatican, and Barth could say with a gesture that, if he followed S. K. in this, he might as well go 'over there'.

Barth was right. He had learnt many things from S. K., but a grateful recognition of his debt did not involve an obligation to follow this master beyond a certain point. S. K. wanted no disciples: he desired only to prompt men to think for themselves.

The most acclaimed and the most detested article of theology that Barth borrowed from S. K. was the assertion of 'the endless qualitative difference between God and man'. This assertion is apt to bring us up standing the moment we hear it pronounced, for we needed to hear it in our day. But second reflection suggests, perhaps, that by this we are cut off from all real relationship with God. It is important as well as interesting to note how cautiously S. K. expresses himself in an entry in his journal for the year 1849:[2]

> This is the law of the relationship between God and man in the God-relationship.
>
> *Divisio*
>
> There is an endless yawning qualitative difference between God and man.
>
> This signifies, or the expression for it is: A man can do nothing at all, it is God that gives all, it is He that bestows upon man faith, &c.
>
> This is grace, and here lies Christianity's first.
>
> *Subdivisio*
>
> Notwithstanding the fact that of course nothing, no work of any sort, any more than the act of faith, can have anything meritorious about it (for in such a case the *divisio* or the principal clause is abolished and we are here dependent upon a subordinate clause)—nevertheless it holds good that we should dare to approach God with childlike confidence. [S. K.'s own prayers are a striking example of this.]

If the *divisio* is the whole thing, then God becomes so endlessly exalted that there is absolutely no real relationship at all between God and the individual man.

Therefore one must pay such careful heed to the *subdivisio*, without which the life of the individual acquires no *élan*.

Generally speaking, one must listen with care to discern who it is that speaks. For the *divisio* or that which is contained in it can be uttered in such a way that it is the expression of the profoundest godly fear, but also in such a way that at bottom it is a deceit which is accomplished by exalting God so highly. Thus it may either be for the sake of getting permission to live just as one wants to, in a worldly view of life, or else for the sake of leading a religious still-life without incurring any danger.

In our time especially it is important to recover the childlike confidence that it is nevertheless permissible for a man, an individual man, to approach God about trifling concerns of his life. For it is after all a conception quite universal that God is something endlessly exalted, so that it hardly could occur to anybody off-hand to treat God with easy familiarity. [This could not be said in our day—especially in Protestantism and more especially in America.] But the misfortune is that the exaltation which has been affirmed of God has become a triviality and actually is a dispensation from the God-relationship. And, as has been said, the strictest orthodoxy can here so easily manage to deceive itself by its doctrine that it is God that does all for us, while we are not able to do anything. For the incommensurability can also be a dispensation.

I do not quote this passage to disparage Karl Barth but only to distinguish between him and S. K.—as he himself has done, clearly and with a good right. And I would add that he has obviously not used this *divisio* as a dispensation either to do as he pleases or to avoid incurring danger. He has not led 'a religious still-life'. In general, this is not the danger to which a Calvinist is especially exposed.

As an example of illegitimate interpretation of S. K. I mention Ibsen's *Brand*. But I hasten to say that this is not meant as a reproach against Ibsen. So far was he from posing as interpreter that he asserted roundly he had 'read little of Kierkegaard and understood less'. In spite of this assertion, it has been shown that Ibsen had not only read several of S. K.'s books but had borrowed phrases from them. I can easily believe, however, that the strongest impression he got of S. K. came to him by a more roundabout way. It appears that in spite of S. K.'s efforts to protect himself against 'the greatest of all misfortunes—a disciple', there was towards the close of his life a group of young men in Denmark who accounted themselves such, and because they were forbidden to approach him they were condemned to misunderstand their master. That seems to me a greater than 'the greatest of all misfortunes'. One of these youths by the name of Lamme was appointed to a pastorate at Skien in Norway, where he deeply stirred his flock by the principles he thought he had learnt from S. K. Ibsen was acquainted with this striking case and made brilliant use of it. No wonder it made upon him a deeper impression than the writings in which he understood so little. But Brand should not be regarded as a picture of S. K., or even as a figure constructed according to his principles. The fact that Brand had no humour marks an essential difference between him and S. K. The possession of that gift would have saved him from being a fanatic. But S. K. was saved from being a fanatic also by his pre-eminent reflection. If we read aright, we discern that even in the heat of his attack upon the Church he was not fanatical, though he employed the exaggeration characteristic of satire. 'All/or Nothing' is not equivalent to 'Either/Or', and it is a phrase which S. K. very rarely used. We may be certain that he would not have condemned Brand for sacrificing his 'all', for that he was ready to do himself; but he would surely have condemned him for sacrificing as he did the lives of his wife and child. That is the gruesome trait in Brand. It is easy to divine what S. K. would have said to him. First of all he would have reproached the young parson for taking a wife and begetting a child when already he bore on his banner this proud device, 'All/or Nothing'. In the second place, he would have denounced him as a murderer of his wife and child—unless, like Abraham, he could appeal to an authentic, direct, and indisputable command of God, justifying the 'teleological suspension of the ethical' and bidding him do what the universal ethical precept forbade.

The amazing thing about S. K. is that a man whose own beliefs were so definite, and whose attitude was so repellent to the modern mind, proves capable of attracting the interest of Ibsen, of arousing the admiration of Brandes, of delighting the voluptuary, of leading Lutherans, Calvinists, and Catholics into new realms of thought, and of starting a new philosophy. Such a case is 'more unique than rare'. And yet the English-speaking world has until now been untouched by this influence and is hardly aware that so interesting a character as S. K. ever existed. I went as far as China to lecture on S. K., and found no response there because China is not inclined to attach any importance to subjects which have not yet emerged in America. In Japan, to my surprise, I found an eager interest because the Japanese are justly proud of learning also from the continent of Europe. For the same reason S. K. is well known in South America, which is not only influenced by Unamuno but has been lately looking to Germany for culture.

Pascal and Nietzsche are the two figures with whom S. K. is commonly compared. The likeness in both cases is striking—with the believer and with the 'Antichrist'. S. K. himself was struck by his likeness to Pascal. Nietzsche has been called 'a pagan Kierkegaard'. In *The Sickness unto Death* S. K. had already diagnosed the tragic case of Nietzsche almost before he was born: 'The despair which is ignorant of the fact that it is despair, or the despairing ignorance of the fact of having a self and an eternal self.' If Brandes, who was a great admirer of both men, had succeeded in making Nietzsche acquainted with S. K.'s works, would he have recognized this description of himself, and would he have perceived that S. K. might have been entirely like him, a hopeless despairer and a defier of God, if he had not been conscious of his despair and 'chosen to despair' (in the sense which S. K. attached to his thought)—and so passed from defiance to the obedience of faith? We cannot know, for the attempt of Brandes to introduce Nietzsche to his prototype came too late, when the recluse of Sils Maria had lost his mind. Both of these comparisons have been drawn in detail by Höffding.

Professor Höffding has taken special pains to enumerate the numerous points of likeness between S. K. and Nietzsche, and others have followed his lead; but no one has done this so well or carried it so far as Karl Jaspers in his most recent book *Vernunft und Existenz*, five lectures delivered at the University of Groningen in Holland in 1935 and published there the same year. I quote from pp. 5 and 94 f. But perhaps he carries it too far, is too subtle in detecting likeness in unlikeness, even to the point of resolving diametrical differences into identity. For example: S. K. denounced modern Christendom as a defection from New Testament Christianity; and Nietsche characterized the same situation by proclaiming, 'God is dead.' It does not seem obvious to me that these two propositions are equivalent. But I can see that they may be regarded as equivalent for the purposes of the 'Existential Philosophy', which attaches itself not to the content of the thought of either of these thinkers but to a formal feature in which they resemble one another to a hair, namely the intrepidity with which they followed 'infinite reflection' beyond the farthest horizons. How much Jaspers makes of Kierkegaard and Nietzsche appears plainly in the following paragraph:

> The present philosophical situation is characterized by the fact that two philosophers, Kierkegaard and Nietzsche, who in their lifetime were ignored and for a long time after were made no account of in the history of philosophy, are now steadily increasing in importance. All the other post-Hegelian philosophers are receding more and more into the background, while to-day these two men already stand out undeniably as the really great thinkers of their age.

Yet in the end we learn from Jaspers that he is unable to follow either of these great thinkers. 'The difficulty of our philosophical situation lies in the fact that we owe to Kierkegaard and Nietzsche the possibility of delving to the deepest foundations, and yet on essential points we resolve not to follow them.' In fact each of these exceptional individuals recognized that his position was unique, and therefore proclaimed that he was not a paradigm for the average man. Jaspers can say with some plausibility that 'the problem is how *one who is not the exceptional* can philosophize *with his eye upon the exceptional*'. Jaspers has need of *both* of these exceptional individuals with an eye to their distinguishing difference. For this defines the limits within which his pendulum swings—between S. K.'s absurdity in believing a revelation of God, and the absurdity of Nietzsche's godlessness. Here the resemblance which unites these two most rational of men is the 'irrational', the 'absurd'. This seems to me reasonable—but I cannot see why the 'Existential Philosophy', which sets out to rescue the irrational from being ignored or devoured by reason, *must* reject the opposite irrational positions of both of the great thinkers it appeals to.

Much more *positive* is the likeness between S. K. and Dostoevski, which often enough has been remarked upon but hardly has been duly appreciated until recently Léon Chestov, the first Russian to notice S. K., has devoted some space to this comparison in his book, which is published only in French, *Kierkegaard et la Philosophie Existentielle* (Paris, 1936).

S. K. makes a many-sided appeal to our generation, and in several respects we are better prepared to appreciate him than were the men of his own age. The history of his inner life, which he himself has recounted in his books as well as in his journals, and which he has illuminated by the profoundest psychological observation, cannot fail to be of singular interest to every age which is aware that the proper study of mankind is man. In our age there is nothing to hinder a prompt appreciation of his aesthetic and philosophic points of view; and even his trenchant criticism of the doctrines of political liberalism are not likely to be superciliously ignored at a time when France is the only country on the continent of Europe which prefers anarchy to the abandonment of the theories of the Revolution. But what S. K. regarded as the conclusion of the whole matter, the religious teaching which he strove so earnestly to impart, will hardly be received with open arms in the English-speaking world, and especially in America. For this involves a criticism of theological liberalism and of our all-too-liberal optimism. I have had opportunity to observe the reaction which S. K. arouses in Protestant circles, especially among professors of theology, and it is evident that if his interpretation of the Gospel, his conception of religion as suffering, is to find access to the American heart, it must 'enter in through closed doors'. Our religiousness has been optimistic in an unexampled degree, and inasmuch as it is optimistic in a finite sense and all but ignores the heavenly hope it has resulted in what Paul Tillich calls 'self-contented and self-contained finiteness'. Again and again I have heard the objection raised that S. K. does not exemplify or express 'the joyous confidence which is so characteristic of the Gospels'. Without admitting the truth of this allegation (for S. K. entitled seven of his Discourses 'Triumphant Notes in the Conflict of Suffering'), I challenge the objectors to investigate their own presuppositions, to inquire fearlessly whether the sacred postulates of American Christianity are actually discoverable in the New Testament. I challenge them to produce from the New Testament a single saying which can be fairly interpreted as an assurance that in this aeon the disciple of Jesus shall enjoy peace 'as the world giveth it', a confidence of faith which is more than 'a fighting certainty', or a hope which has not the disturbing quality of 'hoping against hope'. I grant that much might be quoted to this effect from the Old Testament. But the copy of the New Testament which I possess does not contain the promise or the implication that in this life I shall 'see good days'—and that in addition to this I shall enjoy the calm assurance of life everlasting. Rather it admonishes me to 'Watch!' and it apprises me of the danger and suffering which is associated with that religion which is characterized as the 'following' of Jesus Christ. I note that Jesus addressed his words of comfort only to such as evidently were in need of comfort: the poor, the hungry, those that weep and travail and are heavy laden. In the words of St. John's Gospel he promised peace—but 'not as the world giveth' it. The Apostles as they marched through suffering to martyrdom were able to rejoice in the Lord because they contrived to rejoice in their sufferings. This is a paradoxical joy, and the New Testament holds out no promise of a joy that is more 'immediate'. The Christians of the New Testament are 'pressed on every side, yet not straitened; perplexed, yet not unto despair; pursued, yet not forsaken; smitten down, yet not destroyed'. They live constantly in the apprehension that they have not yet attained, and are disquieted as well as comforted by the thought that God's grace is the paradoxical expression of his righteousness. I can think of no motto more appropriate to all four of the Gospels, more precisely descriptive of the evangelical promises, than the saying reported by St. John: 'In the world ye shall have tribulation; but be of good cheer, I have overcome the world.'

PART ONE

CHILDHOOD

1813–1830

To me it is a prison.

O God, I could be bounded in a nut-shell and count myself king of infinite space, were it not that I have bad dreams.

HAMLET.

I. A TRAGIC BACKGROUND

1813

SØREN AABYE KIERKEGAARD was born on May 5, 1813, in Copenhagen, in the great house on the Nytorv (New Market) which his father had bought after retiring from business with an ample fortune. He was the youngest of seven children born to elderly parents. His father Michael Pedersen Kierkegaard, who was 56 at the time of Søren's birth, had been brought to Copenhagen when he was only 12 by a maternal uncle who employed him in his business of selling the wool of the Jutland heath where, as a little peasant boy, he had tended sheep. Søren's mother, Anne Sørensdatter Lund, also of Jutland peasant stock, was a servant in the house when the first wife died without children, and the master married her before the year of mourning was up. The oldest child was born five months after the wedding—and the stern old man could never forgive himself for his incontinence.

It is natural enough for the Danes to boast that Søren sprang from the most thoroughly Danish stock in Denmark; but I have heard a distinguished Icelander say that he resembles much more *his* race, and that his humour in particular was of a sort that his Danish compatriots could never appreciate. But surely it is vain to seek to explain so singular a genius by racial characteristics. Far more important than his physical inheritance was the tragic background of his history which we must seek in the poor parish of Sæding on the Jutland heath.

We read in the Journal:[1]

> Perhaps I could recount the tragedy of my childhood, the fearful secret explanation of religion, suggesting an apprehensive presentiment which my imagination elaborated, my offence at religion—I could recount it in a novel entitled *The Enigmatical Family*. It ought to begin patriarchally idyllic, so that no one would have a presentiment of the tragedy until that word should ring out and transform all into the dreadful.

There are many entries to this effect. I quote only one more here:[2]

It is terrible whenever for a single instant I come to think of the dark background of my life, from the very earliest time. The anxious dread with which my father filled my soul, his own frightful melancholy, the many things in that connexion which I cannot record—I got such a dread of Christianity, and yet I felt myself so strongly drawn to it. And then at a later time what I suffered from Peter when he became morbidly religious.

I, of course, have made my pilgrimage to Sæding. But except for the old stone church, too poor to have a belfry, nothing is left there that belongs to the days when Michael Pedersen Kierkegaard was a boy. Nothing remains of the house in which his family lived and from which they derived their surname. The word *Kirkegaard* means churchyard, including the cemetery, and is used of the parsonage in particular. The word *Gaard* (pronounced *gor*) is used indifferently, like the German *Hoff*, for a farmhouse or a mansion. This family occupied the parsonage; for since one parson served two poor parishes, the house at Sæding could be let. Surnames were not yet firmly fixed in Denmark, and the next family that moved into this same house were also given the name of Kirkegaard. Michael Pedersen Kierkegaard altered the spelling of his name when he became established in Copenhagen. There is no trace left of the once celebrated 'Red House', the admiration of the whole countryside, which M. P. K. built for his mother and three unmarried sisters, providing that after their demise it should serve as a school-house. Like all the other houses it was roofed with thatch, but it is said to have been built of red brick between timbers painted the same colour—whereas all the other houses of the region were built of mud. But since 1866 the whole region has been changed by Enrico Dalgas and the Heath Society. They abolished the heath and transformed the poorest region in Denmark into rich farmland. Lately I read in the Danish papers that on November 11, 1935, the eightieth anniversary of S. K.'s death, the Bishop of Ribe solemnly dedicated a monument which marks the site of the parsonage where his father was born, as well as a marble tablet in the church in memory of S. K. In the church as I saw it there were two wooden tablets, painted black and inscribed with gilt letters—the only ornaments outside the sanctuary, except a crucifix and a brightly painted pulpit. The earlier of these tablets records the considerable donation made to the parish in 1821 by M. P. Kierkegaard in memory of his uncle Niels Andersen Seding who brought him to Copenhagen and started him on his career. This gift provided for the support of a fit school-teacher at Sæding, for the support of needy pupils (who are required to serve as choristers in the church), and for the purchase of the most suitable text-books. The other tablet was erected to do honour to M. P. K. and to commemorate the gift made by his nephew Michael Andersen Kierkegaard, to whom he had handed over his business. The gift was made partly in behalf of the school and partly in behalf of the poor of the parish. The inscription hails the uncle as 'the guide and aid of my youth, the benefactor of Sæding school'.

Søren too made a pilgrimage to Sæding two years after his father's death. It was his only visit, and the sadness of the occasion doubtless intensified the melancholy impression of the heath. In a journal he kept during that journey he made this note:[1]

> I had it in mind to preach my first sermon in Sæding church, and that must be Sunday next. To my no small wonder therefore I see that the text [i.e. the Gospel for the day] is Mk. 8: 1–10 (the feeding of the four thousand), and I was struck by the word, 'Whence shall one be able to fill these men with bread here in a desert place?' For I surely shall be speaking in the poorest parish in Jutland, in the Heath District.

In another entry of that time he remarks:[2]

> In Sæding parish, it is said, the house still exists where once there dwelt a man who in the time of the pest outlived all the others and buried them. He ploughed deep furrows in the peat and buried his neighbours in long rows.

He registered a less gloomy impression when he said:[3]

> The heath must be singularly well adapted for the production of strong minds. Here all lies naked and exposed before God, and there is no place for the many distractions, the many nooks and corners where consciousness can hide itself and from which it is often difficult even for serious persons to recapture their dispersed thoughts. Here consciousness must

be shut up within itself tightly and decisively. 'Whither can I flee from thy presence?' can truthfully be said here on the heath.

The melancholy impression was lasting, for many years later he wrote:

I sat the other day in a strange mood, self-absorbed, and read an old folk-song which tells of a maiden who expected her lover of a Saturday night, but he did not come, and she went to bed and 'wept so bitterly'; she arose again and wept so bitterly. Suddenly the scene widened out for me—I saw the Jutland heath with its indescribable loneliness and its single larch-tree—and now there rose up before me one generation after another whose maidens all sang for me and wept so bitterly and sank again into their graves, and I wept with them.

We now know why the Jutland heath was charged with such tragic sadness for S. K. The secret which he believed was hidden for ever was revealed almost by accident. In February 1846 he made this brief entry in his journal:[1]

The dreadful case of a man who, when he was a little boy, suffered much hardship, was hungry, benumbed with cold, stood upon a hillock and cursed God—and the man was not able to forget this when he was 82 years old.

He may well have thought that there was nothing here to betray his secret; but 82 was the age of his father when he died, and probably this prompted Barfod, the first editor of his *Papers*, to show the passage to the elder brother Peter, who had resigned the bishopric of Aarlborg when he was an old man and afflicted with a melancholy sense of his unworthiness. As soon as the old Bishop saw it he exclaimed, 'This is our father's story *and ours*.' According to Barfod's report the old Bishop went on to say that his father as a boy of about 11 years tended sheep on the Jutland heath and suffered much from hunger, cold, and loneliness. Once in his desperation he stood upon a stone, lifted up his hands to heaven and cursed the Lord God, who, if he did exist, could be so hard-hearted as to let a helpless, innocent child suffer so much without coming to his aid.

'But the memory of this curse in his childhood never left the boy, the man, the patriarch—and seeing that God's grace from that very moment showered temporal blessings upon him, so that instead of tasting the divine wrath he was overwhelmed with riches, marvellously gifted children, universal esteem—then solemn anxiousness and dread gripped his soul most deeply. God *did* exist, and *he* had cursed this God—was not this the sin against the Holy Ghost which never can be forgiven? It was for this reason the old man's soul continued in anxious dread, for this reason he beheld his children condemned to "the silent despair", for this reason he laid upon their shoulders in tender years the sternest requirements of Christianity—for this reason he was a prey to temptation and in constant conflict of soul.'

There came a moment in the father's life when the long-expected curse seemed to be falling upon the doomed family to exterminate them all. Of his seven children two had died in childhood. Søren Michael was born eight years before Søren Aabye and died four years after the second Søren's birth, being only 12 years of age. It seems odd that there were two Sørens in the same family—really there were three of the children that bore the same name, for one of the daughters was called Petrea Severine, and Søren is the Danish form for Severinus. Their mother was one of three sisters who all were named Anne. The eldest child Maren Christine died in 1822 when she was 14 years of age. Two of the daughters were named Christine. At the close of the year 1832 calamities began to fall upon the old man in quick succession. In September of that year his daughter Nicholine Christine died in her thirty-third year in giving birth to a still-born son. A year later, on September 21, 1833, a son, Niels Andreas, aged 24, died at Paterson, New Jersey. Where is his grave? Where is the house in which he lived, to which proud citizens of Paterson might affix a tablet to record that the brother of the great Danish writer died there? The mother of all these children died after a painful illness on July 31, 1834; and in December of that same year the most brilliant of his daughters, Petrea Severine, married to a distinguished banker and Councillor of Justice, Henrick Ferdinand Lund, died in her twenty-seventh year in giving birth to a son who became famous as an historian and philologist, Peter Severin Lund. Thus in the space of two years M. P. K. lost three of his children and his wife. It is not strange that this melancholy old man, who had regarded his prosperity as an enigmatical sign of God's displeasure because of his childish revolt and his later incontinence, should now behold in these calamities the hand of an avenging God. Yet the youngest son could never forget that the pious old man met these calamities with the words of Job: 'The Lord gave, the Lord hath taken away—blessed be the name of the Lord.' Peter and Søren were the only children left to him, and he had a presentiment that he was destined to outlive them both. That Søren did not escape the infection of this gloomy foreboding is shown by the strange title he gave to a book he published soon after his father's death, criticizing a novel of Hans Andersen: he described it as 'From the manuscripts of one still living'.

Such was the tragic background, at first vaguely apprehended by the child, but all the more terrible because of its vagueness, which darkened S. K.'s youth and affected profoundly his whole life. His nature was thereby sensitively attuned to tragedy, and out of his own experience he was able to understand the idea expressed in the tragic drama of the Greeks and to contrast it, as he does in a famous chapter of *Either/Or*, with the modern idea of tragedy. The feeling he had of solidarity in his father's guilt belonged to the Greek rather than to the modern idea. We are startled to hear him say that, if he were to express the Greek idea of tragedy in one word, it would be: 'It is a fearful thing to fall into the hands of the living God.'

For weal or for woe the father made upon the son a prodigious impression which lasted as long as he lived. As the Benjamin of the family he was kept constantly in his father's company and was encouraged to use a sort of familiarity with the stern old disciplinarian which was permitted to none of the other children. Several stories of his childhood reveal that he was even encouraged to be pert. The mother counted for little in the household. Whereas the father occupies so large a place in S. K.'s books and journals, not a single mention is made of his mother. The fact that as a child he had no mother he could adore is doubtless at the bottom of his own particular tragedy of not being able to 'realize the universal' by marrying. He who wrote so much about woman, and so beautifully but also so despitefully, was able to conceive her only as the counterpart of man, and associated no noble and tender thoughts with woman as a mother. Yet his niece Henriette Lund describes her grandmother as 'a nice little woman with an even and cheerful disposition'. She goes on to say that 'her sons' development was rather over her head; their high flight seemed to her troubled heart like a flight away from the place where she felt herself at home and where she would fain have kept them. Therefore she was never in such high spirits as when a transitory indisposition forced them back for a while under her regimen. Especially was she content when she could put them to bed, for then she wielded her sceptre with joy and kept them as snug as a hen does her chickens.'[1]

The father was undoubtedly a very remarkable man. While he continued to be registered humbly as a 'hosier' he was actually developing a wholesale business in wool. On December 4, 1780, he got permission to deal also in foodstuffs, and on September 19, 1788, he obtained a royal patent to deal in Chinese and East India wares, as well as merchandise from the Danish West Indies, 'such as sugar (refined as well as unrefined), syrup, and coffee beans, and to sell the same at wholesale and retail to all and sundry'. It was probably a morbid melancholy associated with his childish blasphemy as well as his later incontinence which prompted him to give up his business when he was hardly more than 40 years of age. Nevertheless he continued to prosper. During the crisis of 1813, when nearly every one else was impoverished by the failure of the State Bank and the inflation of the currency, he found his fortune relatively augmented by the fact that he had invested the whole of it in a royal loan, and this proved to be the only security which did not greatly depreciate. Søren was born in that year—'when so many worthless notes were put in circulation', as he humorously remarked. Some time before that the father had moved from Hellerod, a suburb of Copenhagen, to the centre of the town, where on the Nytorv, between the old City Hall and Frederiksberg Street, he had acquired a house suitable to his wealth. The bank now built upon that site is marked by an inscription which records that S. K. was born there.

Not many merchants on retiring from business contrive to make such good use of their leisure as did the elder Kierkegaard. He had an exceptionally good mind, not only for business but also for abstract studies. He devoted himself especially to philosophy, and the German philosopher Wolff was his chief admiration. Above all he loved to carry on a discussion with men of talent who frequented his house. It is significant that one of his visitors was Bishop Mynster, Primate of the Church of Denmark. Before his elevation to the episcopate Mynster had been his pastor, and it was he that prepared little Søren for confirmation. The father was a man of deep religious devotion and very scrupulous about his duties towards the Church.

The son cherished the profoundest admiration and reverence for his father. This made it all the more terrible when he first suspected and then discovered his father's guilty secret. The breach was for a while complete. Nevertheless, before the old man's death a perfect understanding was restored. We have a touching testimony to his reverence for his father's memory in the fact that every one of his Edifying Discourses was dedicated in substantially the same terms:

To the deceased
Michael Pedersen Kierkegaard
sometime hosier here in this city
my father
these Discourses are dedicated.

S. K. often regretted his 'crazy upbringing', and yet he could say of his father:[1]

> To my father I owe everything from the very first. It was his prayer for me when, melancholy as he was, he regarded me with a melancholy eye: 'See to it that thou be able to love rightly Jesus Christ.'

He recognized that much of the unhappiness of his life was due to an unwise religious education. Yet the religious impressions he received in childhood were not only indelible but precious to him. He says of the proof of the existence of God that, however cleverly it may be constructed, the principal point has been omitted if the philosopher fails to remark that this faith was taught him in his youth.[2] And about the impression he had received of God's love he wrote:[3]

> 'But still', says the anxious man, 'I do not see God, so I can have no reason to know that He is love; also I do not hear Him say to me that He is love. And at the same time there happen to me things which I cannot in the least understand as good and profitable—how then shall I believe that He is love?'

> Here it is manifest that it really depends absolutely upon a religious education, upon the apriority attained in the fact that from one's earliest age it was a thing absolutely decided that God is love. This proof of the fact that God is love which is founded upon an unaccountable impression, an impression which from the earliest age has been incorporated into one's very being—this is really the principal thing.

Doubtless S. K. inherited from his father a disposition to melancholy, but doubtless it was aggravated by his upbringing. It was a congenital melancholy, but also an infection from his father. It was his great misfortune, and yet we cannot conceive of S. K. without it, nor without it could we have had from him the profit we now experience. He recognized himself that it was his melancholy which made him a copious man, producing in exuberant abundance the material which his imagination employed.

II. AT HOME AND AT SCHOOL

1830

ALTHOUGH Kierkegaard wrote no autobiography, the whole story of his life, including even his childhood and youth, can be told in his own words. His journals were not begun until he was well along in the university, and even then they did not contain a greatdeal of biographical material; but in his pseudonymous works, just because they were pseudonymous, he felt free to describe his own experiences, and because of his lonely life and his morbid reticence he found satisfaction in revealing himself in his books and journals, knowing that the journals would not be seen till he was dead and that the personal references in his books would not be understood. He felt no reluctance whatever to reveal himself to a coming generation, but was rather desirous of doing it. The careful revision of his journals, including the elision of passages which he did not wish to have read, is proof that he expected them to be published. In one place he said:[1] 'Some day not only my writings but especially my life will be studied and studied.' He was confident that his books would some day be understood, and that the personal passages they contain would be understood as a revelation of his own life and experience.

No one ever followed more seriously the Socratic injunction 'Know thyself', and surely no one ever probed more deeply for this knowledge. It was by the study of himself that S. K. became a psychologist. The self-knowledge he attained he was inclined to register in a symbolic or 'poetic' form. In view of the examples which will be given here, this will surely not seem an imperfect or inadequate form.

S. K. for his own part was disposed to value only such books as are a record of personal experience and reflection. He says in his Journal:[2]

> In our day the writing of books has become such a miserable thing, and people write about things they have never thought over, and still less experienced—hence I have determined to read the writings only of the men who have been executed or have been in danger in some other way.

This may seem to limit one's reading too narrowly. Yet Dostoevski is one author who meets this condition, and S. K. conceived that he himself was another. Once feel about, and you discover that there were many. On the title-page of one of his most self-revealing works—Quidam's Diary in the *Stages*—S. K. inscribed the motto: *Perissem nisi perissem* (I should have perished unless I had perished); and three years later he wrote in his journal:[1]

> *Perissem, nisi perissem* is and remains the motto for my life. Hence I have been able to do and endure what another who was not already dead would have been killed by long ago.

In fact he did not begin to write in the great style which was first manifested in *Either/Or* until a great part of him was buried with his disappointed love, and as long as he lived he continued to write like a dying man.

I quote first a vivid picture of the boy's life in his home and at school which he wrote as an introduction to a work which was never published or even completed. It was ascribed to the pseudonym Johannes Climacus, the name which served for his important philosophical books. *Climacus* is Latinized Greek for ladder, and *Ladder of Paradise* was the name of a mystical book of the sixth century. The passage I am about to quote suggests in one place why S. K. was attracted by this name. The work was written to deride the Cartesian maxim that philosophizing must begin with complete scepticism. It is entitled *Johannes Climacus* or *de omnibus dubitandum est*. It is found not among the *Works* but among the *Papers*.[2] Climacus gives a sketch of his youth in the Introduction. I must warn the reader that it does not describe the Climacus we come to know in the later books, but it is evidently a good sketch of S. K.

> In the city of H—— there lived some years ago a young student by the name of Johannes Climacus, who had no craving at all to become conspicuous in the world, but on the contrary found his only joy in quietness and obscurity. Those who knew him more intimately sought to explain his retiring nature, so prone to shun unnecessary contact with men, by the supposition that he was either melancholy or in love. Those who maintained the latter theory were in a sense not far wrong, though they were in error if they supposed that his dreams

were concerned with a girl. Such feelings were totally strange to his heart; and as his outward appearance was delicate and ethereal, so was his soul in the same degree far too spiritually qualified to be caught by a woman's beauty. It is true, however, that he was in love, fanatically in love . . . with thoughts, or more properly with thinking. No young lover can be more deeply moved by the incomprehensible transition through which love awakens in his breast, by the lightning flash in which reciprocal affection emerges in the beloved, than was he by the comprehensible transition through which the one thought fits into the other, a transition which for him was the lucky instant which he had surmised and awaited in quietness of soul. So when his head was heavy with thought and bowed like a ripe ear of corn, this was not because he heard the voice of the beloved, but because he was listening to the secret whispering of the thoughts; when his look was dreamy, this was not because her picture was in his mind's eye, but because the movements of the thoughts were coming into vision. It was his delight to begin with a single thought, from which to climb up step by step along the path of logical consequence to a higher thought; for the logical consequence was for him a *scala paradisi*, and his blessedness seemed to him even more glorious than that of the angels. Then when he had arrived at the higher thought he found an indescribable joy, a passionate rapture, in plunging headlong down along the line of the same consequences until he reached the point from which he had set out. In this, however, he did not always succeed according to his wish. If he did not accomplish exactly as many motions as there were links in the chain of consequences, he became distressed, for then the movement was imperfect. Then he began over again. Then, if he succeeded, his soul shuddered with delight; for sheer gladness he could not sleep at night, but continued for hours making the same movement; for this up-and-down and down-and-up of thought was a delight beyond compare. In his fortunate hours his gait was light, almost a glide; at other times it was anxious and uncertain. That is, so long as he was labouring to climb up, so long as the consequence had not yet proved able to make a way for itself, he was oppressed; for he was fearful of losing track of the many consequences he had ready, without being yet perfectly clear about their necessity. When one sees a man carrying a great number of fragile objects stacked one above the other, one is not inclined to wonder that he walks uncertainly and is every moment clutching after equilibrium; whereas if one does not see the stack, he may smile, as many smiled at Johannes Climacus without suspecting that his soul was carrying a much higher stack than that which amazed them in the other case, that his soul was anxious lest a single consequence should drop out; for then the whole would fall to pieces. He did not notice that men smiled at him, and just as little that at other times an individual turned gladly to look at him as he hastened along the street as light as in a dance. He paid no attention to men, he did not for a moment suppose that they could be paying attention to him, he was and remained a stranger in the world.

Although Climacus's nature must have seemed remarkable to a person who was not well acquainted with him, it was nevertheless by no means inexplicable to one who knew something about his earlier life; as he was now in this his twenty-first year, so, in a certain degree, had he always been. The disposition his soul possessed in childhood had not been thwarted but was developed by favourable circumstances. His home did not offer many diversions, and as he almost never went out, he early became accustomed to occupy himself with himself and with his own thoughts. His father was a very severe man, apparently dry and prosaic, but under this rough coat he concealed a glowing imagination which even old age could not quench. When Johannes occasionally asked of him permission to go out, he generally refused to give it, though once in a while he proposed instead that Johannes should take his hand and walk back and forth in the room. At first glance this would seem a poor substitute, and yet, as in the case of the rough coat, there was something totally different concealed under it. The proposition was accepted, and it was left entirely to Johannes to determine where they should go. So they went out of doors to a near-by castle in Spain, or out to the sea-shore, or about the streets, wherever Johannes wished to go, for the father was equal to anything. While they went back and forth in the room the father described all that they saw; they greeted passers-by, carriages rattled past them and drowned the father's voice; the cake-woman's goodies were more enticing than ever. He described so accurately, so vividly, so explicitly even to the least details, everything that was known to Johannes and so fully and perspicuously what was unknown to him, that after half an hour of such a walk with his father he was as much overwhelmed and fatigued as if he had been a whole day out of doors. Johannes soon learnt from the father how to exercise this magic power. What first had been an epic now became a drama; they conversed in turn. If they went along well-known ways, they watched one another sharply to make sure that nothing was overlooked; if the way was strange to Johannes, he invented something, whereas the father's almighty imagination was capable of shaping everything, of using every childish whim as an ingredient of the drama which was being enacted. To Johannes it seemed as if the world were coming into existence during the conversation, as if the father were our Lord and he were his favourite, who was allowed to interpose his foolish conceits as merrily as he would; for he was never repulsed, the father was never put out, he agreed to everything, and always to Johannes' contentment.

While life in the father's house continued thus to develop his imagination, teaching him to like the taste of ambrosia, the education which fell to his lot in school was quite in harmony with this. The lofty authority of Latin grammar, the divine dignity of the rules, developed a new enthusiasm. However, it was the Greek grammar which especially appealed to him. Absorbed in this, he forgot to read Homer aloud, as commonly he was wont to do for the sake of the beauty of the rhythm. The Greek master taught the grammar in a rather philosophical way. When it was explained to Johannes, e.g. that the accusative signifies extension in time and space, that the preposition does not govern the case, but it is the relationship which does that, then everything widened out before him. The preposition vanished, extension in time and space remained as an enormous empty picture for the intuition. His imagination was again employed, but in a different way than heretofore. What delighted him on the walking tours was filled space, he could not get it thick enough round about him. His imagination was so productive that it was able to get along with little. Outside the window of the sitting-room there grew some ten blades of grass. Here he sometimes discovered a little creature which ran among the stems. These straws became an immense forest which yet had the same denseness and darkness as the bunch of grass. Now, instead of filled space he got empty space, he gazed again but saw nothing except enormous extension.

While there was thus being developed in him an almost vegetative tendency to drowse in imagination, which was in part aesthetical, in part more intellectual, another side of the soul was being strongly shaped, namely, his sense for the sudden, the surprising. This was not accomplished by the magic means which commonly serve to rivet the attention of children, but by something far higher. The father combined with an almighty imagination an irresistible dialectic. When for any reason the father engaged in a disputation with another, Johannes was all ears, and that all the more because the whole thing was conducted with an almost solemn orderliness. The father always allowed the opponent to state his whole case, and then as a precaution asked him if he had nothing more to say before he began his reply. Johannes had followed the opponent's speech with strained attention, and in his way shared an interest in the outcome. A pause intervened. The father's rejoinder followed, and behold! in a trice the tables were turned. How that came about was a riddle to Johannes, but his soul delighted in the show. The opponent spoke again. Johannes could almost hear his heart beat, so impatiently did he await what was to occur.—It occurred; in the twinkling of an eye all was inverted, the explicable became inexplicable, the certain doubtful, the contrary evident. When the dogfish would seize its prey it must turn over upon its back, for its mouth is on the side of the belly; it is dark on the back, silver-white on the belly. It must be a magnificent sight to witness this alternation of colour; it must sometimes glitter so brightly as to hurt the eyes, and yet it is a delight to look upon it. Johannes was witness of a similar alternation when he heard his father engage in disputation. He forgot again what was said, both what the father said and what the opponent, but the shudder of the soul he did not forget. In school life a like experience was not lacking; he saw how a word could alter a whole sentence, how a conjunctive mood in the midst of an indicative sentence could throw a different light upon the whole. The older he grew, and the more the father engaged him in his conversation, the more attentive he became to this inexplicable power; it was as though the father were in a secret correspondence with what Johannes was about to say, and so with a single word could confound it all. When the father was not merely confuting him but was expounding his own view, it was possible for Johannes to perceive how he went about it, how he approached by successive steps the position he wished to reach. Johannes surmised now that the reason why the father by a single word was able to turn everything upside down must be that he himself had forgotten something in the succession in which his thoughts were arrayed.

What other children get through the fascination of poetry and the surprise of fairy-tales, he got through the calmness of intuition and the alternations of dialectic. This was the child's joy, it became the boy's game, it became the youth's delight. So his life had a rare continuity; it did not know the various transitions which commonly mark the different periods of growth. When Johannes grew older he had no toys to lay aside, for he had learnt to play with that which was to be the serious business of his life, and yet it lost thereby nothing of its allurement. The small girl plays so long with the doll that at the last it is transformed into the lover; for woman's whole life is love. His life had a similar continuity, for his whole life was thought.

Climacus became a university student, passed his 'second examination' when he was twenty years old, and yet there was no change in him, he was still strange to the world. Nevertheless he did not shun people, on the contrary he sought to encounter men of like mind. Yet he did not talk out freely, did not give any one to understand what went on in his interior, his eroticism was too deep for that; it seemed to him that he must blush if he spoke of such things, he was fearful of imparting too much knowledge or too little. On the other hand he was always attentive when others talked. Just as a young girl who is deeply in love is not disposed to talk about her love experience, but with a high-strung attention which is almost pain will listen when other young girls are talking about theirs, eager to snatch at every guiding hint, so did Johannes listen to everything attentively in silence. Then when he came home he pondered what the philosophers had said; for this was naturally the society he sought.

It never occurred to him to wish to be a philosopher, to wish to dedicate himself completely to speculation; he was far too light-minded for that. It is true that thinking was his passion, and his soul was not attracted now to this thing, now to the other; but yet he lacked sufficient reflection to discover the deeper connexion. The insignificant and the significant lured him equally to begin his operations with them; the result was of no great consequence to him, what interested him was merely the movements. At times, indeed, he did not fail to notice that starting out from entirely different points he arrived at one and the same place; but this did not seriously engage his attention. His constant delight was just to push through. Wherever he surmised a labyrinth, there he must find a way. If once he began such an enterprise, nothing could make him leave off. If he found it difficult, if after an hour he was tired of the effort, he used to employ a very simple method. He shut himself up in his room, made everything as festive as possible and said then in a voice loud and clear, *I will it.* He had learnt from his father that one *can* what one will; and the father's life had not discredited this theory. This experience had imparted to Johannes' soul an indescribable sort of pride. It was intolerable to him that there should be anything one could not do if only one would. But his pride was not at all indicative of a feeble will; for when he had uttered this energetic word he was ready for anything, he then had a still more lofty goal, namely, to penetrate by his will the jungle growth of difficulty. This was again an adventure which aroused his enthusiasm. So his life was at all times romantically adventurous, although for his adventure he did not need forests and distant travel, but only what he possessed—a little room with one window.

Although his soul was early attracted to the ideal, yet was his trust and confidence in reality in no wise weakened. The ideal which he was nourished upon lay so close to him, all came about so naturally, that this became his reality, and again in the reality around about him he might expect to discover the ideal. His father's melancholy contributed to this. That the father was an extraordinary man was something Johannes got to know later. That he astonished him, as no other man did to the same degree, that he knew; but he was acquainted with so few people that he possessed no scale to measure him with. That the father, humanly speaking, was something out of the ordinary was the last thing he would learn in the paternal house. Once in a while, when an old and tried friend visited the family and entered into a confidential conversation with the father, Johannes would hear him say, 'I am good for nothing, cannot accomplish anything, my one wish would be to find a place in a charitable institution.' That was not a jest, there was no trace of irony in the father's word, on the contrary there was a gloomy seriousness in it which alarmed Johannes. That was by no means an observation carelessly uttered, for the father was capable of proving that the most insignificant man in the world was a genius compared with him. No counter-proof was of any avail, for his irresistible dialectic was capable of making one forget what lay nearest at hand [that such dialectical talent contradicted his thesis], was capable of riveting one's gaze upon the view that he presented, as if there were nothing else in the whole world. Johannes, whose whole view of life was hidden as it were in the father (inasmuch as he himself could manage only to see very little), found himself involved in a contradiction which baffled him for a long time: the suspicion that the father contradicted himself, if not in other ways, at least by the virtuosity with which he could triumph over an opponent and put him to silence. So Johannes' confidence in reality was not weakened; he had not imbibed the ideal from writings which do not leave the man whom they foster unaware that the glory they describe is indeed not to be found in the world; he was not formed by a man who knew how to make his knowledge precious, but rather to make it as unimportant and worthless as possible.

This last outrageous sentence with its four negatives, which comes near breaking my head, I understand as a passionate repudiation of modern idealistic philosophers in general and of Hegel in particular, affirming that his own idealism was derived from the Platonic Socrates, who discovered the ideal in the real and instead of magnifying his wisdom pretends ironically to be ignorant. It cannot be said that this passage furnishes a complete description of S. K., for it dwells only upon the traits which prepared him to be a philosopher, and therefore ignores not only the dissipation of his youth and the tragic disappointment of his love which made him a poet, but also the deep ethical and religious impressions which made him a Christian writer. Fortunately there are other pictures which supply this defect. I quote first from *Either/Or* a passage in which Judge William recounts memories of his youth which we can confidently regard as a part of S. K.'s autobiography.[1]

> Let me illustrate what I mean by an example. I select this one impression which I have retained from my earliest childhood. When I was five years old I was sent to school. Such an event naturally makes an impression upon a child, but the question is, what impression. Childish curiosity is captivated by the various bewildering notions as to what it all means. That this was the case with me also is very probable; however, the principal impression I got was quite another. I made my appearance at the school, was introduced to the teacher, and then had assigned to me as my lesson for the following day the first ten lines of Balle's Lesson-Book, which I must learn by heart. Every other impression was now banished from my mind, only my task stood out vividly before me. As a child I had a very good memory. Soon I had learnt my lesson. My sister had heard me recite it several times and assured me that I knew it. I went to bed, and before I fell asleep I recited it again to myself. I fell asleep with the fixed resolution to read it over again the following morning. I awoke at five o'clock, got dressed, got hold of my lesson-book, and read it over again. It is all just as vivid to me at this moment as if it had happened yesterday. It seemed to me as if heaven and earth might collapse if I did not learn my lesson, and on the other hand it seemed to me that even if heaven and earth were to collapse, that would not excuse me from doing what was definitely prescribed, that I must learn my lesson. At that age I knew so little about duties, in fact I had not yet learnt them from Balle's Lesson-Book; I had then only one duty, that of learning my lesson, and yet I can trace the whole of my ethical conception of life to that impression. I can smile at the little urchin of only five years who took the thing so passionately, and yet I assure you I have no higher wish than that at every period of

life I may take hold of my work with the same energy, with the same seriousness, as at that time. It is true that in later life one has a better conception of what one's work is, but still the energy is the chief thing. That this experience made upon me the impression it did I owe to my father's sober earnestness, and if I owed him nothing else, this is enough to put me in debt to him eternally. This is what counts in education—not that the child learns this or that, but that the spirit is shaped, that its energy is awakened. . . .

In this respect I can say that my childhood has been fortunate, inasmuch as it has enriched me with ethical impressions. Allow me to dwell a moment longer upon a subject which reminds me of my father, and that is the dearest recollection I possess, and it is far from being a poor and unfruitful remembrance which gives me occasion to illustrate once more what I am urging, namely, that the integral impression of duty is the chief thing, not the multiplicity of duties. When this latter is emphasized, the individual is dwarfed and ruined. Now in this respect I was fortunate as a child, for I never had many duties, but commonly only one; this, however, had evident utility. When I was two years older I was sent to the high school. Here began a new life, but here again the chief impression was the ethical, notwithstanding that I had the greatest freedom. . . . For the rest, I enjoyed my freedom, I had only one duty, that of getting along in my school, and that I always took seriously. When I was admitted to the school and the prescribed school-books had been bought, my father delivered them to me and said: 'William, when the month is up you are third in your class.' I was spared all paternal humbug. He never asked me about my lessons, never heard them, never saw my exercises, never reminded me that now it was time to read, that now it was time to stop, never came to the aid of the pupil's conscience, as we see so often done, when noble fathers box their boys' ears and say, You surely can do your thing now. If I had to go out, he asked whether I had time—it was that which decided the matter, not he himself; and he made no great ado about it. I am perfectly sure nevertheless that he was deeply concerned about what I was doing, but he never let me notice it, in order that my soul might be moulded by responsibility. Here again it was the same, I had not many duties. And how many children there are who are spoilt because they are overwhelmed by a whole ceremonial of duties. So I got a sufficiently deep impression of the fact that something exists which is called duty, and that this has eternal validity.

The next passage recalls how his father, desiring to impress upon the child the most poignant truths of Christianity, inserted among his toys a picture of the Crucifixion. He introduces this reminiscence in one of his latest and most serious books, *Training in Christianity*, in order to suggest how we might all of us be affected by this picture and its story, if we were not too familiar with it, if we might see and hear it now for the first time.[1]

> Suppose then such a child and give this child delight by showing him some of those pictures which one readily finds in the shops, which from the artistic point of view are so trivial but to the child are precious.—This one on a snorting steed, with the tossing feather, with the lordly mien, riding at the head of the thousands and thousands you cannot see, with hand outstretched in a gesture of command: 'Forward!'—forward over the crests of the mountains which you see plainly in front of you, forward to victory—that is the Emperor, the unique figure Napoleon.—This one here is dressed as a huntsman; he stands leaning upon his bow and gazes straight before him with a glance so piercing, so self-confident, and yet so anxious. That is William Tell. You now relate to the child something about him and about that extraordinary glance of his, explaining that with that same glance he has at once an eye for the beloved child, that he may not harm him, and for the apple on the child's head, that he may not miss it.—And thus you show the child many pictures, to the child's unspeakable delight. Then you come to one which intentionally was laid among the rest. It represents a man crucified. The child will not at once, nor indeed easily, understand this picture, and will ask what it means, why he hangs on a tree like that. So you explain to the child that this is a cross, and that to hang on it means to be crucified, and that crucifixion in that land was not only the most painful death penalty but also an ignominious mode of execution employed only for the grossest malefactors. What effect will that have upon the child? The child will have a very strange feeling, he will wonder what could have prompted you

to lay this ugly picture among all these other lovely ones, the picture of a gross malefactor among all these glorious heroes. For just as, to do despite to the Jews, there was written above His cross 'The King of the Jews', so that picture, as it comes forth anew regularly every year for a reproof to the human race, is a remembrance which the race never can and never shall be rid of, it shall never be represented otherwise; and it shall ever seem as if it were this present generation which crucified him, as often as this generation for the first time shows the child of the new generation this picture, for the first time explains how things actually go in this world; and the child, the first time he hears this, will become sorrowful and anxious about his parents, about the world and about himself; and the other pictures—yes, they all (as it is said in the poem [of 'Agnes and the Merman']) will 'turn their backs'—so different is this picture. Meanwhile—and we have not yet come at all to the decisive thing, the child has not yet learnt who that gross malefactor was—the child, with the curiosity children always show, will surely ask, Who is he? What did he do? Then tell the child that this crucified man is the Saviour of the world. However, he will not be able to form any clear idea of what that means; tell him therefore only that the Crucified One was the most loving man that ever lived. Oh, in common intercourse, where one can recite all that story by rote, in common intercourse a half-word thrown out as a hint suffices to recall it to every one—so glibly it goes; but truly he must be an extraordinary man, or rather an inhuman man, who does not instinctively cast down his eyes and stand like a poor sinner at the moment he tells this to the child for the first time, to the child who has never heard a word of it before, and consequently never has surmised anything of the sort. But so the parent stands also as an accuser of himself and the whole race!—What impression do you think this will make upon the child—who naturally will ask, But why were people so bad to him then? What?

. . . . . .

But what impression do you think this story will make upon the child? First and foremost surely this, that he forgets entirely the other pictures which you have showed him; for now he has got something entirely different to think about. And now the child will be in the deepest wonderment at the fact that God in heaven did nothing to prevent this being done; or that this was done without God—if not beforehand, at least at the last minute—raining down fire from heaven to prevent His death; that this happened without the earth opening to swallow up the ungodly. . . . That was surely the first impression. But by degrees, the more the child reflected upon the story, the more his passion would be aroused, he would be able to think of nothing but weapons and war—for the child would have made the resolute decision that when he grew up he would slay all these ungodly men who had dealt thus with the Loving One; that would the child have resolved, forgetting that it was 1800 years ago they lived.

Then when the child became a youth he would not have forgotten the impression of childhood, but he would now understand it differently, he would know that it was not possible to carry out what the child, overlooking the 1800 years, had resolved to do; but nevertheless he would think with the same passionateness of combating the world in which people spat upon the Holy One, the world in which they crucify Love and beg acquittal for the robber.

Then when he became older and mature he would not have forgotten the impression of childhood, but he would understand it differently. He would no longer wish to smite; for, said he, I should thus attain to no likeness with Him, the humiliated, who did not smite, not even when he himself was smitten. No, he would only wish one thing, to suffer in some way comparable to his sufferings in the world. . . .

So *can* the sight of this humiliation move one—cannot it also move thee?

All of the descriptions quoted here go well beyond the period of childhood with which we are expressly dealing now; but it is no disadvantage that they enable us to see how the religious impressions of early childhood, though S. K. revolted against them, availed in the end to shape his life. In reading the Journals we find abundant evidence that these descriptions do actually reflect S. K.'s own experience. I quote here only one entry as evidence of this. It was written in 1849:[1]

It was related to me when I was only a small child, and with the utmost emphasis, that *they* spat upon Christ, who yet was the truth, that the *crowd* ('they that passed by') spat upon Him and said, 'Hold thy peace.' This I have treasured deep in my heart (for though there have been moments, yea, hours, when that has been for me as if forgotten, yet have I constantly returned to this my first thought), and so, the better to treasure this under the most opposite outward appearance, I have hidden it in the deepest recesses of my soul; for I was fearful lest it might early escape me, lest it might trick me and become like a blank cartridge. This thought . . . is my life, . . . and though I were to forget everything, yet would I not forget that they told this to me when I was a child, and the impression it made upon the child.

In this connexion I quote one other passage to prove that we are dealing here with an experience which was not only real but fundamental, an experience of childhood which decisively influenced S. K.'s last years and supplied him with courage and serenity in launching his attack upon the Established Church—the ideal of imitating Christ in his suffering and humiliation. It is the beginning of the Introduction to the first of the *Two Minor Ethico-Religious Treatises* ascribed to H. H. The theme of the first treatise is: 'Has a man a right to let himself be put to death for the truth?—The literary remains of a solitary.—A poetical essay.'[1]

Once upon a time there was a man. As a boy he was strictly brought up in the Christian religion. He had not heard much about that which children commonly hear, about the little child Jesus, about the angels, and such like. On the other hand they exhibited to him all the more frequently the Crucified, so that this picture was the only one he had, and the only impression he had, of the Saviour. Although merely a child, he was already as old as a grandfather. This picture followed him throughout his life; he never grew younger, and he never got away from that picture. As it is related of a murderer, that in the anguish of his conscience he could not refrain from looking back at the picture of the murdered man which pursued him, so this man, out of love, did not look away from that picture which drew him to itself, no, not for an instant. What as a child he had piously believed, that the sin of the world required this sacrifice, what as a child he had understood in all simplicity, that the godlessness of the Jews, in the hand of divine governance, was the condition which explained how such a horror could be perpetrated—this he continued to believe unvaryingly, and he understood it unvaryingly.

But later, as he grew older, this picture acquired more and more power over him. It seemed to him as if it was constantly requiring something of him. For he had always felt it to be an impiety that one should venture to paint this picture, and an impiety also to gaze with an artistic eye upon a picture painted like this, to see if it was a resemblance—instead of becoming oneself the picture which resembles Him, and being driven by an inexplicable force to wish to resemble Him, in so far indeed as a man can resemble Him. Of this at least he was fully convinced, that there was no presumption in his longing, as though he could for a moment forget himself to such a degree that he could presumptuously forget that the Crucified was God, the Holy One—and he a sinner. But to desire to suffer for the same cause, even unto death, in that there was no presumption.

Thus was he preoccupied with this picture in quietness of soul; it came ever nearer and nearer to him, the demand it made upon him impressed him ever more and more deeply. Yet to speak about it to any one was impossible. And precisely this it is that proves how deeply the matter concerned him, and it may be taken as a proof that some day it would not be impossible for him to act accordingly. For silence and action correspond to one another perfectly. Silence is the measure of the power to act. A man has never more power to act than he has power to be silent. Every one understands very well that to act is something much greater than to talk about it; therefore if he is sure of himself that he can do it, or if he has resolved that he will do it, he will talk to no one about it. When a man talks about doing a thing, it is a sign that he is not sure of himself. A man who lightly persuades himself to give ten dollars to the poor, and regards that as a perfectly natural thing to do, so that it seems to him (see, here we have the expression!) a thing not worth talking about, he does not talk about it. But perhaps you will hear him talking about his intention of giving a thousand dollars to the poor—alas, the poor will likely have to be content with the ten. A girl who possesses enough inwardness to sorrow all her life over an unhappy love will talk to no one about it. But perhaps in the first moment of her pain you may hear her say that she will take her own life—be calm, she will not do it: because she talked about it, the thought was vain. The consciousness a man has within himself that he can and will is more deeply satisfying than all mere talk. Hence talk deals only with those things that one has no such confidence about. Feelings which one truly has, one does not talk about; only the feelings one does not have, or a degree of feeling one does not have, is matter for conversation. The rule is perfectly simple. In relation to evil it is this. If you have reason to suspect that a man who is dear to you is preoccupied secretly with some terrible thought or another, just try to make him tell it, preferably by way of hoaxing him with the pretence that it is nothing at all, seeing to it that even at the critical moment of communication there shall be no confidential pathos. If you yourself are in that situation, reticent about a terrible thought, by all means tell it to another, but preferably in the form of confidential pathos. For if you should tell it as a pleasantry, it might be taken for one of the clever inventions of your close-mouthed reticence, and the result would be the worse for you. But in relation to the good the rule is the same. If you are genuinely serious about a purpose, say not a word about it to any man. But there is really no need of my saying this, no one is helped by its being said; for he who is truly resolved is automatically silent. It is not as though being resolved were one thing and being silent another; to be resolved means to be silent—as was he with whom this story deals.

He lived on year after year. He had intercourse only with himself and God and this picture—but he did not understand himself. Yet he did not lack willingness or *plerophoria* [full assurance, cf. 1 Thess. 1: 5], on the contrary, he felt an almost irresistible longing to become like the picture. Finally there awoke in his soul a doubt, a doubt wherein he did not understand himself—whether a *man* has a right to let himself be put to death for the truth. Over that doubt then he pondered early and late. His many thoughts are concisely comprehended in this little essay.

What an uncommon doubt! It is no wonder that the preface to this short essay is 'an adjuration to the reader to try to lay aside a part of his customary way of thinking; for otherwise the problem as it is here presented will be non-existent for him—and that strangely enough for the reason that he has already solved it long ago, but in an inverse sense'.

The next passage I quote is entitled 'The Quiet Despair'. I give it in the form of the journal entry of 1844.[1] It was changed somewhat when it was published the following year as one of the stories in Quidam's Diary in the *Stages*, under the date January 5, midnight. We have an opportunity here to see something of the mechanism of S. K.'s art. The tragedy of Dean Swift's old age had a previous history in the *Papers*. It was jotted down for the first time as an example of the irony of fate, among the notes for the book on *The Concept of Irony*, and a couple of years later it was repeated in a more artistic form in the Journal.[2] In 1843 it was published without change as one of the *Diapsalmata* in *Either/Or*. We could be certain that this story preoccupied S. K. because he was fearful of the same fate—even if he had not expressly connected it with his life in the following:

THE QUIET DESPAIR

A Narrative

The Englishman Swift founded a madhouse in his youth and became an inmate of it in his old age. It is related that here he often regarded himself in a mirror and exclaimed, 'Poor old man!'

There was a father and a son. Both intellectually gifted, both witty, especially the father. Every one that knew their home and visited it was sure to find it highly entertaining. Ordinarily they carried on their discussions only between themselves and entertained one another like two clever fellows, rather than like father and son. On a singular occasion when the father looked upon the son and saw that he was sorely troubled, he stood still in front of him and said, 'Poor child, you are living in a silent despair.' But he did not inquire more nearly. Alas! he could not, for he himself lived in a silent despair. For the rest, not another word was ever exchanged about the matter. But the father and the son were perhaps two of the most melancholy people that ever lived, so far as human memory extends.

Here originated that word—quiet despair. It was never used elsewhere, for in general people have a different idea of despair. As soon as the son merely uttered that word to himself, he burst into tears, partly because it was so unaccountably heartrending, partly because he recalled the emotion of his father's voice, since he, like all melancholy men, was laconic, but also possessed the emphasis of melancholy.

And the father believed that he was the cause of the son's melancholy, and the son believed that he was the cause of the father's melancholy, therefore they never spoke to one another [about it]. But this outburst of the father's was an outburst of his own melancholy, so that when he said this he was speaking more to himself than to the son.

Inasmuch as S. K.'s descriptions of his childhood date from later years, it may be that he projected back into this early period a darker melancholy than he actually experienced as a boy. But the attempt of Trols Lund to depict an idyllic childhood for S. K. is without any foundation, and the Journals abound in the gloomiest pictures. I need quote only a few of them, and that only in part.

Such a primitive melancholy, such a prodigious dowry of care, and that in the deepest sense tragical, to be brought up as a child by a melancholy old man—and at the same time with an innate talent for deceiving everybody as though I were sheer life and movement—and then that God has helped me so.[1]

Delicate, slender and weak, deprived of almost every condition requisite for holding my own with other boys, or even for passing as a complete man in comparison with others; melancholy, sick in soul, in many ways deeply unfortunate, one thing I had: an eminently shrewd wit, given me presumably in order that I might not be defenceless. Even as a boy I was aware of my power of wit and knew that it was my strength in conflict with far stronger comrades.[2]

From another entry, written in 1846,[3] under the heading, 'Thus have I understood myself in my whole literary activity', I can quote here appropriately only the first two paragraphs.

I am in the deepest sense an unfortunate individual, who from the earliest time has been nailed fast to one or another suffering, to the very verge of insanity, which may have its deepest ground in a discordance between my soul and my body; for (and just this is the remarkable thing, in conjunction with my infinite cheerfulness) this stands in no relation to my spirit, which anomalously, and perhaps because of the strain and stress between soul and body, has acquired a tensile strength which is rare.

An old man, who himself was prodigiously melancholy (just how, I will not record), has a son of his old age, upon whom all this melancholy falls as an inheritance—but who at the same time possesses sufficient elasticity of spirit to be able to hide this, while at the same time, and precisely because his spirit is essentially and eminently sound, his melancholy cannot acquire a mastery over him, though the spirit is completely unable to cast it off, can at the most succeed in bearing it.

'I was already an old man when I was born', says Kierkegaard in another place—and 'I leapt completely over childhood and youth.' But instead of heaping up more quotations of this sort, of which there are only too many available, I prefer to quote a long passage from *The Point of View.*[1]

For the sake of throwing additional light upon the part divine governance had in my authorship, it is necessary to explain, in so far as I have an explanation at my disposal, how it was that I became an author.

About my *vita ante acta* (from childhood until I became an author) I cannot give here any account in detail, however remarkable it seems to me that from my earliest childhood, and step by step throughout my whole development, I was predisposed to become precisely the sort of author I became. However, for the sake of what follows, I must draw the picture [of my childhood] with a few strokes, which I do with such reluctance as a person must always feel in giving an intimate personal account of himself.

From a child I was in the power of a prodigious melancholy, the depth of which finds its only true expression in the equally prodigious expertness granted me to hide this under an apparent cheerfulness and *joie de vivre*—my only joy almost as far back as I can remember was that no one could discover how unhappy I felt. And this proportionate relationship (the equally great magnitude of melancholy and dissimulation) indicated that I was necessarily thrown back upon myself and upon the God-relationship.—As a child I was strictly and austerely brought up in Christianity; humanly speaking, crazily brought up. Already in earliest childhood I broke down under the impression which the old man that laid it upon me himself sank under. A child crazily travestied as a melancholy old man. Terrible! What wonder then that there were times when Christianity appeared to me the most inhuman cruelty; although I never, even when I was farthest from it, lost my reverence for Christianity, being firmly resolved (especially in case I might not choose to become a Christian) that I would never initiate any one into the difficulties which I knew, and which I have never heard tell of nor read about. But never have I broken with Christianity or given it up; to attack it has never been my thought—no, from the time when there could be any thought of the employment of my powers, I had firmly resolved to employ them all in its defence, or at any rate to present it in its true form. For already at a very early age, with the help of my upbringing, I was in a position to ascertain how seldom Christianity is presented in its true form, how they who defend it most often betray it, and how seldom they who attack it really hit the mark—whereas, as I still think, they squarely hit established Christianity, which rather should be called a caricature of Christianity, or a prodigious quantum of misconception, illusion and such like, tempered with a sparing little dose of true Christianity.—So in a way I loved Christianity: it was venerable in my eyes—it had, to be sure, humanly speaking, made me exceedingly unhappy. That corresponds to my relationship with my father, the man whom I loved above all. And what does this mean? Why, the point is precisely that it was he that made one unhappy—but out of love. His fault did not lie in lack of love, but he mistook a child for an old man. To love him who makes one unhappy is for a reflective man an imperfect definition of love; to love him who malignantly made one unhappy would be virtue; but to love him who out of love, albeit with a misunderstanding, yet out of love, made one unhappy—that is reflection's formula for love, and even though it has hitherto never been stated, so far as I am aware, it is just the normal formula for love.

. . . . . .

So my father died. The powerful religious impressions of my childhood, in a softened and idealized form, acquired new influence over me. Now also I had become so much older that I fitted better to my upbringing, the misfortune of which consisted precisely in the fact that it turns out to be an advantage to me only when I am forty years old. For it was my misfortune almost from birth that I was not a man, and the tragedy was completed by my upbringing. When one is a child—and the other children play and make merry and whatever else they do; oh! and when one is a youth, and the others fall in love and dance, or whatever else they do—then, in spite of the fact that one is a child or a youth, to be spirit! Frightful torment! And all the more frightful if one understands the trick of making oneself seem as if one were the most youthful of all. But the misfortune is already less when one is forty years old, and in eternity it will not exist at all. I have possessed no immediacy, have therefore, in the ordinary human sense, never lived. I began straight away with reflection, not as though I had acquired in later years a little reflection, but I am sheer reflection from first to last. In the two ages of immediacy (childhood and youth) I was able, with the dexterity spirit always possesses, to help myself, was compelled to help myself, with some counterfeit of youthfulness; and without being yet clear in my own mind what the gift was that was granted me, I lived through the pain of not being like others. And of course at that period I would have given all to be able to be that, if only for a short time. A spirit can very well put up with not being like others. Indeed that is precisely spirit's negative determinant. But childhood and youth are related to another determinant, that of the species, the race; and just for this reason it is the greatest torment at that age not to be like the others—or, as in my case, to begin in a topsy-turvy fashion as spirit, which is a determinant some end with in every generation, but the most part never attain, existing as they do merely in the factors of a soul-and-body synthesis. But then in an entirely different sense I have my life before me. Nothing is more thoroughly strange to me and unknown than this pathetic yearning after childhood and youth. I thank my God that I am through with it, and every day I grow older I feel happier, and yet only truly blessed in the thought of eternity, for the temporal is not and never was the spirit's element, but rather in a certain sense its affliction.

An observer will notice here how all was set in motion, and how dialectically. I had a thorn in the flesh, talents of mind (especially imagination and dialectic) and education in abundance, an enormous development as an observer, a truly unusual Christian upbringing, an entirely peculiar relation to Christianity. From childhood I was trained to obedience, obedience absolute, armed with an almost foolhardy faith that I was able to accomplish anything, except one thing only, to be a free bird, if it were only for one whole day, or to slip out of the chains of melancholy in which another power held me bound. Finally I myself was a penitent. I had then the impression that there was another Power which from the very first moment had been observing this and said, as the fisherman says of the fish, Let him run, it is too soon yet to pull him up. And strangely enough there is something that goes very far back in my remembrance, without its being possible for me to say when it began or what in the world put it into my head, that I constantly, that is, every day, prayed to God that he would give me zeal and patience for the work he himself would point out to me.

So I became an author.

The danger of such an education as S.K. received from his father must be apparent to the reader. He himself was keenly aware of it, as we can see in many of his references to it. I quote only one passage from his Journal, written in 1850.[1]

The most dangerous situation for a child
with relation to the religious

The most dangerous case is not when the father is a freethinker, and not even when he is a hypocrite. No, the danger is when he is a pious and godfearing man, when the child is inwardly and deeply convinced of it, and yet in spite of all this observes that a deep unrest is deeply hidden in his soul, so that not even piety and the fear of God can bestow peace. The danger lies just here, that the child in this relationship is almost compelled to draw a conclusion about God, that after all God is not infinite Love.

The conclusion of the *Unscientific Postscript* is so much in place here as the expression of S. K.'s mature reflection about the religious upbringing of children that I cannot refrain from quoting it, in spite of the fact that this whole book is so soon to be published in English. Although the *Postscript* is ascribed to the humorous pseudonym Johannes Climacus, we can confidently regard this passage as S. K.'s judgement, for it happens that he remarks somewhere in the Journal, with regard to this passage expressly, 'Climacus was right.'[1]

Maybe there is one who, candidly understanding himself, might be obliged to confess to the wish that he had not been brought up in Christianity, and so would turn away from it to indifference. Better entire candour than half-measures. But let the confession be made without wrath, without defiance, with a quiet respect for the Power which perhaps, as he supposes, has deranged his whole life, for that Power which might have helped him aright, but did not help him. The case has occurred that a father, even the most loving and careful father, just at the moment when he wished to do the best for his child has done the worst, has done that worst which perhaps has deranged the child's whole life. Shall therefore the son drown filial piety in forgetfulness or indifference, or transform it to wrath when he is reminded of the relationship? Yes, let mean souls do that, such as love God and man only when all goes according to their liking, let them hate and defy ill-naturedly—a faithful son loves unchangeably, and he is unmistakably a mean man who can be separated in wrath and bitterness from him who did him harm, though he knows well that he did it with the intention of doing him good. So perhaps a strict Christian upbringing may have made life too hard for a man, without helping him again; in his heart he may perhaps cherish a wish like that of the inhabitants [the Gerasenes] who besought Christ to depart from their region, because he made them afraid. But a son whom a father rendered unhappy, if he is magnanimous, will continue to love the father. And when he is suffering under the consequences he may well say sometimes, with a disconsolate sigh, Would that this never had happened to me! but he will not surrender to despair, he will struggle against his suffering by struggling through it, and as he struggles his affliction will be mitigated; soon he will be more distressed for the father than for himself, he will forget his own pain in the deep sympathy of the thought how great an affliction this must be for the father, if he understood it—so he will labour, harder and harder, his salvation will be important to him for his own sake, but now almost more precious for the father's sake—so he will labour—perhaps it may succeed. And if it does succeed, he will be almost beside himself with joy and enthusiasm: for what father has ever done so much for his son! and what son owes so much to the father!

So likewise with Christianity. If it has rendered him unhappy, he does not therefore give it up; for it never occurs to him to think that Christianity could have come into the world to harm men, it remains always venerable to him. He does not give it up; and if he sighs disconsolately, Would that I never had been brought up in that teaching! he does not give it up. And his despondency becomes sympathetic sorrow at the thought that for Christianity it may be almost harder to have such a thing come to pass. But he does not give it up. In the end Christianity must make it up to him. 'In the end'—but that does not mean little by little; it is much less than that, and yet infinitely more. . . .

Just as little as Christianity came into the world in the childhood of the human race (for it came in the fullness of time), just so little is it appropriate in its decisive form to every age of life. There are periods of life which demand something which Christianity would simply ignore, something which at a certain age appears to a man to be the absolute, although the same man at a later period may perceive the vanity of it. To stuff a child with Christianity is a thing that cannot be done, for it holds good generally that everyone appropriates only what he has use for, and the child has no decisive use for Christianity. The same law invariably holds which is indicated by the advent of Christianity into the world subsequent to an antecedent stage: *No one begins by being a Christian, but becomes such in the fullness of time—if he does become such.* A strict upbringing in Christianity is a very risky undertaking; for Christianity makes men whose strength is in their weakness, but to force it upon a child with all its solemn earnestness is commonly the way to make a very unhappy youth. The rare exceptions are a stroke of luck.

The Christianity which is taught to a child (or rather which the child pieces together for itself when one employs no violence to force the little existence into decisive Christian definitions) is not, properly speaking, Christianity, but idyllic mythology. It is childhood's idea raised to the second power; and sometimes the normal relationship is inverted in such a way that it is rather the parents who learn from the child than the child from the parents, so that the child's loving misapprehension of Christian truth transfigures father and mother love into a piety which yet is anything but Christianity. It is not without example that persons who themselves have never been religiously moved, become so by means of the child. But that piety is not the religiousness which properly should belong to the elders, and it would be as reasonable for the mother to nourish herself with the milk which nature prepares for the child, as for the parents to find the decisive expression of their religiousness in the childish form of piety. Father and mother love attaches itself so closely to the child, embraces it so tenderly, that this very sentiment of piety discovers a truth which is likewise taught in the Scripture, that there must be a God who embraces little children. But if this feeling constitutes the whole of the parents' religiousness, they are, properly speaking, without religion and merely enjoy the refreshment of a tender feeling of sympathy with child-life and all that this means. Charming and lovable is the piety of the parents, and so too the child's docility and its promptness to understand this bliss; but, properly speaking, it is not Christianity, it is Christianity in the medium of imaginative intuition, it is a Christianity from which the *tremendum* has been withdrawn—one gently leads the *innocent* child to God and Christ. But the very point of Christianity is that it is a sinner who takes refuge in the Paradox. It is very touching and pretty when older people, as is not uucommon, experience a feeling of their own guilt at the sight of a child and tenderly conceive of the child's innocence; but this sentiment is not decisively Christian. For the sentimental appreciation of the child's innocence forgets that Christianity recognizes nothing of the sort in the fallen race, and that qualitative dialectic defines the consciousness of sin more narrowly than we know it in the generic concepts of guilt and innocence. The strict Christian conception of the child as a sinner cannot attribute any advantage to the age of childhood, for the child, having no consciousness of sin, is simply a sinner without sin-consciousness.

[Three paragraphs deal with the sentimental interpretation of Jesus' sayings about little children (Mt. 18: 2; 19: 13, 14) which amounts to 'a satire upon Christianity'.]

The childlike Christianity which is lovable in the little child is in the case of the elders a childish orthodoxy, which finds its blessedness in the fantastic and inserts in it the name of Christ. Such an orthodoxy brings everything to confusion. If it notices that the definitions of faith begin to fall in price, that all wish 'to go farther' and leave faith for dull minds, it realizes that something must be done to boost the price. What happens? Faith becomes something quite extraordinary and rare, not 'everybody's affair'—in short it becomes a distinction of those who have a genius for it ['the religiously minded']. If that is the case, Christianity is totally revoked by this one definition—and that by exponents of orthodoxy! It is quite right for the orthodox to wish to screw up the price, but the value-judgement which posits a difference between one man and another brings everything to confusion, for according to this Christianity is obviously not difficult for the religious genius, and it is impossible for others. Faith is rightly accounted the most difficult thing of all—but with a qualitative dialectic: that is to say, it is equally difficult for all. And it is the ethical qualification of faith which is of help here, forbidding the one believer to be curious and comparative, prohibiting all comparison between man and man, and so making it equally difficult for all.

Such a childish orthodoxy has also emphatically directed attention to the fact that Christ at his birth was wrapped in swaddling clothes and laid in a manger, that is to say, to the humiliating consideration that he came in the lowly form of a servant; and it supposes that this is the Paradox, in contrast to coming in glory. Confusion. The Paradox lies principally in the fact that God, the Eternal, has come into existence in time as an individual man. Whether this individual man be a servant or an emperor is neither here nor there; to be an emperor is no more adequate to God than to be a beggar. One recognizes the childishness of this at once; for just because the child has no developed or positive conception of God (but only imaginative inwardness), he cannot become observant of the absolute paradox, but has a touching understanding of the humorous—that the mightiest of all, the Almighty (here without any decisive definition in thought, and therefore only romantically distinguished from what is on the same plane with it, namely, king and emperor)—that the Almighty should be laid in a manger and born in a stable.... So in the last resort Christianity is humour. Humour diverts attention a little from the prime qualification, God, and then accentuates the fact that the greatest, the mightiest, he who is greater than all kings and emperors, became the poorest. . . . If one would speak about God, let him say, God. That is the quality. If the parson would say eternity, let him say, eternity—but sometimes when he wants to make it seem important he says, To all generations of the age of the ages world without end. But if Christianity is humour, everything is brought to confusion. It ends with my being the best of Christians, for regarded as a humorist I [i.e. Johannes Climacus] am not so bad, yet I am bad enough to perceive the humour in all this, contrasting it with what it means to be a Christian, which I am not. . . .

So when one hears an orthodox person talking continually about childlike faith and the wisdom of children and the woman's heart, &c., he has reason to suspect that this is a humorous character who has mixed up Christianity with childishness. I however, as a humorist, protest that I have no fellowship with him, for his emphasis is false. . . . So much is certain, that if it is a little child that must determine what Christianity is, there will be nothing fearful about it, it will lack that factor which was to the Jews a stumbling-block and to the Greeks foolishness.

When a child is told about Christianity, and the child is not abused, figuratively speaking, by violence, he will appropriate all the gentle, the lovable, the heavenly traits; he lives with the little Child Jesus, and with the Three Wise Men, and with the angels, he sees stars in the dark night, he accomplishes the long journey, now he finds himself in the stable—one surprise after another! He is always seeing the heavens open. With the whole warmth of his imagination he longs for these pictures —but now let us not forget the sweet-meats and all the other splendid things that come in this connexion. The religiousness of childhood is the universal abstract and yet warmly imaginative foundation for all later religiousness.

. . . . . .

The age of childhood is therefore not the true time to become a Christian, but on the contrary the older age, the age of maturity, is the right time when it must be decided whether a man will or will not. . . .

If the child is not allowed, as he should be, to play innocently with holy things, if his existence is sternly forced into the decisive Christian concepts, such a child will have to suffer much. Such an upbringing will either, by inhibiting immediacy, result in despondency and anguished dread, or else incite the lusts of pleasure and the anguish of lust in a measure which even paganism did not know.

Again we have been carried far beyond the period of S. K.'s childhood. He said truly that there was a rare continuity in his life. It is that which carries us on irresistibly. S. K. was so closely knit to his father in childhood that this chapter might have been entitled 'Father and Son'. But in fact the relationship became even closer after a bitter breach and a subsequent reconciliation. S. K. himself recognized that his father's influence over him was greater after his death than in his lifetime. This title, therefore, would be appropriate for the whole book. In this connexion I cannot but think of the book entitled *Father and Son* in which Edmund Gosse incidentally pilloried his parent for the too narrow and severe religious discipline he had been subjected to. The classical instance in English literature of such a mistaken education in religion as that to which S. K. was subjected is the case of J. S. Mill, who was hardened by it against Christianity but did not show disloyalty to his father. S. K. also experienced a period of rebellion against Christianity, but this was transcended, and thenceforth his loyalty to his father was constant and profound.

Having heard what S. K. has to tell about himself, it is interesting to turn to the first edition of the *Papers*[1] where Barfod has taken pains to collect the opinions which S. K.'s surviving teachers and comrades in school were willing to communicate to him. Unfortunately they are not very illuminating. It appears that S. K. was justified in boasting of his ability to deceive people into regarding him as 'the most light-minded of all'. At the age of eight he entered the grammar school which was grandiloquently named the School of Civic Virtue and which at that time had as its rector an estimable man by the name of Michael Nielsen. It was the rector's duty to write a report of each student as he went up to the university. He says of S. K., in the course of his letter, 'He has a good intelligence, open for everything that promises unusual interest, but for a long time he was childish in a high degree and totally lacking in seriousness.' The rector speaks also of 'a desire for freedom and independence, which also shows itself in his conduct by a good-natured, sometimes comical sauciness'. A Latin testimonial accompanied this letter, and in it S. K. is described as *juvenem carum atque jocundum*. Nine years later the same rector wrote a letter recommending S. K. to the Pastoral Seminary:

> The theological candidate, S. Aabye Kierkegaard, distinguished himself as a pupil in this School of Civic Virtue by his industry and intelligence and by his intellectual grasp of the subjects of study in general and of the form and spirit of language in particular. . . . So far as I am competent to express an opinion, he has a far from common mastery of the Latin language, both in its written and in its spoken use. . . .'

It is to be noted that when this was written S. K. had been for some years a teacher of Latin in that school.

The reports of his school-mates would be more valuable if they were not rather contradictory. I will quote only from two of them. Welding, then Dean of Viborg, wrote:

> . . . For the rest of us who led a genuinely boyish life, S. K. was a stranger and an object of compassion, especially on account of his dress, always the same, made of a rough cloth of a dark mixed colour, of a peculiar cut, coat with short skirts [i.e. the other boys had no 'skirts'], always with low shoes and woollen stockings, never boots. This procured him the nickname of Choir-boy. This name was used alternately with Søren Sock—an allusion to his father's earlier business as

> hosier. S. K. was regarded by us all as one whose home was wrapped in a mysterious half-darkness of severity and oddness. . . . Prof. Mathiessen (teacher of German) was an exceedingly weak man who never had any authority over us. Once when the horseplay in his class had gone vary far—it was quite wild in all his hours—when they had made a complete meal, with butter-bread, sandwiches and beer, and had toasted one another with formal *Prosits!* Prof. Mathiessen was about to go out and report the affair to Prof. Nielsen. The rest of us surrounded Mathiessen with prayers and fair promises, but S. K. said only, 'Will you tell the Professor (i.e. Nielsen) that this is what always goes on in your hour?'—whereupon Mathiessen sat down and made no report.

Pastor Anger, recalling proudly that he himself had always stood number one in the class, excluded the possibility that S. K. had ever stood higher than number two. In fact he always was number two or number three, and we may recall that his father had not required more of him. All the writers agree that his fondness for teasing and his rare ability to make an opponent ridiculous cost him many a bloody nose—especially as he was inclined to select the bigger boys as his victims. It is evident that he was 'polemical through and through', as he confessed of himself at a later time. One who knew him as a child affirms that he was 'a regular little wild-cat'. 'In spite of these single combats', says Anger, 'it was always a question which of us two was the weakest in the class and the poorest at gymnastics.'

An account of S. K.'s childhood 'in his own words' cannot properly conclude without mention of the motto he selected deliberately to describe it when he was still a young man and his childhood was not seen in remote perspective. On September 9, 1839, he wrote in his Journal:[1]

> As a motto for my life in childhood I know nothing better than the word in Goethe's *Faust*,
>
> '*Halb Kinderspiel,*
> *Halb Gott im Herzen.*'
> (Half child-play,
> Half God in the heart.)

If this were a casual thought, like many jottings in the Journal which have no great significance for the understanding of his life, we should not stop to puzzle out the meaning of these lines as applied to the childhood of Kierkegaard. But, however casual this thought may have been in the first instance, it commended itself to him upon mature reflection as the most appropriate motto for the years of his childhood, and so it appears again in a document which is important above all others for the deeper understanding of his youth—if only it were not so difficult of interpretation! The difficulty is due in part to the fact that this document no longer exists. After it had been printed in the first edition of Kierkegaard's *Papers*,[1] Barfod lost it, and by this piece of carelessness (not to speak of other losses less serious) the worthy man branded himself as an unworthy editor. He tells us that the six passages in question were 'written on three sheets of fine letter-paper, small octavo gilt-edged'. But as he printed them, and as they are still printed in the last edition of the *Journals*, they are not divided into three approximately equal parts, as we should expect them to be upon the three gilt-edged sheets, but into two very unequal parts, the first three items being poems, each of which is attributed by its title to one of the three ages—'Childhood', 'Youth', and '25 Years of Age'—whereas the three longer prose pieces which follow bear no indication of the ages to which they may be supposed to relate. So this document, as it is now printed, seems to be composed with no more art than the consecutive jottings in the journal which precede and follow it. Yet it is evident that here Kierkegaard was reviewing his whole life up to date. That is not the sort of thing he was likely to do without seeking an artistic expression; and a gesture so solemn and so rare as the selection of three sheets of gilt-edged paper seems to justify the expectation that he would display in a document so elegantly adorned more than his usual art. It is evident now that the external form would be perfect if each sheet was provided with a headline indicating one of the three ages, and under this were placed, first the appropriate poem, and then one of the prose pieces. When we make this hypothetical restoration of the original, taking the prose pieces in the order in which they now stand, we find that it is happily confirmed by internal evidence and becomes exceedingly illuminating. I do not say that the correspondence is at once evident, but the more deeply the document is studied the clearer it becomes. This was not written by S. K. to explain himself to the world, but to explain himself to himself, and before we can decipher it we need to have already almost as much knowledge of him as he had self-knowledge. Nevertheless it is to this document principally that I owe my conception of the story of his youth. This interpretation is due to Professor Hirsch, and it revolutionizes our conception of S. K.'s youth. I must make this acknowledgement here, notwithstanding that the use I make of it is more evident in later sections (see pp. 68 ff. and 185 ff.), and that here we have need only to consider the significance of the two lines from Goethe; because the first prose piece, about 'the great earthquake, the frightful overturning', does not strictly fall within the period of childhood, but is the limit of it, the dreadful experience which brought that period definitely to an end.

'Half child-play'—here we have emphatic evidence that little Søren, different as he was from other boys, knew what it was to play. After all, the rector of the School of Civic Virtue was right in a way when in this favourite pupil he detected 'childishness'—and perhaps, though it surprises us, he was not wrong in reporting that he was 'childish in an extreme degree'. For it has always seemed to me that there was a childlike quality in S. K., even in his maturity, and even up to the end. This is the trait that most endears him to me. He was always humorous, often whimsical, and, in strangest contrast to the grimness of his life and the sternness of his purpose, he was as sensitive as a child and as tender. As a child he was accustomed to play with thoughts, and he continued to play with them even in his serious books—to the scandal of many a serious reader. It has been suggested that this trait, inasmuch as it evidently did not come from the father's side, must have been inherited from the mother, that 'nice little woman with an even and cheerful disposition', of whom we hear so little, and whose moral influence upon her son was so slight. Bearing these considerations in mind, we may perhaps hazard the guess that the extraordinary power S. K. had of deceiving people by making them believe that he was the merriest of all, can be explained very simply by the fact that there was indeed a merry S. K. as well as the melancholy one, but that this 'childish' S. K. was for the most part suppressed, even in childhood.

'Half God in the heart'—we have already seen how large a part religion had in this boy's life, and, however inappropriate this instruction was for a tender age, we have seen that it meant indeed 'God in the heart'. But it was this that suppressed the child in him. S. K. when he came of age clearly divined the factor which had so deeply troubled his life and was to trouble it for a long time to come. His interpretation of the motto for his childhood fits the case exactly, but it is terribly tragic.

Half child-play,
Half God in the heart.

Half/Half is to be understood here in a disjunctive sense—as the most violent disjunction. His life as a child was not a whole, it was rudely sundered in two parts. Because religion was not integrated with child-life—or, to use his own expression, because this child was not 'permitted to play with holy things'—his was a divided personality in childhood, and the reintegration, the unity of mind which 'wills one thing', after which he ardently struggled, he did not attain until the end.

KIERKEGAARD AS A UNIVERSITY STUDENT

By JACOBSEN

PART TWO

YOUTH

1830–1838

And yet, to me, what is this quintessence of dust? Man delights me not: no, nor woman neither.

HAMLET.

I. ENTERING THE UNIVERSITY

1830

So I started out in life, favoured in every way with respect to intellectual gifts and outward circumstances; everything had been done and continued to be done to develop my intellect as richly as possible. Self-confident (yet with a decided sympathy and predilection for suffering and for what suffered in any way or was afflicted)—I can say in a certain sense that I started out in life with an almost foolhardy self-sufficiency; I have never for a single instant in my life been deserted by the faith that one can what one will—only one thing not, but all else absolutely—but that one thing not, not cast off the melancholy in whose power I was. (I know that to others this will seem a vain conceit; but for me it has in truth been so, as truly as the next, which again will seem to others a conceit.) It never at any time occurred to me that there lived a man who was my superior, or that in my time such a man might be born—for myself in my hidden parts I was the most miserable of all. It never for a moment occurred to me that I should not be victorious, even were I to attempt the most foolhardy thing—only in one thing not, but in everything else absolutely—but in that one thing not, not casting off the melancholy from the suffering of which I was scarcely free for one whole day. This, however, must be understood in the light of the fact that I was very early initiated into the thought that victory meant to conquer in terms of the infinite, which in terms of the finite means to suffer. So this again was in conformity with my melancholy understanding in my inward self that (in terms of the finite) I was good for nothing.—What reconciled me to my fate and to my suffering was that I (alas, so unfortunate a man, so agonizingly imprisoned) had acquired this limitless freedom of being able to deceive, so that I had leave to be absolutely alone with my pain. It will be plain that in spite of all my other capacities there was enough here to make me anything but merry.—When this is given (such a pain and such a reticence), it depends upon the distinctive difference of the individual in which direction he will swing, whether this lonely inward torment will daimoniacally find its expression and its satisfaction in hating men and cursing God, or in precisely the opposite direction.[1]

This passage deserves to be pondered at this point where we begin the difficult task of studying S. K.'s youth, which according to his own reckoning was almost exactly conterminous with the ten years he spent at the university. This passage, which we find in that unique confession which he called 'The Point of View for my Work as an Author', was written in 1848 and represents his mature reflection upon his youth—so deeply pondered that it is hard to read. When he says, 'So I started out in life', he was not thinking exclusively, and perhaps not even particularly, of the day when he entered the university, yet this was certainly the first and the most decisive step out of the home and into the world. Youth is not apt to think of the university as a place of cloistered retreat from the world (as the man sees it when he looks back upon it); he is not seeking sanctuary there from a rough world he has not yet known, but rather he is fleeing from the sanctuary of the home and the school, from all the restraints of childhood, to the glorious liberty of youth—or of manhood, as at that time he would prefer to say. On the continent of Europe the liberty of the students is even greater than in residential colleges. The young Kierkegaard, owing to the extreme severity of his home, must have been elated more than others by this sudden emancipation.

When he was something over seventeen years old, on October 30, 1830, S. K. matriculated in the University of Copenhagen after passing his examinations *cum laude*. For Greek, history, French, and an essay in the mother tongue (which his class-mate Anger boasts he had written for him!) he received the qualification *magna cum laude*, or, as they said in Copenhagen, using a more classical phrase, *laud. p. c.* (*laudibilis prae caeteris*). He chose the faculty of theology—doubtless in conformity with his father's wish, but presumably not unwillingly at that moment. His elder brother Peter had already passed his theological examination at Copenhagen and was studying for the degree of doctor of philosophy in Germany. It was to be expected of the sons of such a father that they would seek to enter the Christian ministry. Though Denmark is a small country, it could afford to have one great city and one great university because it was not ambitious to have more.

Copenhagen was then, as it is now, not only the political capital, but the centre of trade and industry and the focus of culture. In later years S. K. was accustomed to speak of it disparagingly as a 'market town' (playing on the name Kjøbenhavn = market harbour), and he accounted it his misfortune as an author that he lived in a place so small and provincial. Certain it is that his genius would have been more promptly recognized and his influence upon the world would have been greater if he had written in any one of the well-known languages of Europe. Yet for a student Copenhagen was not a small place. Of music and art and literature and learning there was enough for him, and the works of German poets, philosophers, and theologians were perfectly accessible.

The 'Second Examination', as it was then called in Copenhagen, must have exacted from the students a certain amount of study during the first year. Young Kierkegaard took the first part of this examination on April 25, 1831, and the second part on October 27 of the same year. He got *laud.* in Latin, Greek, Hebrew, and history; *laud. p. c.* in philosophy, physics, and mathematics. The minimum requirement of liberal study was thus disposed of, and the young man became a 'candidate in theology'. We shall see, however, that for the next seven years he studied but little theology, and a great deal of history, literature, and philosophy. After the Second Examination a student was completely free; he was under no compulsion to attend lectures, and he could postpone his examination until he was inclined to apply for it. So, for reasons which we shall apprehend later, S. K. became 'a student in perpetuity', as he expressed it; and it was not until he had been for ten years at the university that he finally took the examination in theology. To make that decision possible many things had to happen to this 'candidate in theology': several years of dissipation, his lowest fall, his repentance, his conversion, and his father's death.

II. THE GREAT EARTHQUAKE

1830–1

But before we go on to describe the life of a *studiosus in perpetuum* we must stop to reflect upon the factors which determined such a life. For in fact no more than four years had to be passed in the university before taking the theological examination. Peter Kierkegaard had taken it in three and a half years, and while Søren was still a 'candidate' his brother returned from Germany as a doctor of philosophy to teach in the university of Copenhagen. We can imagine the father's dismay at Søren's reluctance to study theology, and the indignation he must have felt when it became evident that this dissolute son had no serious intention of taking his examination and was hardly likely to become a parson. The situation which developed then was different, at least quantitatively different, from the ordinary tension between father and son; the exceeding closeness of Søren's relationship to his father in childhood must have accentuated the distance which grew up between them and stamped it with the character of revolt. We must sympathize with the father—but also with Søren, to whom this tension was all the more painful because Peter played the part of the 'elder brother' in the parable. That the prodigal son was not callous we see clearly from a touching entry in his Journal during the spring of 1837:[1]

> I will turn away from them who are only lurking to spy out if one has done amiss in one way or another—to Him who has more pleasure over one sinner that repenteth than over the ninety-nine wise ones who need no repentance.

What brought things to such a pass? S. K. lets us know—without meaning to tell us. Here we must recall the important document, 'written on three sheets of gilt-edged letter-paper', which was sufficiently described (and reconstructed) on p. 58 f. Here we have to do with the prose piece which matches the two lines descriptive of childhood and tells how that innocent period was brought to an abrupt end by the knowledge of good and evil. Here I translate that piece:[2]

> Then it was that the great earthquake occurred, the frightful

upheaval which suddenly forced upon me a new infallible rule for interpreting all phenomena. Then I surmised that my father's great age was not a divine blessing, but rather a curse; that the distinguished talents of our family existed only to create mutual friction; then I felt the silence of death increasing about me, when in my father I beheld an unfortunate who must outlive us all, a sepulchral cross upon the grave of all his own hopes. Guilt must rest upon the whole family, a punishment of God must be impending over it; it must disappear, be stricken out by God's mighty hand, be wiped out as an unsuccessful experiment. And only now and then did I find a little relief in the thought that my father had accepted the heavy duty of consoling us with the comfort of religion, preparing us all so that a better world would be open to us if we should lose all in this, even if that punishment should fall upon us which the Jews devoutly wished for their foes—that our remembrance should be cut off from the earth and our name blotted out.

This was in the strictest sense a private document and was probably written in 1839, after his reconciliation with his father, and about a year after the father's death. Six years later S. K. recounted the same experience in a still more symbolical form but in a public document, *Stages on Life's Road*, which was published in 1845. It was characteristic of S. K.'s public confessions that they were made in such a form that they could not be understood by his contemporaries. The passage I call attention to now is entitled 'Solomon's Dream'. It occurs in Quidam's Diary, a document which recounts with such realism his own unhappy love that he even inserts in it the letter he wrote to Regina in sending back the ring. The entries in this diary are dated either 'Morning' or 'Midnight'; the former being happy memories of the bliss of a year ago, and the latter tragic reflections upon his present state. Among the midnight entries we stumble upon six narratives, each bearing a striking title: 'Quiet Despair' [see p. 45 f.]; 'The Leper's Soliloquy'; 'Solomon's Dream'; 'A Possibility'; 'To be Learnt by Heart—Periander'; and 'Nebuchadnezzar'. They have evidently nothing to do with Quidam's love affair, and none of S. K.'s contemporaries could imagine that they had anything to do with his own history. That 'Solomon's Dream' is autobiography probably no one would ever have guessed if a brief entry made on the Jutland journey had not been shown to the old bishop Peter Christian Kierkegaard and he had not betrayed the family secret which Søren was scrupulous to keep—'This is our father's history and ours too!' (cf. p. 22). In 1843 S. K. wrote in his journal:[1]

> After my death no one shall find in my papers (that is my comfort) a solitary ray of enlightenment about what has really occupied my whole life—find the writing in my inward parts which explains all and which for me often lends prodigious importance to events which others would call bagatelles and which I should regard as insignificant were I to eliminate the secret note which explains them.

This passage is, of course, provocative to investigators, and many have sought to discover S. K.'s inviolable secret. Brandt is too easily satisfied by the notion that it was his melancholy—which in fact he only too often refers to in his Journals. A much more difficult riddle is 'the thorn in the flesh', about which S. K. speaks often in later life but does not especially associate with his youth. That may be his own guilt. But I am confident that the secret he refers to in the above entry is the guilt of his father and his own sense of solidarity with it. Filial piety prescribed that this should not be revealed, and S. K. could reasonably console himself with the thought that in his books and papers there was nothing that might reveal it. In fact nobody guessed this secret during his lifetime, and all that we know now is the child's defiance of God and a single instance of the man's incontinence. It is not impossible that there may have been more to this secret: it is possible that there was repeated incontinence, and it is certain that the father struggled grimly with a disposition to sensuality which sharpened his moral discipline over his own children, with consequences disastrous to Søren, as we shall see later. Here is the account of[2]

SOLOMON'S DREAM

> The Judgement of Solomon is already well known, which by discriminating truth from deceit made the judge famous as a wise prince. His Dream is not so well known.
>
> Affection knows no greater torture than that a man must be ashamed of his father, of him whom he loves above all and to

whom he owes most, that he must approach him backward with averted face so as not to look upon his shame. But how great is the blessedness of affection when one can love as a son would wish to do and can enjoy the happiness of being proud of the father, because he is the singularly elect, the singularly distinguished man, the people's strength, the nation's pride, the friend of God, the hope of the future, praised in his lifetime, revered in memory! Happy Solomon! Such was thy lot. Of the elect race (how splendid merely to belong to this!) he was the King's son (enviable lot), son of that king who among kings was the elect!

So Solomon lived happily with the prophet Nathan. His father's strength and his father's exploits did not inspire him to emulation, for there was no opportunity left for that [when all was so well established], but it inspired him to admiration, and admiration made him a poet. But if the poet was almost jealous of his hero, the son was blessed in his devotion to the father.

Then on a time the son made a visit to his royal father. During the night he was awakened by hearing movements where his father slept. Terror seized him; he feared it was a villain who would murder David. He creeps nearer—he sees David in heartfelt contrition, he hears the despairing cry of his remorseful soul.

Faint with trembling he seeks again his couch; he falls asleep, but he does not rest; he dreams, he dreams that David is a sinner rejected of God, that the royal majesty is God's wrath against him, that he must wear the purple as a punishment, that he is condemned to rule, condemned to hear the people's benedictions, while the Lord's righteousness holds suspended over the guilty one a hidden and secret doom; and the dream surmises that God is not the God of the pious but of the ungodly, and that one must be an ungodly man to become God's elect, and the horror of the dream is this contradiction.

While David lay upon the ground with a contrite (bruised) heart, Solomon arose from his couch, but his understanding was bruised. Horror seized him when he thought what it is to be God's elect. He surmised that holy intimacy with God, a pure uprightness before the Lord, was not the explanation, but that a mysterious guilt was the secret which explained all.

And Solomon became wise, but he did not become a hero; and he became a thinker, but he did not become a man of prayer; and he became a preacher, but he did not become a believer; and he could help many, but he could not help himself; and he became sensual, but not repentant; and he became contrite, but not upright in posture, for his strength of will was broken by what was beyond youth's strength to endure. And he staggered through life, staggered by life, strong, supernaturally strong, that is womanly weak in the stirring delusions of imagination and marvellous inventions, ingenious in the explication of thought. But there was a rift in his nature, and Solomon was like the paralytic who is unable to support his own body. In his harem he sat like an infirm old man, until passion awaked and he cried out, 'Strike the tambourines, dance before me, ye women!' But when the queen of the East [*sic*] came to visit him, attracted by his wisdom, then his soul was rich, and wise answers flowed from his lips like the precious myrrh which drips from the trees in Arabia.

It is to be understood that the 'great earthquake', inasmuch as it put an end to the period of childhood, cannot be dated later than the beginning of his university career, and of course 'Solomon's Dream' goes along with it. In both accounts such words as 'surmise' and 'presentiment' occur, and it may well be that the child had early begun to question whether all was right with his venerable father; but earthquakes and dreams have at least a definite date, and the word 'sudden' occurs, so that there must have been a decisive moment of revelation which gave body to suspicion, although doubtless it still left room for surmise. It is not necessary to explain these parables here, but we shall see as we go on how closely they apply to S. K. and his relationship to his father. The situation of Solomon was further illuminated by an entry in S. K.'s journal during the course of the year 1843:[1]

I must yet again occupy myself with my 'Antigone'. The task will be to develop and explain the presentiment of guilt.—It was with this in view that I reflected upon Solomon and David, Solomon's youthful relationship to David; for it is perfectly certain that both Solomon's intelligence (the paramount note in him) and his sensuality were consequences of the greatness in David. He has early come to suspect the prodigious perturbation in David, he did not know what guilt might weigh upon him, yet saw this profoundly godfearing man give his penitence so ethical an expression—for it would have been another matter if David had been a mystic. These apprehensions, these presentiments, stifle the energetic qualities (except in the form of imagination) and awaken the intellectual qualities, and this combination of the imaginative and the intellectual, where the factor of will is lacking, is properly what constitutes the sensual.

This last phrase is very characteristic of S. K. and profoundly self-revealing. It appears that with all his acumen as a psychologist he had failed to discover the deep psychological truth enunciated by Baudouin as interpreter of Émil Coué, that 'when the imagination and the will are at strife, the imagination always wins'. Yet he recognized in his father 'a man of prodigious will' along with 'an almighty imagination', and the will did not save him from sensuality. It is very plain that S. K.'s sensuality represented a triumph of imagination over will. So much was it a product of imagination that it had almost no corporeal quality. For he says of himself that he had no immediacy, never 'enjoyed', except indirectly through reflection.

But I must hasten on to speak of his interpretation of 'Antigone' to which he refers in the entry just quoted. For in this he discovered a third way of expressing his relationship to his father without betraying his secret, though he incorporated it in a public document, the third section of the first volume of *Either/Or*, that is, the discussion of the relation between the classical and the modern idea of tragedy. I quote only the part which more especially concerns us here.[1] And before I quote this passage I must remark upon a word which we encounter here for the first time and which we shall frequently have to deal with in the sequel. The word is *Angst* (*Angest* is the older way of spelling it, which S. K. uses) and it has precisely the same significance as the same German word, but we have no precise equivalent for it in English. I use the word 'dread', although I know that it does not adequately translate it. 'Anguish' would not be too strong (Unamuno has used the words *agonia* and *angustia* in Spanish, and *agonie* in the one book he wrote in French)[2] but it fails to indicate the uncanny apprehension of some evil impending, something not purely present but to come, which is proper to the word *Angest.* From time to time I shall say 'anguished dread' to call attention to the fact that the mere word 'dread' is not strong enough to carry the sense of impending tragedy which the original word implies. In one place S. K. says of *Angest*, 'What is it? It is the day to come.'[1]

And now for the story of Antigone:

> So the race of Labdakos is the object of the fury of the angry gods, Oedipos has killed the Sphinx, liberated Thebes, murdered his father, married his mother, and Antigone is the fruit of this marriage. So it is in the Greek tragedy. Here I diverge. In my version everything remains the same and yet all is different. Oedipos has killed the Sphinx and liberated Thebes, so much is known to all, and Oedipos lives honoured and admired, happy in his love for Jocasta. The rest is hidden from men's eyes and no suspicion has ever recalled that horrible dream to reality. Only Antigone knows it. How she came to know it lies outside the tragic interest, and every one is free in that respect to make his own surmise. At an early age, when she was not yet fully developed, dark hints of that horrible secret had at moments gripped her soul, until at last certainty with one blow cast her into the arms of anguished dread.

The rest of the story of Antigone, as S. K. reconstructs it in conformity with the modern ideal of the tragic, I must abbreviate, He supposes that after a time Oedipos dies and his memory is held in singular honour. Antigone then feels more solemnly bound than ever to keep secret the crime which would damn her father's memory if it were to become known. The most serious collision occurs when she falls in love with a man who is also deeply in love with her and who, aware of her love for him, cannot understand why she persists in holding aloof. Here S. K., in a book which was written especially for Regina, explains his own case, and yet disguises it by assigning to a woman the role which he had played. He stresses the fact that Antigone cannot divulge the secret which would bring shame upon her father's memory, and that therefore she cannot marry, for she will not enter into a marriage which is not perfectly open-hearted. The grim secret is her undoing.

S. K. found still another way of speaking about his relationship to his father without revealing the application of the story to himself. This is the fifth narrative inserted in Quidam's Diary, dated May 5, midnight: the story of guilty Periander and his son. It is entitled emphatically 'A Lesson to be Learnt by Heart'.[1] But that story I cannot abbreviate, and it is high time to return to the gilt-edged document we have accepted as a guide. The second sheet (as I have reconstructed it) is what interests us here.

YOUTH

Begging—that's not for us!
Youth hews its own way thus—
Violently seizing the prize.
CHR. WINTHER.

Rent asunder as I was in my inward man, without any prospect of leading a happy life ('that it might go well with me and that I might live long in the land'), without any hope of a happy and snug future—such as naturally issues from and consists in the historical continuity of domestic family life—what wonder then that in disconsolate despair I grasped at the intellectual side of man's nature singly and alone, clinging fast to that, so that the thought of my not inconsiderable mental ability was my only comfort, ideas my only joy, man indifferent to me?

From this record we could learn little if we were not able to read it, as we now do, in its context. The Danish poet when he wrote, 'Begging—that's not for us!' doubtless wished to express the normal independence of youth. But when S. K. chose this as an appropriate motto for his youth he was looking back, not upon a noble spirit of independence which is proper to youth and which he especially sought to inculcate in men (the category of 'the individual', see p. 445), but upon a fierce revolt against all authority, which was first of all rebellion against his father and consequently against his father's God, ending naturally enough with 'indifference to man.' He had already begun to recognize that his attitude was one of defiance—ultimately, defiance against God—and that thus he had repeated in his youth the same sin his father had been guilty of in his childhood. S. K. was peculiarly fitted to enter into sympathy with the classical conception of tragedy because he had a strong sense of the solidarity of the family, of the clan, and of the whole human race. Hence his preoccupation with the dogma of original sin, and hence his readiness to conceive that 'the fathers have eaten sour grapes, and the children's teeth are set on edge', and to give credence to his father's doleful conviction that all his children must die before him, innocently involved in the punishment of his guilt. 'Rent asunder as I was' evidently refers to the experience of the 'great earthquake'. At this point it was not penitence which precluded the 'prospect of a happy life', marriage and a normal human existence, but it was the fate which involved him in his father's guilt. It was too early for him to take refuge in repentance, for he was still innocent; 'the comfort in the thought of original sin' he could discover only after he had become a sinner; and he was still far from perceiving 'the edification of the thought that as against God we are always in the wrong'—the title of the sermon with which *Either/Or* concludes. In the document now before us he reveals the fact that the extravagant self-confidence with which he started out in life was founded upon despair. Upon maturer reflection he understood even more clearly that his youth was defiance and despair. Despair is one of S. K.'s most prominent themes, and his reflections upon it, though sometimes paradoxical, are always illuminating. It is prominent in the Second Part of *Either/Or*, where S. K. through the mouth of Judge William registers his conviction that the 'aesthetical' life inevitably ends in despair—indeed that despair, open or disguised, conscious or unconscious, is the constant characteristic of such a life. Therefore it is plain to him that any honest account of it indicates bankruptcy. Therefore Judge William counsels his young aesthetical friend to 'choose to despair' as the first honest step towards the ethical life. But despair is also the theme of *The Sickness unto Death*, published in 1849, and there it is brought into relation with the religious life.

III. *STUDIOSUS IN PERPETUUM*

1830–6

WE have seen how vividly S. K. describes the period of his childhood. At first sight it seems as if he tells us next to nothing about his life at the university. For his journals, which later grew to such stupendous size, leave us here in the lurch. They do not begin until 1834, and until June of the following year, when his mind was stirred by a walking-tour in north Seeland, they contain hardly any entries that are self-revealing. From that date they begin to reveal his mind to us, but until the spring of 1838 they are valuable chiefly as an indication of his historical and literary interests—and negatively as a proof of his lack of interest in theology. The archives of the university furnish no evidence that he was diligent in attending lectures, though we gather from his note-books that he elected to hear a few which he thought were worth while. The items classified as 'Theology' by the editors of his *Papers* occupy 21 pages, as contrasted with 98 pages of 'Aesthetics', for his first six years at the university. During the next four years 'Exegesis' and 'Dogmatics' occupied more space, but 'Philosophy' predominated. Yet during the last year of this period S. K. was seriously studying for his theological examination, which he passed with honour on July 3, 1840. This evidence indicates in a general way that during his first years as a student he was interested chiefly in aesthetics, and during the last years in philosophy. The subjects which engrossed him especially were the legends of Faust, Don Juan, and the Wandering Jew (Ahsverus), which he began to study in the spring of 1835. With this he included a study of fairy-tales and the popular legends of famous robbers like Robin Hood. He had in mind a grandiose plan, a history of the middle ages illuminated by its secular ideals as they are exhibited in the predominant interests of the common people. Faust, Don Juan, and Ahsverus, though they seemed to S. K. to coalesce in a measure, he regarded as representatives of 'life outside religion in its three typical aspects: doubt, sensuality, and despair'. The plan he had in mind must have been singularly attractive to this versatile young man because it combined history, literature, aesthetics, and philosophy. For it was to have been a philosophical work in the manner of Hegel, whose influence at that time predominated among the intellectual youth of Copenhagen and from whom S. K. was not yet emancipated. This great work was never accomplished, perhaps because his favourite professor, Paul Møller, who evidently was acquainted with this plan, sent to him as he was dying a last message through Professor Sibbern: 'Tell little Kierkegaard not to undertake too big a task, for that was what did me harm also'; perhaps because he had revolted against Hegel's method of dealing with history, or perhaps because he heeded Paul Møller's suggestion that he should take up the subject of irony, which eventually he chose as the theme of his dissertation for the master's degree. The study of the use of satire by the ancients was another occupation. Any one who is acquainted with S. K.'s works will recognize how large a part all these studies play in his literary production. The seemingly idle years of the student in perpetuity were not altogether wasted. The legends and fairy-tales greatly embellish his works, and he would hardly have become such a master of irony and satire without these early studies. The Don Juan *motif* predominates in *Either/Or*. If Faust appears less often than we might expect, it may be because S. K.'s category was not doubt but despair. Ahsverus is never named in his writings, but despair unpersonified is a thought that pervades them from first to last.

A recent book by Frithiof Brandt[1] calls attention to the fact that we really have from S. K.'s own pen a great abundance of information about his youth of which no writer hitherto has availed himself. He refers especially to the descriptions of 'the young friend' to whom the letters of Judge William are addressed in the Second Part of *Either/Or*. When we take account of all these passages it is astonishing to find that there are nearly two hundred pages which may be taken to describe young S. K. It is clear enough that he satirizes himself, and yet Judge William's affection for the young man does not seem to be misplaced. He must have had charm. It is no callow youth we see depicted here, but a student in his last years at the university who ought to have been out of it long before. I quote here a few passages, and they must be long, because the characterization of the young friend needs to be seen in dark relief against the background of the Judge's ethical counsel. Even the Judge's ethical position gives us, in a sense, a picture of Kierkegaard. It depicts the ethical side of him which was then suppressed but was struggling for mastery and ultimately triumphed. For clearly the Judge's arguments for the moral life must have been the arguments S. K. was using against himself.[1]

My Friend,

What so often I have said to you I say now once again, or rather I shout it at you: Either/Or! . . . [There follows a solemn discourse on the vital importance of resolute and decisive choice.]

As for you, this phrase is only too often on your lips; it has almost become a by-word with you. What significance has it for you? Simply none. You, according to your own expression, regard it as a wink of the eye, a snap of the fingers, a *coup de main*, an abracadabra. You know how to employ it on every occasion, and never without effect. You are affected by it as a neurasthenic is by a strong drink; it exalts you to a sort of intoxication which you call the higher madness. 'It is the compendium', you say, 'of all human wisdom, and a good gospel for suffering humanity; but no one has ever stated it so pithily as that great thinker and true practical philosopher who said to a man who had knocked off his hat: Pick it up, and you will get a licking; don't pick it up, and then too you will get a licking—now you can choose.' You take great delight in 'comforting' people when they turn to you for counsel in critical situations. You listen to their account and then you say: 'Yes, I clearly perceive that two alternatives are possible, you can either do this or that. My sincere opinion and my friendly counsel is this: Do it or don't do it, in either case you will regret it.' He, however, who makes sport of others makes sport of himself, and your use of this by-word is not a trivial thing but a sad proof how slack your soul is when your whole philosophy of life is concentrated in the single sentence, 'I say only either—or.' If this were really your serious meaning, there would be nothing more to be done for you, one must let it go at that and bewail the fact that melancholy or frivolity had weakened your mind. But on the contrary one knows very well that such is not the case, and one is not disposed to lament over you, but rather to wish that life may some day apply the thumbscrew and compel you to let out what is really in you, that it may subject you to the more stringent examination which mere talk and witticism will not enable you to pass. Life, you explain, is a masquerade. This gives you inexhaustible matter for amusement, and as yet no one has been able to recognize you in your disguise; for every self-revelation, you say, is a deceit, and only in this way [behind a mask] can you breathe freely and prevent others from pressing closely upon you and making respiration difficult. Your whole occupation consists in keeping yourself hid, and in this you are successful, for your mask is the most enigmatical of all. In yourself you are nothing, you are all the time in a relationship to others, and what you are you are through this relationship. To a pretty shepherdess you stretch out a languishing hand, and in the same instant you assume the mask of bucolic sentimentality; you betray a reverend spiritual father with a brotherly kiss, &c. You yourself are nothing, an enigmatical figure on whose forehead is written, Either—Or. 'For this is my motto, and these words are not, as the grammarians suppose, disjunctive conjunctions; no, they belong inseparably together and therefore ought to be written as one word, inasmuch as in their union they constitute an interjection which I shout in the ears of mankind, just as boys shout Hep! after a Jew.' Now in spite of the fact that nothing of that sort makes any impression upon me, or, if it has any effect at all, it is only to stir up a well-justified indignation, nevertheless for your sake I shall answer you. Do you not know that there comes a midnight hour when all must unmask? Do you suppose that life will for ever suffer itself to be treated as a joke? Do you suppose that one can slip out a little before the midnight hour? Or does this fail to frighten you? In the course of my life I have seen men who have so long deceived others that finally it has become impossible for them to reveal themselves. I have seen men who have so long kept in hiding that finally in sheer lunacy they have felt a compulsion to intrude inopportunely upon others their most secret thoughts, which hitherto they had proudly concealed. Or can you think of anything more dreadful than that your nature might be resolved into a multiplicity, that you might literally become many, that like that unhappy demoniac you might become Legion, and that thus you would lose the most inward, the most holy thing in man, the uniting power of personality? Truly you ought not to jest with that which is not serious only but dreadful. There is something in every man which hinders him from becoming perfectly transparent to himself; and this may reach such a degree, a man may be so inexplicably woven into the involved relationships of life that it is next to impossible for him to reveal himself. But he who cannot reveal himself cannot love, and he who cannot love is the most unfortunate of all. And you wantonly play this part, you practise yourself in the art of making yourself a riddle to everybody. My young friend, suppose there was nobody that troubled himself to guess your riddle—what enjoyment would you have in it then? But above all, for your own sake, for the sake of your salvation—and what is perdition if it does not aptly describe the state of your soul?—put a stop to this wild flight, to this nihilistic passion which rages in you. For this is precisely what you wish, you wish to reduce everything to nothingness; the hunger of doubt within you you are fain to satiate at the expense of existence. To this end you train your faculties, to this end you harden your heart; for you are quite ready to admit that you are good for nothing and that the only thing that amuses you is to walk seven times round existence and blow the trumpet and then see the whole thing collapse so that your soul may be pacified, sweetly sorrowful, at calling forth an echo—for echo sounds only across empty space.

This, however, is not the way to come to close quarters with you. Besides, my head is too weak, if you will, to hold out, or, as I prefer to think, too strong to find it agreeable to see everything dizzy before my eyes. I will therefore take up the matter from another side. Figure to yourself a young man, at the age when life is just beginning to assume significance for him. He is in good health, pure, happy, talented, rich in hope for himself, and the hope of every one that knows him. Suppose (yes, it is a hard thing I have to say to you)—suppose that he was mistaken in you, that he took you to be a serious, tried, and experienced man to whom one could confidently turn in seeking an explanation of life's riddles; suppose that he turned to you with the charming confidence which is youth's adornment, with frank assurance that he will not be gainsaid, which is youth's privilege—what would you answer him? Would your answer be, 'I say nothing but either—or'? Would it really? Or, as you are wont to express yourself when you wish to indicate your aversion to having other people vex you with their personal troubles, would you stick your head out of the window and say, Try next door? Or would you treat him as you treat others who come to take counsel with you or get information, whom you dismiss just as you do the man who comes to collect the church rates, by remarking that you are only a transient lodger in life, not the possessor of property or the head of a family? A young man of talent is the sort of thing you prize only too highly. But in this case your relationship to him was not exactly what you would have wished it to be, you were not brought into contact with him by an accidental encounter, you were not tempted to employ your irony. Although he was the younger, you the older man, yet the fine quality of his youth made the moment serious. It is true, is it not, that you yourself would wish to be young again, that you feel there is something beautiful in being young, but also something exceedingly serious, that it is by no means a matter of indifference how one employs one's youth, that it requires a decisive choice, a real either/or. You will feel that the important thing after all is not the training of one's intellect, but the ripening of one's personality. Your good-natured sympathy was aroused, in that spirit you would talk to the young man, you would seek to strengthen his soul, to reinforce his trust in life, you would assure him that there is a power in man to make front against the whole world, you would very emphatically counsel him to employ his time aright. All that you can do, and you can do it handsomely when you have a mind to. But now attend to what I have to say, young man—for though you are not young, one is always compelled to speak of you as such. What did you do in this case? You recognized what you are so much disinclined to recognize, the significance of either/or. And why? Because you were moved by love for the young man. And yet in a way you deceived him, for he will perhaps meet you on another occasion when you may not find it convenient to recognize the either/or. Here you see the pitiful consequence of the fact that a man's nature is inhibited from revealing itself harmoniously. You meant to do the best, and yet perhaps you have done the young man an injury; perhaps he might have been better able to assert himself in opposition to your distrust of the world than to find secure repose in the subjective and deceitful trust you conveyed to him. Suppose that after the lapse of several years you were to meet this young man again; he was lively, witty, intellectual, bold in his expression, but your sharp eye easily discovered doubt in his soul, you had a suspicion that he also had acquired the questionable wisdom: I say nothing but either—or. It is true, is it not, that you would be sorry for him, that you would feel that he had lost something, a something which is very essential? But you will not be sorry for yourself, you are satisfied, even proud of your questionable wisdom, so proud indeed that you cannot suffer another to share it, you would prefer to be alone with it. And yet from another point of view you find it deplorable, and it is your honest opinion that it is deplorable for the young man to have attained the same wisdom. What a monstrous contradiction! Your whole nature contradicts itself. But the only way to escape from this contradiction is by an either/or. And I who love you more sincerely than you loved that young man, I who in my life have experienced the significance of choice, am ready to congratulate you that you are still so young, that although there is always something to lose, yet if you have energy enough—or rather have the will to have it—you stand to gain what is the principal thing in life, to gain your own self, to inherit yourself.

. . . . . .

From the argument I have been developing above you will see that my conception of choice is essentially different from yours— if indeed I can speak of 'your choice', seeing that yours is so different a thing that it actually hinders you from choosing. For me the moment of choice has the utmost seriousness, not so much on account of the rigorous cogitation required for the estimation of the possibilities involved in choice, and not so much on account of the multifarious thoughts which attach themselves to the single question at issue, but rather because danger is imminent, because the very next minute a choice may no longer be available to me, for the reason that something has already been experienced in life which must be lived over again backwards. If any one thinks that for a certain time he can keep his personality blank and empty, or that in a strict sense he can break off and bring his personal life to a standstill, he is very much in error. The personality is already interested in the choice before a man chooses, and when one defers the choice, the personality chooses unwittingly, or rather the choice is made by obscure forces within it. When one tardily makes the choice (which, as I remarked before, one is not always required to do) one then discovers that there is something which must be done over again, some way which must be retraced, and that is often exceedingly difficult. There is a fairy-tale which tells of a man whom fabulous creatures, half man and half woman, drew into their power by means of their demoniac music. To overcome this magic it was necessary for the enchanted person to play the same piece backwards without making a single mistake. This is very profoundly thought out, but very difficult to perform; and yet it is true, he has assumed the error as part and parcel of himself, and this is the way he must extirpate it, and every time he makes a mistake he must begin all over again. See, therefore, how important it is to choose, and to choose in time.

You on the other hand have a different method—for I see clearly that the polemical side you turn to the world is not your true nature. If the proper task of human life were to ponder and cogitate, you would come pretty near to perfection. I will take an example. To suit your case it must, of course, be a glaring contrast: either a parson / or an actor. Here is the dilemma. Now all your passionate energies are aroused. Reflection with its hundred arms seizes upon the thought of being a parson. You find no rest, day and night you think about it; you read all the writings you can lay your hands on, go to church three times a Sunday, strike up friendships with parsons, write sermons yourself and deliver them to yourself. For half a year you are dead to the whole world. Now you are ready; you can now talk about the clerical calling with a deeper insight and apparently with more experience than many a one who has been a parson for twenty years. Your resentment is aroused when you meet such people, because they cannot expatiate so eloquently as you. Is that what is called enthusiasm? you say; I who am not a parson, who have not consecrated myself to this calling, speak with angels' voices in comparison with them.

That perhaps is true enough—however, the fact is that you have not become a parson. Then you behave in the same way about the other problem [that of becoming an actor], and your enthusiasm about art almost surpasses your spiritual eloquence. You are now ready to choose. However, one can be sure that in the meantime, considering the prodigious amount of thought you have been doing, many things must have occurred to you by the way, many incidental remarks and observations. At the moment therefore when you should make the choice there comes life and movement into this residuum; a new either/or presents itself: jurist, or perhaps advocate, which has something in common with both sides you have been considering [lies somewhere between the cure of souls and the theatre]. Now you are lost. For at that moment you are already advocate enough to prove that it is reasonable to take the third possibility into consideration. So your life passes. After you have wasted another half-year upon these deliberations, after you have exhausted the powers of your soul by an amazing energy, you have got not one step farther. Then the thread of thought breaks, you become impatient, angry, ready to destroy and burn it all; and now you go on: either a barber or a bank clerk: I say only either—or. What wonder then that this word has become to you a stumbling-block and foolishness, that it seems to you like the arms of the iron maiden whose embrace was the death-penalty! You survey men, you make sport of them, and what you have become is just what you most abhor—a critic, a universal critic in all faculties. Sometimes I cannot help laughing at you, and yet it is a great pity that your really distinguished talents are thus wasted by dispersion. But here again there is the same contradiction in your nature; for you are well able to perceive the ludicrous, and God help the man who falls into your hands, if his case is like yours.

. . . . . .

What is it then that I distinguish in my either/or? Is it good and evil? No, I would merely bring you to the point where this choice has significance for you. On that everything depends. If only a man can be brought to stand at the cross-roads where there is no escape for him but to choose, he will choose aright.

. . . . . .

> My either/or does not first of all designate the choice between good/or evil; it designates the choice of choosing between good and evil/or excluding such an alternative.[1]

After considering at length and illustrating by many examples the case of the favourites of fortune who fall into despair, and more briefly the case of men whose despair might plausibly be attributed to misfortunes, the judge concludes that despair is the natural and inevitable concomitant of the aesthetical life, that, consciously or unconsciously, it is inherent in it always. Then he proceeds:[2]

> So we have reached the conclusion that every aesthetical view of life is despair, and this might seem to be the right moment to accomplish the movements whereby the ethical is brought into evidence. However, there remains still one more stage, an aesthetical view of life which is the most refined and superior of them all, and that I shall discuss with the utmost care—for now comes your turn. You can follow with composure the argument I have developed hitherto, for in a sense it is not you I have been addressing, and it would have been of very little use indeed to address such words to you, to explain to you that life is vanity. That you know very well, and in your own way you have tried indeed to adjust yourself to the situation. I have propounded all this for the reason that I wish to protect my rear and would prevent you from springing suddenly back [into one of the positions which now have been closed]. This last view of life is despair itself. It is an aesthetical view of life, because the personality retains its immediacy; it is the last aesthetical view of life, because to a certain extent it has accepted the consciousness of the nullity of such a view. However, there is a difference between despair and despair. . . . [You have not suffered from the misfortunes which come from without, &c.] and yet you are in despair. It is not despair about any actual thing, but a despair in thought. Your thought has hastened ahead of you, you see through the vanity of all things [before you reach them], but you have not got any farther than this. Occasionally you plunge down into pleasure, and when for a single moment you abandon yourself to it you are aware in your inner consciousness that it is vanity. So you are constantly above and beyond yourself—in despair. This

accounts for the fact that your life lies between two prodigious contradictions: at times you have enormous energy, and at times an indolence just as great.

. . . . . .

Here I have your view of life, and believe me, much in your life will become explicable to you when you regard it with me as thought-despair. You hate activity in life. Reasonably enough [from your point of view], for ere there can be any meaning in life it must have continuity, and that is what your life lacks. You occupy yourself with your studies, it is true; you are even diligent in that way; but it is only for your own sake, and it is carried on with as little teleology as possible. Apart from this you are idle, like the labourers in the Gospel you stand idle in the market-place. You thrust your hands in your pockets and look on at life. At one time you repose in despair, nothing arouses you to activity, you won't go out into the streets—'If they should tear the tiles from the roof, I won't go out.' You are like a dying man, you die daily, not in the deeply serious significance which commonly attaches to that word, but life has lost its reality, and you 'reckon your life-periods according to the number of times you get notice to quit [your lodgings for failure to pay your rent]'. You let everything pass you by, it makes no impression—but then comes the sudden something which grips you. Perhaps it is an idea, a situation, the smile of a young girl—and then you are in the game. For though there are times when you are distinctly not in the game, there are other times when you distinctly are in it and in every way 'very much at your service'. Wherever something is happening, there you are at hand. You behave in life as you are accustomed to do in a crowd. You work your way into the thickest group, trying if possible to be thrust up by the others, and as soon as you are up you make yourself as comfortable as you can—and in like manner you let yourself be carried through life. But when the crowd is dispersed and the event is over you stand again at the street corner and look out upon the world. It is well known that a dying man possesses supernatural strength, and so it is with you. If there is an idea to be thought out, a work to be read through, a plan to be put into effect, a little romance to be experienced—yes, if it is even a question of buying a hat—you take the matter up with prodigious energy. You work indefatigably, a day, a month, according to the circumstances; you find pleasure in the proof that your vigour has not diminished, you take no rest, 'Satan himself could not hold out with you.' If you work in company with others, you work them to exhaustion. But when the month is past—or the half-year which you regard as the maximum—you break off and exclaim, 'Here the story ends.' You retire and let the others carry the burden of it; or, in case you alone are involved in the affair, you utter no word to anybody about it. You pretend to yourself and to others that you have lost the inclination, and you flatter yourself with the notion that you could have continued to work with the same intensity, if only you were inclined to. But this is a monstrous deception. You would have succeeded as others do, if you had patiently willed the completion of the thing; but then you would have learnt by experience that this requires an entirely different sort of perseverance from that which you possess.[1]

. . . . . .

You soar high up above yourself, but this higher ether in which you float, the finer sublimate in which you are absorbed, is the nothingness of despair. And far beneath you your eye beholds knowledge in its multiplicity, various insights, studies, observations, which for you have no intrinsic significance, but which you employ capriciously and contrive to combine into tasteful decorations for that voluptuous palace of the soul's delight in which you occasionally reside. What wonder then that for you existence is a mere fairy-tale—'that you are often tempted to begin every speech with the phrase, Once upon a time there was a king and a queen'. . . . Having got the suggestion that 'life is a fairy-tale', you are capable of spending a whole month reading nothing but such literature. You make a profound study of it, comparing and proving, and really getting at some results. And what do you use it for? To divert your mind—then you let the whole thing off in a brilliant display of fireworks.

You soar high up above yourself, and what you behold far beneath you is a multiplicity of moods and situations which you employ as interesting points of contact with life. You can be sentimental, heartless, ironical, witty—in that respect one must admit that you are well schooled. So soon as something crops up that is capable of rousing you out of your indolence, you at once become passionately engaged in your special line of activity. And in the practice of your line it cannot be said that you lack art, for you are only too well equipped with wit, agility, and all the seducing gifts of the mind. You are wont to say, with arrogant self-complacency, that you are not so ungallant as to appear in company without a sweet-smelling, freshly plucked bouquet of wit....

... So you crave nothing, you wish for nothing; for the only thing you could desire is a magic wand which would give you all things—and that you would use to scrape your pipe with. So you are through with life and 'do not need to make a will, because you have nothing to leave'. But you cannot hold yourself upon this point in a permanent balance, for though your thought has taken everything from you, it has given you nothing in its place. The next moment some insignificant thing captivates you. You regard it indeed with the proud superiority which your arrogant thought supplies, you disdain it as a paltry toy, you are tired of it almost at the moment when you take it in your hand, yet you busy yourself about it nevertheless, and although it is not the thing itself which concerns you (that is never the case with you), yet you are interested in the fact that you are willing to condescend to it. In this respect, whenever you come into association with other men, your nature suggests a high degree of faithlessness—which nobody can reproach you for, because your life lies quite outside of ethical determinants. Fortunately you are not much disposed to enter into sympathetic relations with others, and so this trait is not often remarked upon. You come to my house often, and you know that you are always welcome to me, but you know too that it never occurs to me to invite you to sympathize with me in anything whatsoever. I would not even take you for a drive in the forest—not because you are too merry and entertaining, but because your sympathy is always false. For if you happen to be pleased, one can always be sure that it is not with something that pleases the rest of us, but with something you have *in mente*; and if you are displeased, it is not because something unpleasant has occurred to put you out of sorts (for that could happen as well to the rest of us), but because the very moment you got into the carriage you discerned the nullity of this diversion....

. . . . . .

What do I advise you to do? ... I advise you to despair.... Choose then despair, for despair itself is a choice, for one can doubt without choosing to do so, but without choosing to despair one cannot do it. And when any one despairs he chooses again. What then does he choose? He chooses his own self—not as it is in its immediacy, not as this fortuitous individual which he is, but himself in his eternal worth.[1]

. . . . . .

But what is it that I choose? Is it just this or that? No, for I choose absolutely, and the only way I can manage to choose absolutely is by not choosing this or that. I choose the absolute. And what is the absolute? It is myself in my eternal worth. Nothing else but myself can I ever choose absolutely, for if I choose something else, I choose it as something finite, and so I do not choose it absolutely....

But what is this self of mine? At first sight, and as the first expression for it, I would answer: It is the most abstract thing of all, and yet in itself it is at the same time the most concrete thing—it is freedom.[2]

It is evident that the young friend was very far from being a hermit. He was always on hand where anything was going on. It was true of S. K. that, though he shared his secrets with no one, he threw himself violently into the social life of the university. He took an active part in the Student Association, which served as a debating society; and he took part in the organization of the 'Academica', which was a secession of elect spirits from the larger organization. On November 28, 1835, he delivered a long address before the Student Association on the subject of *Our Journalistic Literature*, 'a study from nature under midday illumination'.[3] On another occasion he had the responsibility of presiding over a plenary assembly of the Association when a political question of immediate interest was tumultuously discussed. When it seemed that the decision might go against the conservative position which he espoused, he defied his brother and other advisers by proclaiming peremptorily that the meeting was adjourned. Years later, on a visit to Christian VIII, he was surprised to learn that the king was informed about this meeting and the part he had played in it. At a time when S. K. was generally blamed for showing no interest in public affairs, the king required his visits and expected to learn much from a man who was so constantly in the streets and in contact with all sorts of people.

About this time (at the turn of the year 1835/6) S. K. wrote four articles for the *Flying Post*, the organ of the great Heiberg, arbiter of literary elegance in Denmark. This first literary venture won for him enthusiastic applause. Before it was known who the author was, Paul Møller supposed that Heiberg was the writer and congratulated him on the best articles that had ever appeared in his paper. All of these articles were political except the first, which was ironically entitled 'Another Defender of Woman's Lofty Qualities'. S. K., who knew so well how to distinguish things that are different, was impatient at the indiscriminate adulation of woman which ignored her specific difference as a female of the species and so failed to accord her the praise she deserved. The political articles were strongly conservative. S. K. remained a conservative to the end of his days—even when he was attacking the Established Church. His polemic was directed against the rule of the masses, the futility of endeavouring to discover truth by means of the ballot, and against the right divine of mobs to govern wrong. He was not opposed to change as such, but contended against the effort to impose upon Denmark the abstract ideas of the French Revolution, without taking into account the character of this northern race, the history of the nation, and the institutions which had grown up in conformity with the genius of his people. In his day the Jews (men without political attachments) were prominent as instigators of liberal reform in Denmark, as they were also in other lands, and as they are to-day. In an early entry in his journal S. K. wrote:[1] 'The present age is the age of despair, the age of the Wandering Jew (many reforming Jews).' Among the reforming Jews, Goldschmidt was the most conspicuous a few years later. The modern development of the Scandinavian nations, with the most liberal government in the world, but with institutions peculiar to themselves and appropriate to their situation, has amply justified S. K.'s position. What his positive political notions were, or what they developed into, may be learnt from the last part of *A Literary Review*, which has been translated by Mr. Dru and may soon be published.

In 1838 S. K. wrote a satirical play for the students.[1] It was never finished, but the hero Willibald was evidently S. K. himself and throws some light upon his activities. A little while later, only a few months after his father's death, he published his first book,[2] strangely entitled: *From the Manuscripts of One Still Living*—'Published against his will by S. Kierkegaard'. We have already remarked that this title indicated his surprise at surviving his father, in defiance of the doom which seemed to impend over the family. The second part of the title, 'published against his will', is explained by the fact that it was a rather cruel criticism of Hans Christian Andersen. The actual content of the book had to be expressed in a second title, printed on a page immediately following the Preface: 'About Andersen as a Novelist, with constant reference to his last work *Only a Fiddler*.' Brandt seeks to show that Andersen was for a while his intimate companion in a boarding-house, and although S. K. was ready enough to rag him then, he felt some compunction at launching against him a whole book of criticism, and therefore preferred to pose not merely as an editor without responsibility for what was said, but as an editor who reluctantly made such criticism public. It cannot be said, however, that he seemed reluctant to wound when once he was launched and in full swing of criticism. Andersen, who proved himself a genius by his *Tales*, was really deplorable as a novelist and as a playwright. Only his Italian novel, *The Improvisatore*, has charm, and that is partly due to its autobiographical elements. But what principally aroused S. K.'s wrath was poor Andersen's plea that genius needs favourable circumstances for its development. Andersen's own life belied this thesis, for no genius was ever more disadvantageously placed in his youth. The truth is that now, when he was recognized as a genius, he was pathetically eager to be coddled. It was S. K.'s opinion that 'genius is like a thunder-storm which comes up against the wind'.[3] His reply to Andersen was: 'Genius is not a penny dip to be blown out by the wind, but a conflagration which the storm only challenges.' We may suspect that the following motto, quoted by Hertz, was originally a rejoinder of S. K. to Andersen at the boarding-house table: 'The human spirit is not to be likened to a hen's egg'—that is to say, it does not need warmth to hatch it. Naturally, Andersen's softness was hateful to S. K. His own independent attitude is strikingly stated in an entry of July 28, 1839:[1]

> I was painfully impressed by a suggestion of my singing-master, Pastor Ipsen, about the convenience of a position in the Prince's Court. . . . That I who believed my whole life spent in God's service would not be enough to atone for the excesses of my youth, that I should hear again that I ought to take the first step on a path where all is lost if one cannot shine. The old siren song,—No, thank you, Herr Pastor! When I sit alone like a Greenlander in my kayak, solitary upon the great sea of life, one moment under, another over the water, always in God's hand, there from time to time, as I happen to feel like it, I will harpoon a sea-monster—to be *captain of a flag-ship* is not for me.

But the value of this book is not to be found chiefly in the criticism of Andersen. It reveals the intellectual maturity of this young man of 25 years, and Emanuel Hirsch is justified in making much use of it in his study of S. K. as a writer. We can discover in it some of his most characteristic trains of thought. It shows that while he was still a student at the university, and nearly four years before he began to write his most famous book, *Either/Or*, he was already a vigorous thinker and an approved writer. The ten years he loafed at the university had not been wasted.

Brøchner gives this description of S. K. in his youth:[2]

> There could be something infinitely tender and affectionate in his glance, but there could be also something piercing and teasing. With one glance at a passer-by he was able to put himself irresistibly *en rapport* with him, as he himself expressed it. The person who encountered his glance was either attracted or repelled, thrown into embarrassment, uncertainty, or irritation. I have walked through a whole street with him, hearing him explain how by putting oneself *en rapport* with another, one could make psychological experiments, and while he explained his theories he put them into practice with almost every person we encountered. There was not one upon whom his glance did not make an impression.

> At that time, says Brøchner, he was twenty-three years of age, had something very irregular in his whole figure, and a striking way of wearing his hair [it rose high above his forehead].... It was always interesting to walk with him, but in one respect it had its difficulties. Because of the irregularity of his movements, due doubtless to his spinal curvature, one could never keep to a straight line in walking with him; one was constantly pushed against the houses or the cellar stairs or over the curb-stone. When at the same time he was gesticulating with his arms or his cane, it became still more like an obstacle-race. And one had to seize the opportunity now and then to get on the other side of him so as to gain room.

Brøchner was one of the few men in Denmark capable of appreciating the greatness of S. K. in his maturity. His description of the difficulty of walking with him is admirably illustrated in a painting by Janssen, now in the Frederiksborg Museum, which represents him in his maturity crossing the Nytorv, the public square on which his house fronted, in lively conversation with a well-known artist of that day. It is reproduced here opposite the title-page of Part Four. A famous caricature by Marstrand also represents him in the street and shows only too plainly the crooked back, which S. K. attributed to a fall from a tree when he was a small boy. It is likely that his father's children were not robust enough to engage in the rougher sorts of play. An elder brother, Søren Mikael, came to his death in his twelfth year as a result of butting his head in play against the head of another boy. The records of the hospital ascribe S. K.'s paralysis and death to some trouble in the spinal column, which they do not define more precisely. It is plausible to ascribe to this cause instances which occurred from time to time of an acute pain which compelled him to fall impotently upon the floor. He was loath to have any one witness this weakness and was prompt to pass it off with a piteous jest. On one occasion he fell from the sofa, and when his companions hastened to help him to rise he said, with bitter humour, 'Leave it there till the morning, when the housemaid will sweep it up.' On a similar occasion his jest was 'Little Ludwig will pick himself up.' We shall later have occasion to remark upon the fact that for some reason or another he associated the name Ludwig with himself.

In this connexion we mention a brief but significant episode in S. K.'s career. No sooner had he entered the university than he was also enrolled in the Royal Bodyguard—and after three days he was dismissed as 'unfit for service'. This is only one of the many indications of his physical unfitness.

Goldschmidt (who as owner of the *Corsair* played an important part in S. K.'s life) describes him as he was when he first knew him in 1838, his eighth year at the university:[1]

> He had at that time a fresh complexion, but was rather thin, rather stoop-shouldered, eyes shrewd, lively and masterful, with a mixture of good nature and archness. [Then, speaking of a later time and a conversation with him on the street:] There was a long pause, and then he took a little skip and smote his cane against his leg. There was something foppish about this gesture, yet not at all like the foppishness one sees elsewhere in the world. The action was droll, yet it gave me pain, . . . making the impression that this erudite man would like to enter into the joy of life, but could not or must not.

It appears that in his youth S. K. was foppish in an ordinary worldly way. He may well have felt an exuberant sense of relief at being able to cast off the peculiar dress his father had inflicted upon him as a boy, which subjected him to the ridicule of his comrades. On his tour in north Seeland he described himself complacently as 'dressed in the latest fashion, with a cigar in my mouth'. In those days he carried a cane—instead of the umbrella which became a favourite theme of the caricaturists, in spite of his protest that it served as a protection not only from the rain but from the sun, and that he had a peculiar distaste for heat. The bills of his tailor are known to us because they were recorded on the occasion when his father decided to pay his debts, and they give colour to the report that he was elegantly dressed. Brøchner recalls that when he first saw him in a small company he took him to be a clerk in a business house. That, I suppose, is a proof that he was dressed more fashionably than students are apt to be; for it is notorious that clerks are obliged to dress more smartly than scholars or dukes. We learn incidentally that he often wore spectacles. A jotting in his journal makes a pathetic reference to this custom: 'For spectacles hide much—even a tear in the eye.'

Frithiof Brandt, in a recent book describing 'The Young Søren Kierkegaard', displays an amazing industry, and an acumen which any detective might envy, in ferreting out the minutest details of S. K.'s life while he was a student in the university. He has succeeded not only in filling up the gaps in our knowledge but in presenting a new picture of the young man which is not altogether lovely. Such a work cannot be summarized. But I must refer to some of Brandt's discoveries. By connecting S. K. with the poet Hertz he has opened a new vista into his life as a student. It appears that Hertz was so realistic in his method of constructing his works of fiction that for one of them[1] he relied upon notes he took of conversations which were carried on in a 'clique' of young men who took their meals at a common table in a boarding-house and used the back parlour for their reunions. He made so much of S. K.'s conversations that he earned the nickname of Echo. For S. K. was a member of this clique, and so also, according to Brandt, were Hans Christian Andersen and P. V. Jacobsen (who became the model for Judge William) and P. L. Møller (who was to figure later as 'the Seducer' and who later provided the occasion for S. K.'s assault upon the *Corsair*). There seems to have been a business man of sorts incongruously grouped with these young poets and authors owing only to the fact that he took his meals at the same table; and this may explain why the Ladies' Tailor figures among the guests at the Banquet in the *Stages*. From the conversations which Hertz reports in his book and from the descriptions he gives of the several members of the clique, it is possible to identify all these characters with a good deal of plausibility. It appears that S. K. was not so much welcomed in this circle as tolerated, that he was admired for his wit and his prodigious knowledge, but also feared, especially by those who were the butt of his terrible sarcasm. The sentimental Andersen, a defenceless giant, was his favourite target, P. L. Møller was the only member of the party who could return his blows effectively, and Jacobsen the only one whom he treated with respect. We get the impression here, as we do also from the judge's description of the 'young friend' and from S. K.'s own account of himself in the Journals, that he was a talented but insolent youth who used his wit to wound his comrades and triumph over them, had no apparent fellow-feeling, but stood aloof from life and superciliously observed it. In later days he often described himself as 'an observer'. His works prove that he was an acute observer and did not vainly describe himself as 'a police detective'. It seems that in the days of his youth he was a cynical observer. He reports of himself that he never in his life confided in any one or expected any one to confide in him. Yet in spite of the fact that he was essentially unsociable, he liked in his youth to mix with all sorts and conditions of men—evidently for the sake of conducting his 'psychological experiments'. In later life he did not abandon the character of an observer and the habit of being frequently in the street, but his relations to people became more sympathetic. His talent as an observer he learnt to employ as 'a spy in a higher service'.[1]

The question of S. K.'s sanity has been so often raised that we cannot escape it and may as well face it here. There is no doubt that physically he was a sick man, and when we say that he was melancholy we confess that he had a psychic ailment. He often said of himself that he had been 'on the verge' of insanity, and he was fearful of becoming actually insane. It may well seem to us a marvellous thing that he was able to keep his balance. Nothing can be plainer than the fact that in this he did succeed, and in part we can see that what saved him was first of all the habit of thinking clearly and honestly, and then his Christian faith. In *Fear and Trembling* Johannes de Silentio quotes from Seneca a saying which he in turn had from Aristotle: *Nullum unquam extitit magnum ingenium sine mixtura dementiae* (there never existed great genius without an admixture of madness). Then he goes on to say:[2]

> For this madness is the suffering genius is compelled to undergo in the conditions of existence, it is an expression of the divine envy (if I may make bold to speak thus), whereas the gift itself of genius is an expression of the divine favour.[3] Thus from the very beginning the genius is disoriented with respect to the universal, and is brought into relation with the paradox, whether, in despairing revolt against the confines which hedge him in and which in his eyes seem to transform his power into impotency, he will seek a daimoniac comfort which he will admit neither to God nor man, or whether he will comfort himself religiously with love for the Divinity. Here lies a psychological task to which, it seems to me, a man might well consecrate his whole life, and yet one hears so seldom a word about it. In

what relation does mental derangement stand to genius? Can the one be construed out of the other? In what sense and in what degree is a genius master of his madness? For it goes without saying that he is master of it in some degree, for otherwise he would be actually crazy. For such observations, however, ingenuity is requisite in a very high degree, and also love. To make critical observations upon the superior man is exceedingly difficult. But if a man, with attention to these conditions, were to read completely through the works of just one eminent genius, it might perhaps be possible, though not without great pains, to discover a little.

This may be regarded as S. K.'s invitation to study his case. But surely it is not an enticing invitation. Several Freudians have rashly undertaken to psychoanalyse S. K. without observing these very exacting conditions. Hjalmar Helweg, Director of the Hospital for the Insane at Oringe, Denmark, is the only alienist who has taken the pains to read every word S. K. ever wrote, and has studied him with sympathy.[1] He modestly concludes his preface with these words: 'However well one may think that he has managed to say a thing, he will always discover that S. K. has said it better.' I have no fault to find with his verdict, except that it is not very illuminating. He concludes that S. K. suffered from a condition of depression alternating with, but more commonly blended with, a condition of exaltation. The reader will be given here ample opportunity to judge whether S. K. has not said it better. He became a psychologist by analysing his own pathological condition, and thereby he anticipated much we are familiar with now in the so-called 'deep psychology' of Freud, Adler, and Jung.

When we normal, common-sense people busy ourselves about the question of S. K.'s sanity, he is quite capable of turning the tables on us. In the *Repetition* S. K. pits one side of his character against the other—and each comes to the conclusion that the other is mad. Constantine Constantius, the pseudonymous author of the book, represents, as the name is intended to indicate, the quality of cool reflection, unmoved by changing moods and feelings, whereas 'the young man', who elects to confide in Constantine his harrowing love problem, is swayed so completely by feeling that he cannot muster up resolution to follow the shrewd and cold advice of his counsellor—

which was exactly the advice S. K. had given to himself and followed in his dealings with Regina.[1]

> Great God! [Constantine exclaims.] Such a melancholy I have never before encountered in all my practice. That he was melancholy, I knew full well—but that a love-affair could have such an effect upon him! Yet how logical even an abnormal condition is when it is normally present. People often advise that a melancholy man should fall in love, with the assurance that then all the trouble will vanish. But if he is really melancholy, how could it be possible that his soul should not busy itself in a melancholy fashion about the thing which to him is the most important of all?

Later[2] the young man writes to Constantine:

> I admire you, and yet at times it seems to me as if you were deranged. Or is it not a sort of mental derangement to subject in such a degree every passion, every emotion of the heart, every mood, to the cold discipline of reflection? Is it not mental derangement to be so normal, to be a mere idea, not a man, not like the rest of us, pliant and yielding, capable of being lost and of losing ourselves? Is it not mental derangement to be always awake, always sure, never obscure and dreaming?

This is not the only case where S. K. seeks to get a better understanding of himself by parcelling himself out among several pseudonyms, each of which represents only a single aspect of his character; but let the reader beware of jumping to the conclusion that therefore he can be understood as an instance of multiple personality. For S. K. was always conscious of being a whole personality. In this case he was both Constantine and the young man; he was pre-eminently reflection, but also pre-eminently a man of feeling; he was able to give himself cold advice and take it; but on the other hand his thought was prompted by feeling, and he emphatically insists that thought, if it is to be good for anything, must be 'passionate thought'.

It is said that S. K. was profoundly influenced by Romanticism of the German type, and the assertion is often made that from this he liberated himself more tardily than from Hegel. On the other hand, it is affirmed quite as often, and by authorities equally good, that he totally lacked appreciation of the beauties of nature. Neither of these contradictory opinions seems to me to be true. On the occasion of his first long vacation in the country he abandoned himself to the charms of nature in the spirit of Romanticism. That is true—and it may seem the more significant because the beauties Denmark has to offer are rarely of a sort that would stir the enthusiasm of the characteristic romanticists. It is a matter of course that S. K. as a youth would be influenced by the German romantic movement, which was one of the most vital factors of his time. There is sufficient evidence that he read the works of this school, yet where he comments upon them his attitude is always critical. Almost a year before he made his tour in north Seeland he set down in his diary a reflection which definitely puts him outside the ranks of Romanticism:[1]

> The reason why I cannot rightly say that I distinctly enjoy nature is that I cannot succeed in making it clear to my reflection *what* I enjoy. A work of art, on the other hand, I can grasp; I can (if I may so say) find its Archimedian point, and so soon as I have found that, everything clears up for me. . . . The mind of the author is akin to mine; it may perhaps be far superior, but it is limited like mine. The works of the Divinity are too great for me; I find myself lost in the details. Hence it is that the utterances people give vent to on beholding nature are so insipid ('Splendid!' 'Wonderful!' &c.), for they are all-too-anthropomorphic; they are arrested by the outward aspects, the inmost things and the depths they are unable to express.

And an entry of December 2, 1837 (i.e. more than two years after the excursion), shows that if ever he had abandoned himself to Romanticism, he had thoroughly recovered himself:[2]

> . . . Yes, Echo, thou great master of irony, thou who canst parody the highest and the deepest things on earth. . . . Yes, Echo, take vengeance upon all the nonsense which conceals itself in forest, in meadow, in church and theatre, and which now and again breaks loose and drowns out everything for me. I do not hear the trees in the woods relating to me old legends, &c.—no, they whisper to me all the twaddle they have so long been witnesses of. I beg you in God's name to hew them down, so as to free us from those prating nature-worshippers.

Would that all these praters' heads sat upon one neck; like Caligula, I should know what I had to do about it.

In S. K.'s writings one frequently meets with sarcastic references to the people who 'see God in Nature'. We understand very well that he would scorn this as a particular instance of the presumption he so hotly condemned, that one can 'prove the existence of God'. But we must recognize here that he regarded it as a particularly flagrant instance, for the fact that it implied on God's part the use of 'direct communication' in making Himself known to men through nature, that it conceived of God as 'immediately present in nature', as revealed in it and not hidden. Karl Barth attaches himself to S. K. at this point when he insists that God is the Unknown God. How much anguish our generation might have been spared had we been sober enough to imitate S. K. in his Socratic ignorance: if the scientist had been sober enough to draw no inference from the fact that he had searched the whole heaven with his telescope and found no God (or examined the human body with his microscope and found no soul); and if religious people had been sober enough not to see God in nature—and so avoid the sting of the reflection that 'nature lends such evil dreams'. We have seen that even in his youth S. K. was sober enough to confess that he could not fully enjoy nature because he could not clearly make it out. Charles Darwin alleged a reason the exact opposite of this to account for the fact that in his later years, after he had developed his theory, he was no longer able to enjoy the beauties of nature—the peacock's tail, &c.—because he understood it too well, knew so precisely how it had come about, in the service of an all too finite teleology. S. K.'s ignorance had this advantage over the knowledge of Darwin, that it left open to him the possibility of experiencing, in every intuition of natural beauty—not indeed a proof of God or a vision of God, but—what Fries calls 'a presentiment of the eternal in the temporal', which is the only legitimate enjoyment of the beauty of nature.

The *Diapsalmata*, which are an introduction to *Either/Or*, give us a deep insight into the spiritual emptiness and essential despair of the aesthetical life, that is, of S. K.'s own life as a student—just at the time when he appeared to be the merriest of all. His life as a youth did not exemplify the *Weltschmerz* which Goethe had exalted as a token of greatness of mind. On the contrary it was an entirely unheroic weariness and disgust with life. The personal character of these diapsalms is proved by the fact that several of them were lifted bodily out of the Journals. It is misleading to speak of them as aphorisms, though the polished form suggests that name, for only a few are maxims of universal validity, and by far the greater number are personal expressions of the feelings of the heart. In that sense they are psalms—not sacred psalms, such as men 'roll to wintry skies' in the belief that God will hear them, but psalms which S. K. could declaim only to himself. Therefore at the bottom of the title-page is written (in small letters) '*ad se ipsum*', which was a title he had inscribed in one of his early journals. I will give a few examples. They searchingly illuminate the young man's deplorable state of mind. I begin with expressions of mere disillusionment with the world, but there crops up one which affirms sheer hatred of men; and then in the last quotations we perceive how deep was the sorrow, how sharp the pain, how dark the melancholy which prompted his revolt and separated him from the world.

I feel like a piece on the chess-board when the opponent says of it, 'That piece cannot be moved.'

I don't care for anything. I don't care to ride, that involves too much movement; I don't care to walk, that is too fatiguing; I don't care to lie down, for either I must remain there, and that I don't care for, or else I must get up again, and that I don't care for at all. The sum of it all is, I don't care.

As it was in the case of Parmenicus, according to the legend, who in the Trophonian cave had lost the faculty of laughter, but in Delos regained it again at the sight of a formless lump which was reputed to be the image of the goddess Leto, so was it in my case. When I was very young I forgot in the Trophonian cave how to laugh; when I grew older, when I lifted up my eyes and beheld reality, then I fell to laughing, and since that time I have never left off. I saw that the meaning of life was to make a good living, its aim to become a Minister of State; that it was love's rich satisfaction to get a well-to-do girl for a wife; that it was the blessedness of friendship to assist one another in money difficulties; that to make a speech signified enthusiasm; that it was courage to dare to be fined ten dollars;

that it was heartiness to say, 'Your health!' after dinner; that it was godfearingness to go once a year to the altar. That I saw, and I laughed.

After all, Nature does recognize the dignity of man; for when people want to keep birds away from the trees, they set up something which is supposed to resemble a man, and even the distant resemblance to man which the scare-crow has suffices to instil respect.

Life has become a bitter drink to me, and yet I must take it, slowly, in counted drops.

Time passes, life is a stream, men say, &c. It doesn't seem so to me: time stands still, and I with it. All the plans I devise fly straight back again upon me; when I want to spit, I spit in my own face.

One must be very naïve to believe that it helps to shout and scream in this world, as though thereby one's fate might be altered. Let a man take it as it comes and refrain from much speaking. In my youth when I entered a restaurant I was accustomed to say to the waiter, 'A good piece, a very good piece, from the loin, not too fat.' Perhaps the waiter did not hear my shout, let alone pay attention to it, and my voice would not likely carry as far as the kitchen and influence the carver—and even if all that happened, there was perhaps not a good piece in the whole roast. Now I shout no more.

Most men pursue pleasure in such great haste that they hasten by it. Their case is like that of the giant who guarded in his castle a princess he had carried off. One day he took his midday nap. When he awoke after an hour she was gone. Hastily he put on his seven-league boots—with one stride he was far beyond her.

The best proof for the wretchedness of existence is that which is derived from the observation of its glory.

Of all laughable things the most laughable, it seems to me, is to be busy in the world, to be a man that is brisk to his dinner and brisk to his work. So when I see a fly settle at a critical moment upon the nose of such a busy man, or if he is splashed with mud by a wagon which passes him in still greater haste, or the railway gate closes on his nose, or a tile falls from the roof and kills him, then I laugh from the bottom of my heart. And who indeed could help laughing? What, after all, does he accomplish, this busy hurrier? Is not his case like that of the woman who was all in a flurry because a fire had broken out in the house—and rescued the andirons? What more indeed does he rescue out of life's great conflagration?

At the theatre it chanced that a fire broke out behind the scenes. Pierrot stepped out to inform the public of it. People thought it a joke and applauded; he repeated the warning, they applauded all the more. Thus, I suppose, the world will come to an end to the accompaniment of the universal jubilation of wits who take it to be a joke.

Wine no more gladdens my heart; a little of it makes me sad, much of it, melancholy. My soul is languid and powerless, in vain I dash the spurs of pleasure in her side, she is exhausted, she can no more gather herself for a royal jump. I have lost all my illusions. In vain I seek to abandon myself to joy's infinitude, it cannot lift me up, or rather I cannot lift myself. Erstwhile, when it but beckoned, up I climbed, light and sound and buoyant. When I rode slowly through the woods, it seemed as though I were flying; now, when foam is on the horse and it almost drops with fatigue, it seems to me as though I were not moving. I am alone—that I have always been, forsaken, not by men (that would not pain me) but by the happy genii of joy which in multitudinous bands surrounded me—I who everywhere met acquaintances, everywhere discovered an opportunity. As a drunken man collects about him youth's frolicsome swarms, so about me there flocked elves of joy, and my smile was meant for them. My soul has lost the possibility. If I were to wish for anything, I should not wish for myself kingdom or power, but the passion of the possibility, the eye which, always young, always blazing, beholds the possibility. Enjoyment disappoints, the possibility never. And what wine is so foaming, what so fragrant, what so intoxicating!

Never have I been joyful, and yet it has always appeared as if joy were in my train, as if the genii of gladness were dancing around me, invisible to others but not to me, whose eyes shone with delight. So when I pass men by, as happy and joyful as a god, and they envy me my good fortune, then I laugh; for I despise men, and I revenge myself. Never have I wished to do any man wrong, yet it has always seemed to me as though every man that came near me remained mortified and injured.

For when I hear others boast of their fidelity and their integrity I laugh, for I despise men, and I revenge myself. Never has my heart been hardened against any man, but always, even when I was most moved, I have given the impression that my heart was closed to every feeling and estranged. For when I hear others praised for their good heart, see them loved for their deep and rich feeling, then I laugh; for I despise men, and I revenge myself. When I see myself execrated and held in abhorrence for my coldness and heartlessness: then I laugh, for my resentment is sated. If it should be possible for the good men to bring me to the pass where I really was in the wrong, did really do wrong to any one—then indeed I should have lost.

My figure is badly proportioned in the fact that my fore-legs are so small. Like the hare from New Holland [i.e. the kangaroo] I have very small fore-legs but endlessly long hind-legs. Commonly I sit quite still; when once I make a movement it is a prodigious leap—to the terror of all those to whom I am bound by the tender ties of kinship and friendship.

My sorrow is my feudal castle, which is perched like an eagle's nest high up on the peak of a mountain, among the stars. No one can take it by storm. Thence I swoop down into the realm of reality and seize my booty; but I do not remain down below: I bring my booty home, and this booty is a picture, I weave it into the tapestries which adorn my castle. There I live like a departed soul. All that I have experienced I plunge into the baptism of forgetfulness to consecrate it to the eternity of remembrance. There I sit pensively, like an old grey-haired man, and explain the pictures in a soft voice, almost whispering, and besides me sits a child and listens, although he remembers all before I tell it.

What is it that binds me? Out of what was the chain forged by which the Fenris Wolf was bound? It was fashioned out of the noise made by cats' paws travelling over the ground, out of the beards of women, out of the roots of rocks, out of the grass bears eat, out of fishes' breath and birds' spittle. So am I bound with a chain forged out of dark imaginings, out of alarming dreams, out of uneasy thoughts, out of fearful forebodings, out of inexplicable dreads. This chain is 'exceeding pliable, soft as silk, yields to the strongest strain, and cannot be torn asunder'.

Something marvellous has happened to me. I was caught up into the seventh heaven. There sat all the gods in assembly. As a special grace there was accorded to me the privilege of making a wish. 'Wilt thou,' said Mercury, 'wilt thou have youth, or beauty, or power, or long life, or the most beautiful maiden, or any other glorious thing among the many we have here in the treasure-chest?—then choose, but only one thing.' For an instant I was irresolute, then I addressed the gods as follows: 'Highly esteemed contemporaries, I choose one thing, that I may always have the laugh on my side.' There was not a god that answered a word, but they all burst out laughing. Thereupon I concluded that my wish was granted, and I found that the gods knew how to express themselves with good taste; for it surely would have been inappropriate for them to answer seriously, 'This is conceded to thee.'[1]

It is evident that many of these *Diapsalmata*, perhaps all of them, belong more properly to our next chapter, which describes 'the path of perdition'. But in such a case as this, where is the line to be drawn? Is not the recklessness of 'a student in perpetuity', without aim, without direction, precisely what is meant by the warning 'Broad is the way'?

If we were to read the *Diapsalmata* as S. K.'s contemporaries read them, and as men continued to read them until the Journals were published and studied, we should call them witty, or perhaps humorous; but now, when they are brought into such a personal connexion with him, we perceive how sarcastic was his humour and how bitterly he satirized himself. It is only too true that the wit of the young Kierkegaard was of a sort that burnt and seared, whereas in later years the humour which sparkles everywhere in his books is frequently warm and tender and illuminating.

At this point the contemporary entries in the Journals begin to be a help to us. One may say that the Journals were not seriously begun until the summer of 1835, when his father gave Søren a sum of money to pay for a tour of some months in the north of Seeland. Doubtless he was eager to have the youth separated for a while from the sort of persons he consorted with in Copenhagen, and was hopeful that a summer spent in the country might work a change in him. It did indeed, but hardly in the way his father hoped. For the first and only time he abandoned himself to the charms of nature in the spirit of German Romanticism. Also he found himself enough alone and at leisure to review his past life and plan seriously for the future. And so it is that the journal of this tour, which is the very beginning of his serious Journals, contains the fullest and most perspicuous account of his state of mind that he ever wrote in his youth. Because these entries deal with one of the most critical periods of S. K.'s life, it is necessary to quote them at considerable length.

First of all, however, we need to remark about the Journals that they are not diaries. We speak properly of 'The Diary of the Seducer' and of the diary of the young man in *Guilty?/Not Guilty?* where the element of time was essential; but the entries in S. K.'s Journals were timeless, they were the records of his thoughts, things he wanted to remember, some of them thoughts he would use ultimately in his writings, very few of them being essentially related to particular dates, and few of them actually dated, except during the first years. The first name he gave these compilations was 'Miscellanies' (*Blandinger*); then, in 1846, in the midst of the first 'NB-Journal' he began (March 9) what he called 'Report', followed by 'Report—Result'; and from that time the successive volumes up to the time of his death were designated Journal-NB^2, &c., concluding with Journal-NB^{36}.

In the midst of the journal of the Seeland excursion he records a letter of June 1 addressed to the scientist Peter Wilhelm Lund, whom he had known at the house of his sister Petrea as her husband's brother, but who now was permanently settled in Brazil in pursuit of the study of palaeontology. Doubtless S. K. admired him, but it is likely that he selected him as a confidant for the reason that he was so far away, and knowing Søren's reticence we may wonder if such a letter was ever posted. I quote here a few selections from this letter:[1]

> ... [Comparing the fruitfulness of a man's life with the growth of plants, he says:] The first and foremost requisite is to get established in that particular part of the earth's surface where one belongs; but that is not always so easy to find. In this respect there are some happy natures which have so decided an inclination to a particular direction that they steadily labour on in the way which once for all was indicated to them, without

ever pausing to think that it was perhaps another way they ought to be treading. There are others, too, who suffer themselves to be governed so entirely by their surroundings that they never get a clear notion whither they are tending. . . . But how few there are in the first class, and to the second I would not wish to belong. Greater is the number of those who try to test in life what this Hegelian dialectic is all about. It is entirely in order that the wine should ferment as it clears, but nevertheless this situation is often disagreeable in certain of its phases, although taken as a whole it has agreeable aspects in the fact that within the general attitude of doubt it succeeds in attaining relative results. . . . Every man naturally desires to work in the way indicated by his talents, and from this again it follows that he desires to cultivate his talents in a particular direction, that, namely, which is best adapted to his individuality. But what is this? Here I stand before a huge question-mark. I stand here like Hercules, but not where two roads cross—no, here there is manifest a far greater multiplicity of paths, and so it is all the more difficult to grasp the right one. Perhaps this is precisely the misfortune in my existence, that I am interested in far too much and not decisively in anything; my interests are not subordinate to a single aim, but they are co-ordinate.

I will try to show how the matter stands with me.

1. *Natural Sciences*. . . . I have been enthusiastic about the natural sciences, and I still am, but it seems to me that I shall not make them my chief study. [This subject, however, is discussed in no less than two pages.]

2. *Theology*. This seems to be what I have come closest to choosing; but here, too, great difficulties present themselves. Here in Christianity itself there are contradictions so great that they hinder at least a clear view. I have grown up, so to speak, in orthodoxy, as you surely know; but so soon as I began to think for myself the huge colossus began to totter. . . . I could very well agree with it in particular points, but these are to be regarded as the sprouts which one finds growing in the crevices of the cliffs. On the other hand I could very well perceive distortion in particular points—but I must for a while let the fundamental basis remain in doubt.

It appears that the chief reason he has for pursuing the study of theology is 'that thereby I could give my father a great pleasure'. He dismisses rationalism from consideration because of its intellectual duplicity. We learn in other connexions that he had tried Schleiermacher and found him wanting, and that the zealous religious movement led by Grundtvig in Denmark, which his brother had embraced, was not at all to his liking. These were not casual judgements, and throughout his life they were never reversed. He never was friendly to conventional orthodoxy, or to rationalism, mysticism, or pietism.

S. K.'s head-quarters on the tour of Seeland was the small town of Gilleleie at the northern apex of the island. From this town was dated on August 1 a long entry in which he reviewed his situation even more candidly than he had ventured to do to a friend in Brazil.[1]

> ... What I especially need is to become clear about myself, what *I ought to do*—not what I ought to know, except in so far as knowledge must go before doing. The thing is to understand my destiny, to perceive just what the Deity would have *me* do. The first requisite is to find a truth which is truth *for me*, to find *the idea for which I am willing to live and die*. And what use would it be to me if I were to find out the so-called objective truth? ... I will not pretend to deny that I recognize an imperative of the understanding, and that this properly exercises an influence upon men; *but this has to become vitally a part of me*, and this is what I now recognize as the chief thing. This is what my soul thirsts after as the African deserts thirst after water.... But to find that idea, or rather I should say to find myself, it avails me nothing to plunge any farther into the world. And that is just what I did before. So I believed that it would be good for me to throw myself into *jurisprudence*, so as to be able to develop the sharpness of my wits with the many complications of life. Here especially a great mass of detail is presented in which I could lose myself; here perhaps I might be able to construct out of the given factors a totality, an organism of the life of thieves, and pursue it on its obscure side (here also a spirit of association is manifest in a high degree). I could wish to be a prosecuting attorney, partly for the reason that by putting myself in another's place I could, so to say, acquire a substitute for my own life and find in outward change

a certain diversion. What I lacked was this, to lead a *complete human life* (and not alone a life of understanding) so that thereby I might succeed in basing the development of my thought not alone upon—well, not upon something one calls objective, upon something which in any case is not my own, but upon something which hangs together with the deepest roots of my existence, whereby I grow as it were into the divine and cling fast to it even though the whole world should collapse. How near man is to madness, in spite of all his knowledge! What is truth but a life lived for an idea? In the last resort everything must be based upon a postulate, but the moment this is no longer extraneous to a man but he lives in it, at once it ceases to be for him a postulate. Behold, this is what I lack, and thereafter I strive. . . . Only when a man has learnt thus inwardly to understand *himself* does his life attain repose, only then is he delivered from that troublesome and mischievous travelling companion, his life's irony, which manifests itself in the sphere of the understanding and requires that all understanding begin with non-understanding (Socrates), just as it was out of nothing God created the world. But especially is this the case in the fairways of morality, for one who has not caught the trade-wind of virtue. Here a man is tossed about in the most dreadful manner; at one moment it allows him to feel happy and content with the resolution to journey on in the right way, the next moment it plunges him into the abyss of despair. Often it lulls a man to sleep with the thought that 'it simply couldn't be otherwise', only to awaken him again suddenly to the sternest accounting. . . . So let the lot be cast—I pass the Rubicon! It is true that this path will lead me *into conflict*, but I do not flinch. I will not sorrow over the time past—for to what use is sorrow? Forcefully I will make my way and not waste time . . . I will hasten on in the new-found way and cry out to every one I meet, not to look back like Lot's wife, but to hurry on because there is an eminence we are striving to climb.

Much of this expresses merely the experience which is common to youth in the face of the perplexing problem of choosing one's profession. But there is a great deal that is profoundly characteristic of S. K. The phrases which he has underscored (here printed in italics) indicate perceptions which he never relinquished and which later (especially through the mouth of Johannes Climacus) he developed fruitfully, under such rubrics as 'existential thinking', 'reduplication', 'inwardness', and 'truth is subjectivity'. Partly because of his father's wealth, and partly because of his own various talents, S. K. was put to the embarrassment of facing a greater multiplicity of choices than are visible to most young men. We can understand why he remarked, in a later entry in his Journal,[1] that in Gribs-Skov, the great forest north of Hillerød, 'There is a place called The Nook of the Eight Paths. The name pleases me immensely.' As this had also the advantage of being a beautiful spot, it was often the goal of S. K.'s carriage-drives. To understand the attraction the legal profession had for him, we must remember that he had played very seriously with the idea of composing a romance about 'The Master-Thief', and began at the university to study the popular legends about famous robbers like Robin Hood, accounting this a theme worthy of attention alongside the legends of Faust, Don Juan, and the Wandering Jew, supplemented by fairy-tales of all sorts.

The last paragraph quoted above announces a heroic decision, but does not disclose what it was. We might suppose that it was the noble purpose of preparing for the theological examination, both because it would please his father and because this was his ostensible reason for being at the university. But from the next passage I shall quote we learn that 'crossing the Rubicon' meant anything but that, and it appears that the danger he was prepared to face with so much courage meant only a conflict with his father. There is no indication that he made a choice of any one path out of the many which were visible to him; but his decision not to take the path which lay straight before him filled him with an exuberance which for a while blinded him to the fact that he had really made no definite choice at all, except to follow his own inclinations—in defiance of his father and of God. Without plainly perceiving it, he was in reality facing, not 'eight paths', but an either/or. And since no definite decision had been made with regard to a profession, we need not be surprised to discover that his soul did not attain repose.

Soon after S. K.'s return to Copenhagen an entry[2] dated October 17 states roundly the conclusion he had come to: '*Philosophy and Christianity cannot, however, be united.*' This is what S. K. often asserted in later years, meaning to say, 'Away from speculation!': Christianity remains, but philosophy must go by the board. It would be a great mistake, however, to suppose that he means the same thing here. For here he means to say that, inasmuch as Christianity cannot be reconciled with philosophy, Christianity must be rejected. This is made only too plain by what follows in this entry, and still more from the following entry[1] from which I am about to quote:

> I have now sought to show why Christianity and philosophy cannot be united. In order to justify this separation I have considered how Christianity, or rather the Christian life, must appear from the standpoint of reason. I shall now confirm this by describing how man as man, outside of Christianity, appears to the Christian. For this purpose it will suffice to recall how Christians regarded the pagans, considered their gods the invention of devils, their virtues splendid vices, how one of their coryphaei declared that man was merely a clot and a stone before the coming of Christ, how they declined to relate the preaching of their Gospel to man as such, how they constantly began with 'Turn ye and be converted', and how they themselves declared that their Gospel was to the pagans foolishness and to the Jews a stumbling-block. . . . And what brings it about that there are actually so many who, as they say, find in their consciousness Christian impulses, yet on the other hand neither are nor profess to be Christians? It is surely because Christianity is *a radical cure* which one shrinks from; and without having precisely the same formal conceptions which led many Christians in the earliest times to defer the decisive step until the last minute, it is surely for this reason such persons lack strength to take the desperate *leap*. In addition to this there is the strange stuffy atmosphere which we encounter in Christianity and which exposes every one, until he has been acclimatized, to a very dangerous climatic fever. If we look towards life here on earth, they rise up against us and declare that everything is sinful, man as well as nature; they talk about the broad way in contrast to the narrow. If we look toward the other world, we first discover there, as the Christians teach, the untying of the knot (Act V). And though the Christians have not had so grandiose an imagination as that which led the northern peoples to depict Loke chained to a cliff with poison

dripping down upon him, while they afforded him the comfort of placing his wife by his side—the Christians on the other hand have known how to deprive the unfortunate of every alleviation—not even a drop of water to quench his burning tongue. Almost always where the Christian employs himself about the world to come it is desolation, punishment, destruction, eternal torture and pain which he envisages; and, exuberant and extravagant as his imagination is in this regard, just so meagre is it when it is a question of the blessedness of the believers or the elect, which is depicted as a blessed intentness of gaze with fixed and vapid eyes, with great staring pupils, or with a gaze so suffused with moisture that clear seeing is impeded. . . . Very much more beneficent, it has always seemed to me, is the notion of seeing assembled together the great, distinguished, talented men of the whole world, such as have set their hand to the wheel of human progress. My enthusiasm has always been aroused by the thought of such a veritable high-school of the human race, such a republic of science and learning, in which we (in strife ever with contradictions) would be growing every moment in knowledge. . . . The Christians, however, have been loath to grant these great men entrance into their society, in order that it might not become too mixed and that only a single accord might be struck, so that the Christians might sit like a Chinese assembly of mandarins and rejoice that they had brought to completion that high, insurmountable wall against—the barbarians. And why all this? Not to blame the Christians, but to show the contradictions which are *de facto* recognized in the Christian life, to warn every one whose breast is not yet tight-laced in a spiritual corset of this sort against subjecting himself imprudently to such a thing, to protect him from such narrow-breasted asthmatic conceptions. It is certainly hard to dwell in a land where the sun never shines above the horizon, but on the whole it is not particularly agreeable to dwell in a place where the sun stands so directly over your crown that it does not let you or any of your surroundings cast a shadow.

Perhaps there is nothing more significant in this passage than the aloofness with which S. K. speaks of 'the Christians'—as though this young candidate in theology had already definitely severed all relationship with them. Not only does he state with passionate vigour the worst that can be alleged in disparagement of Christianity (involving even the words of Jesus in his criticism), but he plainly prefers the humanistic ideal in its most extravagant form. There is nothing in this whole passage which the later Kierkegaard would not have repudiated—and which he did not repent of and do penance for—except the conception that 'Christianity is a radical cure' and that it requires a 'desperate leap'. He recognized also at a later time that a Christianity which is not 'to the Greeks foolishness and to the Jews a stumbling-block' is evidently not Christianity. Clearly this passage indicates a deliberate revolt against Christianity and the resolution to renounce it. This followed as a natural consequence upon his revolt against his father. How closely the two were bound together we shall see in the next chapter. At this moment S. K. was not only in rebellion against Christianity, but in rebellion against God. So he interpreted the situation at a later date. He recognized that essentially it was an attitude not of doubt but of defiance. And yet, remembering the solemn assertion he made thirteen years later in *The Point of View*,[1] 'I never gave up Christianity', I do not venture to say here that he renounced it, but only that he had resolved to do so. Just as he failed to carry out the noble purpose of moral reform which he so eloquently registered in the entry quoted just before this, so he failed to realize the liberation he promised himself in this act of defiance. Defiance, unlike doubt and disbelief, implies necessarily that the object we defy is existent and real. We cannot defy what is non-existent for us, and for S. K. Christianity still remained existent. In that sense he might properly say, in looking back, 'I never gave up Christianity'; but perhaps it would be more true to say that Christ never gave him up. The last sentence of this defiant passage betrays a certain lack of confidence on the part of the defier: 'It is certainly hard to live in a land where the sun never shines.' In fact that darkness was not broken until the day of his conversion two and a half years later, when he experienced the 'indescribable joy' (see p. 170).

Try as we may, we cannot succeed in interpreting S. K. so profoundly, at any rate not so tersely, as he has interpreted himself, especially in *The Point of View*. So here I quote from that confession again. This time it is a passage which lies exactly between the citations to be found on pp. 66 and 49.[2]

Thus I set out upon the journey of life—initiated into all the possible enjoyments of life, yet never really enjoying, but rather (for this was the pleasure I had in conjunction with the smart of melancholy) labouring to give the impression that I enjoyed—having intercourse with all possible men, yet never for a moment supposing that in any of them I had a confidant, as surely it never occurred to any of them to confide in me—that is to say, I was obliged to become and I became an observer, and as such (being also spirit) I became enriched with experiences, got a vision at close range of the whole aggregate of pleasures, passions, moods, feelings, &c., acquired practice in understanding men through and through, as well as in imitating them; my imagination and dialectic had always material enough to work on, and yet I had time enough free from all labour to be idle. For long periods I have been busy about nothing else but the performance of dialectical exercises with a seasoning of imagination, trying out my spirit as one tunes an instrument of music—but I did not really live—I was tossed about in life, sorely tempted by much, and by wellnigh the most various temptations, also unfortunately drawn into errors, and, alas! also into the path of perdition. So in my twenty-fifth year I was for myself an enigmatical, complicated, extraordinary possibility, the significance and the definition of which I did not myself understand, in spite of the most eminent reflection. I understood one thing, that my life should be most properly employed in doing penance. But properly speaking I had not lived—except under the determinant of spirit. Man I had not been, and least of all child or youth.

So then my father died.

IV. THE PATH OF PERDITION
1836

At the moment when S. K. was preparing to 'cross the Rubicon' (p. 110) he recognized clearly that this step must involve a breach with his father. He scouted that 'danger', for his defiant attitude meant that he was already in revolt against his father and the strict régime in which his father had brought him up. In that mood he was not likely to reflect much upon the practical consequences—the inconveniences which this might involve for himself. It is possible that he left home at this time (the beginning of the winter term of 1835) and lived henceforth in boarding-houses. The fact that he had at this time no regular allowance from his father seems not to have troubled him much, for he was determined, in any case, to live as a rich man's son—and he succeeded in doing this by running up bills with the shopkeepers and getting loans from his friends. His debts continued to roll up, and the situation was not much relieved when on September 1, 1837 (the date of his definite exclusion from the home), his father resolved to give him an annual allowance of 500 Rigsdaler. This does not seem too meagre an allowance for a student when we reflect that it was equivalent to more than $1,000 in U.S. currency and was about half the average salary of a university professor. But at the end of that year his father found himself obliged (or was moved, as some say, by the intervention of Søren's elder brother) to pay his son's accumulated debts, which by that time amounted to 1,262 Rdl. (about $3,000). The creditors had become impatient, and Søren was hard pressed. He had even been posted for exclusion from the Student Association if before a certain date he did not pay his accumulated dues.

It is instructive to scrutinize some of the debts that were at that moment paid off. The debts of honour to fellow students amounted to 170 Rdl. ($400). A debt of 44 Rdl. ($105) to Madame Frey was for tobacco—which meant a great many cheap cigars and still more fillings for the pipe. There was a debt of 235 Rdl. ($560) to a coffee-house (*Conditori*), about which we shall have something to say later. The items for tailors and haberdashers were of course large. But the largest item was for books—

331 Rdl. ($794)—which proves that in the midst of his dissipation S. K. had not abandoned the intellectual life. He said of himself, quite justly:[1]

> I have tasted of the fruit of the tree of knowledge and often had delight in its flavour. But this delight was only in the moment of apprehension and did not leave any deeper mark in me. It seems to me that I have not drunk of the cup of wisdom but fallen into it.

I am not so fanatical as to cite these instances of lavish expenditure as a proof that S. K. was walking in 'the path of perdition'. It must be confessed that even after he had leapt over into the ethical stadium, and even after he had become a religious man, he was anything but frugal in his tastes. He himself provides me with the title of this section. I am not so stern a moralist as to count it an evident sign of perdition that S. K., like so many students, was frequently drunk among the drunken,[2] or that he was sure of finding 'the honoured company' of his boon companions in the wine-cellar singing the obscene words they had learnt from Goethe's *Faust*:

> *We feel so cannibalically well,*
> *Just like five hundred sows.*

But to me it does not seem a mitigating circumstance that some of his symposia may have displayed such refinement of taste as is suggested by his description of the famous Banquet in the *Stages*. For according to Judge William (who registers here, I suppose, the opinion of S. K.)[3] aestheticism is more dangerous just in proportion as it is more refined—a variation of Burke's 'Vice gaining more of evil by losing half its grossness'.

Brandt[4] essays to prove, with enough evidence to convince me, that the banquet described in the *Stages*, under the title *In Vino Veritas*, was not altogether imaginary, that some of S. K.'s companions in the boarding-house clique reappear in it, and that S. K. not only planned the whole but generously met the cost of the entertainment. The story represents clearly enough that Constantine Constantius (who impersonates one side of S. K.) planned the whole thing and carried it through in the face of the scepticism of his comrades. It might seem as if all the participants shared in the expense; but in S. K.'s sketch for a student play (p. 92) it was Willibald (= S. K.) who paid for the banquet. We may suppose that this banquet was the same as that described more idyllically in the *Stages*, and that in the later story S. K. modestly hints that he himself was the provider of all this luxury, as well as the planner, by the fact that he gives to the person who recounts his embellished 'recollection' the significant name of William Afham—*af ham* = by him—and so we might render this name in English as William Byhim. It was like the rich man's son to do such a lavish thing. But where did he get the money to pay for it? Brandt points to the *Conditori* debt of 235 Rdl. ($560). Such a banquet as that described in the *Stages* would have been cheap at that price.

Constantine Constantius prescribed that at this banquet every member of the party should make a speech about love, and that no one should speak until he was under the influence of wine. S. K. remarks with reference to the first part of *Either/Or* that he could not introduce there any instance of true love, because that did not belong properly in the aesthetic stage. It was for this reason, perhaps, that he did not include in *Either/Or* an account of his own experience of love, which he had purposed to put there and afterwards introduced in the *Stages*, in the form of Quidam's Diary, *Guilty?/Not Guilty?* At all events, it is obvious that, under the conditions prescribed, the speeches at the banquet might deal with every sort of love except true love. Brandes remarks that one can almost see blue flames issuing from the mouths of the speakers. The daimonia which characterized the banquet was plainly devilish. If this was characteristic of S. K.'s parties, and particularly if this party was planned and paid for 'by him', it cannot seem extravagant to speak of 'the path of perdition'.

We seem to be far advanced in this path, if the Seducer who figures in this banquet was P. L. Møller, one of S. K.'s familiar companions. In *Either/Or*, where this personage first appears as the author of *The Seducer's Diary*, S. K. seems inclined to idealize him, inasmuch as he all but hides the vulgarity of his loves (which appears only in the interesting episode of the serving-maids, tastelessly omitted from the recent English translation by Fick) and their multiplicity. At that time he could treasure a hope of his reformation. But in the *Stages* the Seducer is plainly a lost soul. It is significant that Møller, as a literary critic, while he delighted in condemning S. K.'s works, had nothing but praiser of the Seducer and the philosophy of life which he represents. Years later it was partly S. K.'s contempt for Møller which drew him into conflict with the *Corsair*. His contempt was deserved. If any man ever went to perdition in an earthly sense, it was P. L. Møller. He came to an early and miserable end in France, befriended only by two women whom he had seduced. The sentimentality of our day forbids us to speak absolutely of perdition. But perhaps there never was an age when the fact of it is more common and more evident—if in this life only we have hope. In our age we have not enough imagination to conceive of such a thing as 'gaining the whole world', and we have not enough courage to face the possibility that a man may 'lose his own soul'.

The banquet described in the *Stages* was made to end idyllically by the fact that the guests, returning in the early morning from the country restaurant where the scene was laid, stumbled into a garden and witnessed the conjugal felicity of Judge William and his beloved wife as they sat at breakfast in a summer-house. But perhaps this beautiful ending was invented to obliterate the memory of a very dreadful sequel. For it is possible that this was the drunken banquet which preceded S. K.'s fall and in a sense occasioned it. William Afham introduces the story of the banquet by a disquisition upon the distinction between memory and recollection, making it plain that the function of recollection is to idealize the crude content of memory.

'Broad is the way that leadeth to destruction', and surely no way could be broader than that along which we have seen young Kierkegaard travelling as 'a student in perpetuity'—if indeed that can be called a way which has apparently no direction. We have seen him wandering on an exceedingly broad plain, facing in turn all the points of the compass. Here we are to see that this plain had a slant which sloped perilously to the depths.

S. K. was soon to discover that the choice he had made with so prodigious an expenditure of reflection after his vacation in North Seeland was, properly speaking, no choice at all. He had resolved to put aside Christianity and be free from the restraints of religion—that is, from ethics. But, strictly speaking, this was not an ethical choice—nor an unethical. He had chosen the aesthetical life; but he had not chosen it as the evil. He had chosen it as a life indifferent to the distinction of good and evil. Judge William, in the second part of *Either/Or*, insists that the real choice, the genuine either/or, is not a choice between this and that, and not even the more fundamental choice between good and evil, forasmuch as this does not constitute a dilemma, seeing that a man who is plainly confronted with this choice has no alternative but to choose the good. The essential either/or is the question whether one will choose to make this choice—that is, to choose between the evil and the good. This primary choice is of course always involved in the choice of the good. But this primary choice young Kierkegaard did not make: he simply chose the aesthetic life, as in itself neither good nor evil but indifferent. But with this he made no decisive choice. He shrank from it. Judge William warns his young friend that he who declines to make a choice as an act of freedom will discover that the choice is made for him by obscure movements in the unconscious, impersonal self—that is, by necessity. It may be said that S. K. did not even choose with what the judge calls 'aesthetic seriousness', for this implies the choice of something in particular, the decision to be something definite—'a Don Juan, a Faust, or a pirate'. He simply chose in general the aesthetic life, and he was soon to discover that this was really no choice at all. In the characteristic language of *Either/Or*, he had not chosen to despair, and so he had not chosen himself, and he had not chosen absolutely, for there is no absolute choice except the choice of one's own self according to its eternal worth.

I have summarized here a great part of the argument of the second part of *Either/Or*. Some of the passages which have here been exceedingly compressed will be quoted *in extenso* in the next section. Any one who reads *Either/Or* without having any acquaintance with S. K.'s life will very naturally conclude that the subtle distinctions made by Judge William are merely an exhibition of dialectical gymnastics. Thus were S. K.'s contemporaries condemned to read it. But now we understand that it is all a passionate analysis of his own poignant experience, all of it drawn from his very entrails, that it is existential philosophy, at the farthest remove from speculation. Knowing this, one will not dismiss it petulantly because it contains terms strange and new; and one will not count it too laborious a task to study and scrutinize every definition, in this and in the other works where S. K. reveals himself. For it is all real and it is all honest. I have never encountered a man so honest as S. K.

We are to see that the 'path' upon which S. K. set out afresh pitched suddenly downward, and that before a year was passed he was carried far beyond the bounds his reflection had set for him, and finally slid into an abyss. This situation was the more tragic for him because, in spite of all appearances to the contrary, he had not renounced morality. This was the one absolute value that remained to him from the impressions of his childhood. Religion in general and Christianity in particular he regarded with critical aloofness. He had decided to leave the question of the truth of Christianity undecided for the moment. It is to be noted, however, that he never slumped into the position so common to-day (or at least yesterday) which treats religion as a 'value'—thereby seeking to avoid any possible conflict between religion and philosophy (or science). Christianity for S. K. was either true or untrue, it was either the absolute truth it claimed to be, or it was not truth at all. Hence he regarded it as a competitor of philosophy, and at that moment it seemed to him an unequal competitor. However, we can see that he was becoming less and less confident of discovering absolute truth through philosophy—all the more because he was profoundly dissatisfied with the Hegelian system, which was the philosophy then in vogue. That system was condemned in his eyes because it had no ethics. So at this time religion was challenged, and philosophy was challenged, but ethics was unchallenged. The ethical was his one absolute—only he did not 'choose' it. He had not yet learnt from Judge William that this choice cannot safely be deferred, because the individual is all the time moving on, like a ship while the helmsman defers the decisive act of putting her about. And so he went on the rocks. Like all aesthetic individuals he was 'living in the moment',[1] and had not yet learnt the solemn significance of the instant of choice, 'the instant', which is 'not an atom of time but of eternity'. And so, while recognizing the ethical as the absolute, because he did not definitely choose it he fell.

Christianity was certainly not his absolute at this time. He stood apart from it as an observer—and not a friendly one. And yet we have no right to reject or to discount the solemn affirmation he made in *The Point of View* [cf. quotation on p. 48], that even though 'there was a time when Christianity seemed to me the most inhuman cruelty . . . yet, even when I was farthest from it, I never have broken with Christianity or given it up, . . . it was venerable to me'. We must make what we can of this declaration, in spite of all that appears to belie it in the youth of S. K. Certainly at this time he was 'far from it'. Yet we can see at least that it still existed for him. Just before the note (cf. pp. 112 ff.) which registered his determination to prefer philosophy to Christianity he wrote this entry in his journal, on the date October 9, 1835:[1]

> The case of Christianity, or this thing of becoming a Christian, is like every radical cure—one postpones it as long as possible.

We see that even at this time he had the feeling that Christianity was put aside but not discarded. In the important entry which he dated 'Gilleleie, August 1, 1835' (cf. p. 109 f.), he said:

> With a feeling of dim apprehension I have sought to avoid coming into too close a contact with the phenomena whose attractive force might perhaps exercise too great a power over me. I have sought to appropriate much from them, have studied their character and their significance in human life, but yet at the same time I have been on my guard not to come like moths too near the flame.

How coolly he could observe Christianity is shown by another entry of about the same time:[3]

> Christianity was an imposing figure when it first stepped out into the world and uttered its message; but from that moment on when it sought through a pope to prescribe limits, or would throw the Bible at people's heads, or finally [referring to Grundtvig] the creeds, it is like an old man who thinks now that he has lived long enough in the world and would make an end of it. Therefore it naturally occurs to its illegitimate children (the Rationalists) that it may be pronounced incompetent and put under a guardian, whereas on the other hand its true children think that, like Sophocles, it will in the decisive moment rise up in its full power.

An entry already quoted on p. 19 speaks of his 'offence at religion' even in childhood.[4] Looking back upon his childhood from the year 1850, he describes his distaste for religion thus:[5]

> Take an analogy. Describe to a child the family doctor as an

awfully nice and kind man, &c. Then what happens? The child will naturally put it this way: Yes, it is perfectly possible that he is such a nice man, I am quite ready to believe it, but I very much prefer nevertheless to have nothing to do with him, for to become the object of his special kindness means that I am sick—and to be sick is not a nice thing, and therefore I am very far from being delighted at the thought that he will be summoned. Suppose there is an invalid in the family who is indefatigable in praising the physician's kindness. The child thinks thus: Yes, that is all very well—when one is sick.

But in fact the 'offence' and stumbling-block which he found in Christianity was far deeper than this would lead us to suppose. Several of his own expressions[1] incline us not to dismiss as incredible one of Levin's bits of gossip, to the effect that S. K. once said to him that it was lucky for him that he (as a Jew) was *free from Christ.* If he himself were free from Christ, he would enjoy life in an entirely different way and have a good time. Sometimes when he read to Levin passages from the New Testament he broke out in tears and sobs. Some light is thrown upon this by an entry in the Journal which says: 'With God the Father I could get along easier than with the Son, for he is the example that must be followed.'

At this point we need to have in mind the experience hinted at in 'Solomon's Dream' and in 'The Great Earthquake' (p. 68 f.), and the description (p. 75) of the disconsolate spirit with which S. K. began his youth and entered the university. Despair was evident in these documents, but now we begin to discern a note of defiance. In later years S. K. expressly understood his youth as defiance. It was defiance of his father, first of all, but also defiance of God. From his own experience he learnt to regard defiance of God as 'slave-revolt'—an interesting contrast to Nietzsche's description of obedience to God as 'slave-morality'. In the title of one of the sections of *The Sickness unto Death* (which is a study of despair) he describes his particular sort of despair as 'In despair at willing to be one's self, defiance'.[2] S. K. acknowledges that 'this sort of despair is seldom seen in the world'. 'Nevertheless', he adds, 'it still does occur in actuality'—that he knew well from his own experience. The whole section, which analyses this sort of despair, must be read if one would thoroughly understand

S. K.'s experience. Here, however, I can quote only the following passage:

> In order to will in desperation to be oneself there must be consciousness of an infinite self. This infinite self, however, is indeed only the abstractest form, the abstractest possibility of the self. And this is the self that he wills in desperation to be, detaching the self from every relationship with the Power which has posited it, or detaching it from the conception that there exists such a Power. By the aid of this infinite form, the self in desperation wills to dispose of his own self, or to create his own self, to make his own self into that self which he desires to be, to determine what he will admit as a constituent of his concrete self and what he will not admit. His concrete self, or his concretion, is characterized of course by necessity and limitations, it is this perfectly definite thing, with just these talents, disposition, &c., in the concretion of this relationship, &c. But by the aid of the infinite form, the negative self, he will first undertake to refashion the whole so as to make out of it such a self as he desires, brought about by the aid of the infinite form of the negative self—and thus it is he wills to be his own self. That is to say, he wishes to begin a little earlier than other men do—not by and with the beginning, but 'in the beginning' —he will not clothe himself in his own self, will not see his task indicated in the self that is given him, he will construct it for himself by the aid of the infinite form.

I could wish as heartily as any reader that S. K. did not so often express his thoughts in the terminology of the speculative philosophy which he decried and opposed—and yet I cannot quite see how he could have expressed the same thoughts in everyday language.

But here is a figurative expression of the same thought which may please the reader better. It occurs at the conclusion of the section from which I have just now quoted:[1]

> To describe it figuratively, it is as if an author were to make a clerical blunder, and this [blunder] were conscious of being such—though perhaps it was not really a blunder but was in a higher sense an essential constituent of the whole exposition—it is then as if this clerical blunder were to revolt against the author, out of hate for him were to forbid him to correct it, and

were to say to him in mad defiance: No, I will not be erased, I will remain as a witness against thee that thou art a mediocre author.

Knowing that S. K. is here describing his own case, we discover a deep pathos in the phrase, 'Perhaps it was not really a blunder', &c. 'An essential constituent of the whole' means the 'pinch of spice', the 'corrective', p. 587. It must be confessed that philosophical terminology could not describe so vividly what it means for a man to defy his Maker.

We have seen that S. K.'s defiance of God was intimately connected with his defiance of his father. The story[1] of Periander, Tyrant of Corinth, which is introduced in Quidam's Diary with the emphatic title, *A Lesson to be Learnt by Heart*, and dated on May 5, midnight (which was Søren's birthday), must certainly refer to his own history and to his defiance of his father. Periander was one of the Seven Wise Men of Greece—and yet in his actions the most foolish of men. The gods who had blessed him with wisdom and power were moved by a secret offence against them to lay upon him the curse that his actions should shame his wise words. He had murdered his beloved wife out of jealousy. The two sons learnt who the murderer of their mother was. The elder was not greatly moved by this knowledge, but the younger refused to speak to his father, preferring exile in a remote village, where the father, who secretly admired him for his courage and believed that he alone was capable of succeeding him, eventually sought him out. But they parted as enemies, never to be reconciled. Only this last trait is foreign to S. K.'s history—even the elder brother is remembered.

Another of the six stories introduced in Quidam's Diary (in *Guilty?/Not Guilty?*) is 'The Leper's Soliloquy', dated February 5, midnight.[2] Simon the Leper revolts against the God of his father Abraham—with a protest as violent as that of Job. Simon had discovered a salve by which the appearance of leprosy might be concealed—without diminishing its contagion. Manasses, his only companion, who dwelt with him among the tombs, departed, carrying the salve with him, to live again among men and put them in danger. Simon in the end is resigned to his horrible fate and reconciled to his God. The 'salve' means of course S. K.'s extraordinary talent for hiding his melancholy; and if the word 'melancholy' be put in the place of 'leprosy', this is clearly enough S. K.'s own story.

We cannot account for the gravity of S. K.'s condemnation of his life at this time unless we recognize that he understood it as defiance and rebellion against God. That made the sins he committed infinitely heinous. To use the Old Testament term, he 'sinned with a high hand'. His own language has led some of his commentators to suppose that there weighed upon him the unutterable guilt of blasphemy, that on some occasion or another he had cursed God. I am not at all inclined to seek for any definite or outward expression of S. K.'s defiance. For he himself has said of that sort of defiant despair which characterized him—'despair at willing to be oneself'—that it has 'no corresponding outward expression'. That is to say, any deed, even the most insignificant, can serve equally well to express defiance of God, and in itself the outward expression is indifferent. But here I feel bound to quote from *The Sickness unto Death* a long passage in which he has analysed himself with the utmost care:[1]

> This sort of despair is seldom seen in the world. Such figures hardly occur except in the writings of the poets, that is to say, the real poets, who always lend to their creations a daimoniac ideality (taking this word in its purely Greek sense). Nevertheless, such a despair does also occur in actuality. What then is the corresponding outward expression? Well, the fact is, there is nothing 'corresponding' inasmuch as an outward expression corresponding to reservedness is a self-contradiction, for, if it is corresponding, it is in fact revealing, but in this case the outward expression is always indifferent—here especially where reservedness, or what one might call inwardness clogged up, is the phenomenon in question. The lowest forms of despair, where there is no inwardness, or at least not enough to speak about,—the lowest forms of despair one might represent by describing or remarking upon the outward form of such despair. But the more spiritual despair becomes, and the more its inwardness becomes a world for itself in reservedness (*Indesluttethed*), just so much more indifferent is the question of the outward form under which the despair conceals itself. But just in proportion as the despair becomes spiritual, just so much more is it attentive to the dai-

moniac shrewdness of keeping the despair shut up in reservedness, and just so much more attentive therefore to transpose the outward expression into the irrelevant, making it as insignificant and indifferent as possible. As in the fairy-tales the troll vanishes through a crack which no one can discern, just so is the despair, in exact proportion as it is more spiritual, the better able to take up its dwelling in an outward expression behind which it would hardly occur to any one to seek for it. This concealment itself is something spiritual, and it is one of the safety-devices for assuring oneself of having as it were behind reality a safe enclosure, a world exclusively for oneself, a world where the despairing self is engaged as restlessly as Tantalus with willing to be its own self.

In 1836–7 S. K.'s thoughts were continually circling about the problem of sin and guilt. No occupation could be more dangerous for a young man who was resolved not to come into intimate contact with Christianity. He was indeed like a moth fluttering round the candle-flame. He did not then realize his danger, but later, out of this very experience, he learnt to recognize the truth that the only way of entering into Christianity was through the consciousness of sin. He did not at first realize that his 'dread of the Good' was an example of daimonia, or that it was a 'sympathetic antipathy'. He was aware, however, of the ambiguity of his 'dread of the Evil', that he was at once repelled and attracted by evil. In 1842 he formulated his experience in these terms:[1]

People have often enough explained the nature of original sin, and yet they have lacked a principal category—namely, dread, which is the real determinant of it. For dread is an attraction to what one fears, a sympathetic antipathy. Dread is an alien power which lays hold of an individual, and yet he cannot tear himself loose from it, and also will not; for one fears, but what one fears also attracts one. Then dread renders the individual impotent, and the first sin always occurs in impotence; apparently therefore he lacks accountability, but this lack is precisely what ensnares him.

This does not go far beyond his understanding of the matter early in the year 1837:[2]

A certain presentiment commonly goes before everything

that is to occur (cf. a scrap of paper[1]); but just as that can have a deterrent effect, so also it can be tempting, when the thought is awakened in a man that he is as it were predestinate, he sees himself brought as it were to some point by a chain of consequences, but they are consequences upon which he is able to exert no influence. Hence one must be so careful with children, never believe the worst, lest by an untimely suspicion, by a remark carelessly thrown out (a firebrand from hell which kindles the tinder that is in every soul) one may produce an anxious consciousness, whereby the soul which is innocent but not strong might be tempted to think itself guilty, come to despair, and thereby take the first step to reach that end which the anxious presentiment foreboded—an utterance whereby the kingdom of evil is given an opportunity to reduce him, by the snake-like fascination of its eye, to a state of spiritual impotence. Also to this situation we can apply the word: Woe unto him from whom the offence cometh.

All that S. K. experienced and reflected upon in the years of his temptation and fall, he formulated more precisely in *The Concept of Dread*, and there also he integrated his earlier conceptions in a more mature philosophy. In this connexion the titles of the chapters cannot seem strange to us—as they must to one who approaches the book without any knowledge of S. K.'s experience: Dread as the Presupposition of Original Sin; Dread as the Consequence of Original Sin; Dread as the Consequence of that Sin which Consists in the Lack of the Consciousness of Sin; Sin's Dreadful Anguish, or The Consequence of Sin in the Individual. It should be noted that in Danish the name of original sin is 'inherited sin', and S. K. could not but think of the last link in the chain, inheritance from his father. Though one may feel remote from the affirmation of the New England Catechism, 'In Adam's fall we sinned all', one cannot lightly dismiss S. K.'s experimental apprehension of the fact that 'the sin of the whole world combined to make him guilty'.[2] The last chapter of the book, Dread as a Means of Salvation in Conjunction with Faith, could of course not have been written until he had had the happy experience which it describes. And yet in a way this was an experience he did not attain until the end. Until the end he did not think of himself as a Christian, but spoke emphatically of the task of 'becoming a Christian'. In 1850 he realized that his 'stern education from innate dread to faith' was still far from complete:[1]

> Dread is the most frightful of all trials. He in whose soul there is an innate dread, though he may very well have an enthusiastic conception of God's love, cannot make his God-relationship concrete. . . . For the dread continues to be too strong for him and hinders him from viewing dangers, trials, temptations, &c., from the proper side, as tests for him to sustain—whereas he can hold all the tighter to the thought, Yes, but God is love nevertheless.

Here he is speaking, not of the dread which goes before sin and entices one into it, but of 'the dreadful anguish which is the consequence of sin in the individual'.

In a few brief quotations I present some of the outstanding definitions of *The Concept of Dread*:[2]

> Dread is a qualification of the dreaming spirit, and as such it belongs to the province of psychology. . . . So soon as we have regard to the dialectical qualifications of dread, it appears that this has precisely the ambiguity which is characteristic of psychology. Dread is a sympathetic antipathy and an antipathetic sympathy.
>
> The qualitative leap itself is beyond all ambiguity; but he who becomes guilty through dread is in a way innocent, for it was not he himself, but dread, an alien power, which laid hold upon him, a power which he did not love but dreaded—and yet he is actually guilty, for he sank in the dread, which he loved even while he feared it. . . .
>
> Everything depends upon dread coming to evidence. Man is a synthesis of the soulish and the bodily. But a synthesis is unthinkable where the two are not united in a third. This third is the spirit. . . .
>
> One can compare dread with dizziness. One whose eye chances to behold the yawning depth becomes dizzy. But his eye is as much the cause of this as the abyss is, for he might not have gazed down. So is dread the dizziness of freedom, which occurs when the spirit is about to compose the synthesis, and freedom then gazes down into its own possibility and grasps at finite things to hold itself by. In this state of dizziness freedom sinks. Psychology can go no farther than this. In

that very same moment all is changed, and freedom when it again raises itself up perceives that it is guilty. Between these two moments lies the leap, which no science has explained or can explain. He who becomes guilty in dread becomes as ambiguously guilty as it is possible to be. Dread is a womanish impotence in which freedom swoons. Speaking psychologically, sin always occurs in impotence. But dread is at the same time the most selfish thing, and no concrete expression of freedom is so selfish as the possibility of every concretion. This again is the overwhelming thing which determines the individual's ambiguous, sympathetical and antipathetical relationship. In dread there is the selfish infinity of the possibility, which does not tempt like a choice, but guilefully causes dread by means of its sweet apprehension. . . .

Just as dread is posited in the sense of shame, so is it present in all erotic enjoyment, not because this is sinful, by no means —wherefore it is no use for the priest to bless the pair ten times over. Even when the erotic experience itself is as beautiful, as pure and as moral as possible, undisturbed in its joy by any sensual reflection, dread is nevertheless present—not always disturbingly, however, but as a concurrent factor.

In this instance it is exceedingly difficult to make observations. Here especially one must take the precaution which the physicians take, never to observe the pulse but in such a way as to ensure that they will not feel their own pulse instead of the patient's, so here one must take care that the movement one observes be not the uneasiness of the observer himself in the face of the observation. However, this at least is sure, that all poets describe love (however pure and innocent they represent it) in such a way as to associate it with dread (*Angest*). To establish this in detail is the business of the aesthetical writer. But why this dread? Because in the culmination of the erotic the spirit cannot take part. I will speak like a Greek. The spirit is present indeed, for this it is which constitutes the synthesis, but it cannot express itself in the erotic, it feels foreign to it. It says as it were to the erotic, Excuse me! Here I cannot be a third person, therefore I will conceal myself for a while. But this precisely is dread, and at the same time it is shame. For it is a great stupidity to suppose that the blessing of the Church and the faithfulness of the husband in keeping only to his wife is enough. There is many a marriage profaned, though it is not done by an outsider. But when the erotic is pure and innocent and beautiful, then the dread is friendly and mild; and hence the poets are justified in speaking of a sweet uneasiness (*Beængstelse*). It goes without saying, however, that the dread is greater on the part of the woman than on the part of the man.

What is said here about dread emerging at the moment when the spirit is about to constitute the synthesis of soul and body is closely related to Judge William's explanation of the origin of melancholy:[1]

> What is melancholy? It is hysteria of the spirit. There comes a moment in a man's life when his immediacy is as it were ripe, and the spirit demands a higher form in which it can apprehend itself as spirit. Man as spirit merely in immediacy is bound up with the whole earthly life, and now the spirit would as it were collect itself out of this dispersion and transfigure itself into itself. The personality would become conscious of its eternal worth. If this does not occur, if the movement is brought to a check, if it is reversed, melancholy results.

I reflect that if this explanation of melancholy is as true as it is interesting, it is inconsistent with S. K.'s later tendency to represent that his whole youth and even his childhood was clouded by the deepest melancholy.

We must always remember that S. K. learnt his deep psychology first of all by reflection upon his own experience. When he entered the university he already knew 'dread as it is dialectically qualified by reference to fate' (after the Great Earthquake). For while he was still innocent he had a presentiment of the obscure fate which impended over his family and felt a solidarity with his father's guilt. But it did not have its full effect in a moment: he was to learn that 'it is not sudden like a dart, but gradually bores its way into the heart'. At the moment we are now approaching he was to have the experience of 'Dread as dialectically qualified by reference to guilt', and of 'Freedom lost somatic-psychically', which he calls 'The Shipwreck of Freedom'. (I quote here the titles of three sections of the book.)

I must not delay any longer to state in brief terms a theory of the character of S. K's sexual fall which is now very commonly accepted. It was first suggested by P. A. Heiberg, the principal editor of S. K.'s *Papers* until his death a few years ago. In 1912 he published a book called *An Episode in Søren Kierkegaard's Youth*. His theory is that, some time during the month of May 1836, after a night of bacchanalian debauch, young Kierkegaard, in a state of complete inebriation, not knowing what he did, was taken by his companions to a brothel and there lay with a harlot. Heiberg's argument is not only ingenious but convincing, so far as the main thesis is concerned. He consolidated it further in 1918 by a larger work entitled *A Segment in Søren Kierkegaard's Religious Development*.[1] These two books must be ranked with the primary sources for the study of S. K.

I need not recite Heiberg's ingenious proof of this thesis, for in this section I have assembled all the relevant material, so that this conclusion seems to spring to the eye as soon as attention is drawn to a story entitled *A Possibility*, which is incorporated in Quidam's Diary on the date of April 5, midnight. This is one of the six stories in the Diary. Inasmuch as we have already dealt with four of them (pp. 45, 70, 125 f.) and found that not only are they essentially autobiographical, in spite of the fantastic terms in which they are couched, but reveal S. K.'s deepest secrets, we approach this story with a strong presumption that it too must be a confession—but, like the others, a confession incognito, cunningly designed to hide the identity of the subject.

The story is beautifully embroidered; but, baldly told, the substance of it is this. A man of good talents, highly competent as an accountant, but with an extraordinary innocence and simplicity, something like a mild insanity, falls in with bad companions, who on one occasion make him drunk and take him to a brothel. He never remembered clearly what had happened, but he broke completely with these companions and became more solitary than ever, devoting himself entirely to his work. During the course of an almost fatal illness he conceived the fixed idea that as a consequence of his barely remembered escapade 'another being owed its life to him'. This was 'the possibility' which preoccupied him ever after, prompting him to carry out the most careful study of physiognomy, especially of children and of their inherited traits, and to scrutinize every child he passed in the street in the hope of discovering his own offspring.

And what made his mental derangement so dialectical was that he did not even know whether this [notion that he had visited a brothel] was a consequence of his sickness, a delusion of his fever, or whether death (by approaching him so nearly) had really come to the help of his memory with a recollection of reality.

The scene of this story is a quiet quarter of Copenhagen, which three years earlier S. K. had planned to describe for its own sake.[1] This therefore is clearly a part of the embroidery. After the lapse of a year he recurred to this theme again, and then he inserted in it the figure of the gently deranged man with his secret who appears in the finished story. All this we learn from the Journal.[2] In the end S. K. has so perfectly embellished this tale that it appears to me the most beautiful thing of the sort he ever did, a perfect model of a short story.

How are we to distinguish between the embroidery and the autobiographical kernel? For my part I cannot agree with Heiberg in ascribing to S. K., a man of such eminent reflection and such sound intelligence, a delusion which he himself ventures to attribute only to an insane man. The notion that he might have been parent to an unknown child certainly did not preoccupy S. K. long, for at the end of his short life he boasted that at least he was not responsible for bringing a child into the world. So far as this part of the story is concerned, the only similarity I can admit is S. K.'s affectionate interest in children. He says of himself that because he had never been a child he had a peculiar interest in childhood, and at a time when he was directing his daily walks towards the quiet quarter which he afterwards described so beautifully, he said,[3] 'I am intent at this time to make every child I meet smile at me.' It is clear that the simple tale of a night of dissipation (which I believe is the autobiographical kernel) is far too simple and too common to make good 'copy', even for a newspaper. To make a beautiful story of it, S. K. had to embellish it, and doubtless he was glad to disguise his confession by distracting attention from his real tragedy and fixing it upon a romantic but fictitious detail.

But we cannot lightly dismiss the presumption that the core of this story is autobiographical. For we know that S. K. had a secret which he jealously guarded, a sin of his youth which haunted him all his life long. The Accountant, too, was sly enough to keep his secret—making his simple neighbours believe that his strangeness was due to the fact that he had been hopelessly in love with a queen of Spain. In an entry closely related to the 'plan' of this story S. K. proposes another 'plan':[1]

> A man who had gone about with a jealously guarded secret became insane. Here one would suppose that his secret might come to light; but behold, in spite of his insanity, his soul clung fast to its place of concealment, and his neighbours are more than ever convinced that the false story with which he deceived them is the truth. He is cured of his insanity, gets to know everything, and perceives that he had betrayed nothing. Now, was that a joyful discovery for him or not? Perhaps he could have wished to be rid of his secret through his insanity; it was as though a hostile fate compelled him to keep his secret and will not suffer him to let it out. Or was it not a fortunate thing, was it not a good genius which helped him to keep his secret?

Any one who follows in the Journals S. K.'s agitated reflections upon his secret sin, noting how on the one hand he longed to be rid of his secret, yet on the other hand jealously guarded it and trembled at the possibility of its discovery, will perceive that in the passage just quoted he was thinking about himself and planning another story about himself—another story in which he could in a way unbosom himself without betraying himself. Several entries in which he anxiously ponders the maxim of canon law, *de occultis non judicat ecclesia* (the Church law does not sit in judgement upon secret sins), must be dealt with in a later chapter if at all; but here it is in place to remark upon two of them, belonging respectively to the years 1845 and 1846. In the first[2] he reflects upon 'the dialectical contradiction as to whether he profits others by keeping silent about his guilt and seeking to work in a quieter way [i.e. not as a parochial pastor], or whether it were better to come out with it all'. In the second[3] he raises the question: 'Dare I conceal the guilt? And yet dare I on my own initiative make it known? If God wills that it should be revealed, he is quite able to bring that about, and this self-denunciation could also be a way of playing the part of providence.'

According to S. K., 'the ethical requires revelation', frankness, openness; but he himself was close, reticent, secretive, unable to reveal himself. He knew very well that in this respect he suffered from an irrational inhibition, a daimonia. In the chapter of *The Concept of Dread*, which describes the daimonia of reservedness (*Indesluttethed*),[1] he describes himself—in unsparing terms:

> He can desire revelation up to a certain point, but hold a little remainder back, so as to begin the morbid reserve all over again. (This is the case with the minor spirits who cannot do anything *en gros*.) He can desire revelation, but incognito. (This is the shrewdest contradiction of reservedness. However, examples are to be found among poetically minded persons.) Revelation can already have conquered, but at the same moment reservedness boldly makes its last effort and is artful enough to transform revelation itself into a mystification, and reservedness has conquered.

Then S. K., in order to give concrete expression to the algebraic abstractions he has been dealing with, seeks to make the introvert's monologue audible—by describing his own case more nearly, but still incognito:[2]

> Meanwhile I will indicate a collision the contradiction of which is as dreadful as morbid reserve itself is. What the reserved man jealously guards in his morbid reserve may be something so dreadful that he dare not utter it even to himself, because it seems as if by the mere utterance he would be committing a new sin, and as if it were tempting him again. In order that this phenomenon may occur, the individual must exhibit a mixture of purity and impurity which seldom is seen. It is therefore most likely to occur when he who did the dreadful deed was not master of himself. Thus, in a state of intoxication, a man can have done something which he only dimly remembers, and yet may know that it was so dissolute that it is almost impossible for him to recognize himself. . . . What decides whether the phenomenon is daimoniac is the individual's attitude towards revelation, whether he will permeate this fact with freedom, accept it in freedom. The moment he does not will this, the phenomenon is daimoniac. One must hold this steadily and sharply in view; for even he who wills it is essentially daimoniac. That is to say, he has two wills, the one subordinate, impotent, which wills the revelation, and a stronger

which wills reservedness; but the fact that this is the stronger shows that he is essentially daimoniac.

S. K. was unable to 'permeate with freedom' the gross fact which became his troublesome secret. He had an innate indisposition to frankness. But this case was peculiarly difficult because of the sheer vulgarity of his fall. 'It was in one of those places where, strange to say, one gives money for a woman's despicableness'—so he said in telling of the Accountant's 'loss of purity'. He deplored 'the shipwreck of freedom', 'freedom lost somatic-psychically'. He felt that he was a leper, like Simon in the story lately referred to, and that for the rest of his life he must be distinguished from innocent men by 'the penitent's garb'. He told nobody what his sin was, but he often announced, to the amazement of his acquaintances, 'I am a penitent.' He confessed to his friend Boesen that he was very erotic, and doubtless he thought so; but good Pastor Boesen protested that he was the purest man he had ever known. Goldschmidt[1] says that 'when P. L. Møller went to pieces morally as a consequence of his collision with S. Kierkegaard, the deepest ground for this was that Kierkegaard stood in a finer, purer, and higher relationship to women'. We have seen that he thought of himself as an unusual 'mixture of purity and impurity'.

For my part, I have no doubt that Heiberg has discovered the sin which hindered S. K. from marrying Regina and from seeking a parochial charge. We have seen that he confessed his secret many times—but always with so much mystification that he himself was not eased of it, his contemporaries had no suspicion of it, and it has required in our day extraordinary acumen to ferret it out.

An entry of May 17, 1843, in which he reviews the breaking of his engagement to Regina, concludes as follows:[2]

> But if I had explained myself, I must have initiated her into terrible things, my relationship to my father, his melancholy, the eternal night, my aberrations from the truth, my lusts and excesses, which yet perhaps in God's sight were not so atrocious, for indeed it was dread (*Angest*) which caused me to go astray, and how could I seek refuge and support when I knew or surmised that the only man I had admired for his force and strength was himself tottering?

I have remarked that the six stories in Quidam's Diary not only illuminate S. K.'s own history, but have to do precisely with his deepest secrets, which, now that we have the key to the enigma, are clearly enough revealed to us. This is sufficiently evident, I think, when we compare these stories with the secrets S. K. could not reveal to Regina. 'My relationship to my father' corresponds to *Solomon's Dream* and *Periander*; 'his melancholy' to *The Silent Despair*; 'my lusts and excesses' to *A Possibility*; and 'my aberrations' to *Nebuchadnezzar*. S. K. planned but did not carry out a seventh story for July 5, midnight. It was entitled *Abelard*, and therefore must have dealt with the secret of his relationship to Regina.

If in our day we have come to understand S. K. a little, this is not merely because his journals are open to us, but because we have learnt to discover him under the strange disguises in which he paraded his deepest secrets with the intent of hiding them. To quote from *Hamlet*, his favourite drama, we have learnt 'by indirections to find directions out'.

'It was dread which caused me to go astray.' This was written in 1843, but entries made in the Journal not long after his fall show that S. K. soon acquired this wisdom. Early in 1837 he wrote:[1] 'All sin begins with fear, just as fear of a sickness is a disposition for it.' Søren, of course, like all children, knew very well the sense of shame associated with sex, and perhaps this exquisitely sensitive child was also in this respect more sensitive than most children. He recalled certain occasions when a devastating impression was made upon him by casual remarks of his elders:[2] as when mention was made of an awful sin which was expressly covered by an ecclesiastical indulgence (*etiam si matrem virginem violasset*); and once when he approached his father with the query whether the Master-Thief (that figure which so much employed his imagination) did not represent a misuse of inherent strength, so that there might be a possibility of his reformation, he received the solemn reply, 'There are crimes which one can contend against only by God's constant assistance.' Knowing as we do the old man's weakness, we can understand that this solemn reply came from his heart, that he was not thinking of the hypothetical case of the Master-Thief, but of his own conflict with sensual temptation. Young Søren must have had a presentiment of this, for he says, 'I rushed down to my room and looked at myself in the glass.' In this same connexion he recalls the singular impression made upon him when, as he says, 'I often heard my father say, what a good thing it would be after all if one had such a venerable old father confessor to whom one could thoroughly open one's mind.' These entries were written in 1837, when S. K. was beginning to struggle up after his sexual fall. But this was a topic he continued to refer to. In 1845 he wrote:[1]

> In case one had told a child that to break a leg was a sin, in what anxious dread he would be living, and perhaps often breaking a leg, and the mere fact that he came near to it would seem to him a sin. Suppose that it was impossible to live down that impression of childhood, so then, out of love for his parents, and in order that this misconception might not become dreadful through his own ruin, he would hold out as long as possible. Just as when one draws the reins too tight on a horse, pulls him back with all one's might—then he falls.
>
> And indeed one can find now and then just such misguidance with respect to what sin is, occasioned most likely by one who has the best intentions. As when a man who had been dissolute and wished to deter his son from the same sort of life, interpreted the sexual instinct itself as a sin—and forgot that there was a difference between himself and the child—that the child was innocent and therefore must of necessity misunderstand. Unhappy is he who already as a child is harnessed to pull and toil through life like a slave.

Evidently this is Søren's own history. He was harnessed all his life long to the misconception his father had instilled in him. And yet when he reflected upon the concrete sins of his youth he was not fanatical in his judgement about them, and it was not fanaticism which prompted him to call himself a penitent. We have seen that he could say even of his 'lusts and excesses' that 'perhaps in God's sight they were not so atrocious'. In 1848[2] he spoke of 'the melancholy which at one time precipitated me into sin, and yet humanly speaking was almost more insane than guilty'. His own experience had taught him that 'presentiments, even when they are without foundation, if only they find favourable soil in a family environment, exhibit the consuming power of inherited sin, are capable of producing despair, and are far more frightful in their effects than the actual fact'.

It was not as an 'actual fact' that S. K.'s sin tormented him so dreadfully. The Journal gives no indication that he was greatly distressed about it until a long time afterwards. For a long period he seems to have been able to forget it, like the Accountant. When he recalled it from time to time he was able to idealize it. But on October 8, 1836, he wrote:[1]

> It is notable the amazing way in which something long past can suddenly spring up into consciousness, e.g. the memory of something wrong, of which perhaps one was hardly conscious in the moment of action—a flash of lightning announcing a violent storm. They do not step forth but actually leap forth with prodigious power, demanding to be heard. Surely it is in this enormous sense that the passage in the Gospel is to be understood, that on the Day of Judgement man must give account for every idle word he has spoken.

Likewise the Accountant did not remember his deed until a long while afterwards. And the experience S. K. here registers was only the lightning which presaged the 'great thunderstorm' which was to break upon him at the moment when he first saw Regina, fell in love with her at first sight, and reflected with agony that for him, as a penitent, marriage was out of the question.

We do injustice to S. K.'s intelligence if we suppose it was merely the 'actual fact' which tormented him so deeply and so long. The significance of the fact was immensely enhanced by reflection. We have learnt to understand that he had a sense of solidarity with his father's guilt—a solidarity which was not modelled so much after the primitive Greek conception as after the Hebrew idea of a God who visits the iniquities of the fathers upon the children unto the third and fourth generation. But he also believed (and it does not seem an unreasonable belief) that he had exactly repeated his father's sins, both in his sexual fall and in his defiance of God. Not as though these two things were separable, for according to his notion (and who could know better than he?) his dissolute life itself was a gesture of defiance. It was devilish, therefore. A sin which, regarded as a mere fact, another man could easily forget, became for him 'something that never can be forgotten'.[2] In the end he was able to believe that it was forgiven by God; but this was not enough for him, he wanted it also to be 'forgotten by God'—and that was not so easy to believe.

We are able to perceive now that when S. K. defended in

Either/Or the bold proposition that 'Christianity brought sensuality into the world', he was not wantonly playing with paradox, but was reflecting most seriously upon the grievous wounds he had received in childhood and youth from his father's stern repression of the sexual instinct. He represents that in his childhood Christianity was abhorrent to him in a way, although at the same time it was venerable to him. At that time the only stumbling-block he could know was the sexual inhibition which is characteristic of Christianity. Even at a later age he often sighed to think how pleasant it would be to be a pagan. Christianity excluded sensuality. But, in the very fact of excluding it, it posits it. It must have been in the world before it was excluded, but it is brought into evidence by the fact that it is excluded.

> As a principle, as a power, as a system in itself, sensuality was first posited by Christianity. I might perhaps adduce a further qualification which maybe shows most emphatically what I mean: it is by Christianity that sensuality is first posited under the qualification of spirit. . . . So sensuality has existed before in the world, but not as spiritually qualified. How then did it exist? It existed as soulishly qualified. Thus it was in paganism, and if one will seek the most perfect expression of it, thus it was in Greece. But sensuality soulishly qualified is not contradiction and exclusion, but harmony and accord.[1]

'Drive the devil out of the door with a pitchfork, and he will come back by the window. If there were no devil, we should be obliged to invent one.' Both of these witty sayings are grimly true. And he who has for so long been nameless in cultivated society, or has been named only in jest, is now again becoming familiarly known by the more neutral Greek name of *daimon*. The notion of daimonia as a widely prevalent influence in human life has become current in modern thought (on the Continent) from two sources: S. K. and Dostoevski. At this period of his life S. K. had abundant opportunity of observing this influence, both in his own experience and by observation of his companions. But he recognized that this influence followed him also in later life, when he was walking in the ethical path, and even when he was definitely in the religious stadium. He used the word sometimes in a neutral sense, but we have seen that he applied it in a bad sense to his morbid disposition to reservedness, and to that rare sort of defiant despair which characterized him.[1] He applied it also to the 'indirect communication' which he confessed was 'instinctive' to him.[2] It was clearly a morbid disposition to reticence which not only inhibited him, until his last years, from making direct communication of his thought, but seemed to treat his whole life as a guilty secret, even when it was innocent and beneficent. The chapter which deals expressly with daimonia is that which in *The Concept of Dread* is entitled 'Dread of the Good',[3] from which we have made several quotations. But in Chapter III of this book, the third section, dealing with 'Dread dialectically qualified with reference to guilt', shows how much S. K. had been reflecting upon the factor of daimonia (known by its old name of devilishness) in the medieval legends which he was studying at that time with so much interest—particularly, of course, in the legend of Faust. The Journals show that these medieval notions led him to observe the signs of the potency of 'the kingdom of evil here in this life'.[4] With Faust he associated the Gnostic sect of the Carpocratians whose principle was to 'pass through every vice just to get experience of life'.[5] Many entries show that this principle had a strong attraction for him. He was even inclined to admit that as a theory there was some truth in it—if only one did not try to live up to it. He says of Faust:[6]

> Faust did not desire to learn to know evil in order to congratulate himself that he was not so bad (this only Philistines do), but on the contrary he wished to feel all the sluices of sin open in his own bosom, the whole interminable realm of possibilities—all this will not suffice him. He desires the illusion of his expectations.

S. K. himself understood the attraction of the medieval fancy of selling oneself to Satan.[7] His imagination was very well able to soar to the high mountain where the devil could show him all the kingdoms of the earth and the glory of them, with the promise that 'All of these things shall be thine'. That was the dream of Faust, of all the alchemists, of all who sought the philosophers' stone. In our age imagination has no such wings. A man can conceive of possessing only a very little bit of the earth—and for that he is ready to sell himself to the devil. But on the other hand he cannot conceive of any loss so great as the loss of his own soul, the loss of himself. There is no passage in the Scripture S. K.

more often referred to than that which speaks of gaining the whole world and losing one's own soul.

There was one trait of daimonia in S. K.'s own life which very particularly preoccupied him at this time. It was what he called 'the devil of wit'. He recognized that his scorching wit was devilish and that it separated him from sympathetic companionship with men—and more especially from good women. He asked himself in his Journal,[1] 'In how far is it true that I must not laugh at my own witticisms?' And immediately after that he registers the laconic entry: 'The omnipresence of wit.' Omnipresence is a divine attribute. The use of the word here clearly implies something superhuman but devilish. In the Second Part of *Either/Or*[2] Judge William confides to his young friend that his wife, though she has a genuine liking for him, is troubled by the suspicion that he laughs when he is alone. In his laughter she detected derision of men. 'Believe it or not,' said the Judge, 'but I regularly take your part against her, seeking to explain that it perhaps is not exactly as she supposes, but that it is in an infinite comparison you undervalue men, that the restlessness with which your soul presses after the infinite makes you unjust to men.'

> Do not suppose that I would intrude upon your secrets, but I have only one question I should like to ask you, and I believe you can answer it without committing yourself too deeply. Answer me that question candidly and without circumlocution: Do you really laugh when you are alone? You understand what I mean; I do not inquire whether once in a while or even frequently it may happen that you laugh when you are alone, but whether you find your satisfaction in that lonely laughter. If you do not do that, I have won, and I shall be able to convince my wife of it.

Inasmuch as the young friend made no candid answer to this question, we may suppose that young Kierkegaard found daimoniac satisfaction in lonely laughter as an expression of his contempt for men.

Here I refer again to Brandt's study of S. K.'s youth. Building upon P. A. Heiberg's conclusions, he furnishes, as he says, 'a series of new conclusions'. I have made use of many of them, but I present his argument in detail only at the point where he corrects the misapprehension which naturally arises from Heiberg's emphasis upon *one* 'episode' in S. K.'s youth. It seems very clear to me that the sexual fall was not nearly so diabolical (even in S.K.'s eyes) as his nihilistic wit. Brandt describes how that culminated and how it was cured—by the intervention of his admired teacher Paul Møller.

S. K.'s admiration for Paul Møller is well known, but Brandt was the first to remark upon the close intimacy which grew up between these two men, and upon the fact that S. K. found in this teacher deep sympathy and comprehension. Paul Møller was prepared to understand young Kierkegaard at this period of his full revolt against the world, because he himself had passed through just such a phase and only recently had found repose in Christian faith. Among Paul Møller's papers is found a collection of cynical aphorisms ascribed to Ahsverus, the Wandering Jew, who typifies despair. Brandt argues plausibly that these fragments (which might have been entitled 'Thus Spake Ahsverus') were modelled upon S. K. and his satirical epigrams. This suffices to show how intimate was the tie between these two friends and how thorough was the understanding.

But the most ostensible proof of this friendship is the fact that in 1844, six years after Paul Møller's death, S. K. dedicated to him *The Concept of Dread*. This is the more significant because, with this solitary exception, he dedicated his books only to his father and to Regina—and to 'that Single Individual' whom he addresses as 'my reader'. The terms of the dedication, as it appears in the book, express the highest admiration; but it is very significant to note that the preliminary drafts[1] contain six expressions which S. K. eventually discarded because, presumably, they imply a degree of intimacy and affection which he did not think fit to express in a public document. I quote the dedication below, putting the rejected phrases in brackets. The phrase 'far travelled' signifies here that his friend is dead and far away, but he was prompted to use it because it occurs in a song composed by Møller which was sung at a public commemoration of him at which S. K. was present and was struck by these words.[2]

To the Deceased

PROFESSOR PAUL MARTIN MØLLER

The fortunate lover of Greek literature, Homer's admirer, Socrates' intimate, Aristotle's interpreter—Denmark's joy in 'Joy over Denmark', far travelled, always 'remembered in the Danish summer',—my [youth's enthusiasm] admiration; [the mighty trumpet of my awakening, my sentiment's desired object, the confidant of my beginning, my departed friend], my loss [lost reader], this work is dedicated.

What especially interests us here is his salutation of Paul Møller as 'the mighty trumpet of my awakening'. What can that mean? That S. K. was eventually awakened we know full well; but we should very much like to know *when* and *how*.

Heiberg places the fall in the month of May 1836. There is not much room for difference of opinion about that. It is clear from the Journal that S. K.'s moral life was at its lowest ebb about that time. There is a complete gap in the Journal from April 18 to June 6, and while the entries immediately preceding this gap are desperate almost to the verge of insanity—showing that S. K.'s alcoholic excesses were part and parcel of what might be called an intellectual inebriation—we are surprised on the other hand to find that the first entries after the gap are of a religious nature, the first of this sort to occur in the Journal since nearly a year before. The first entry on June 6 begins:[1] 'Therefore it is necessary to assume an assistance of God in order to amend oneself.' The next comments upon Mt. 11: 12. A third, dated 'June 12, Josty' (the famous coffee-house in the Frederiksberg Garden), deals with the significance of praying 'in Christ's name'. As religious utterances they are cold, yet they clearly enough show an intention to reform.

The entries which immediately precede this gap in the Journal are the following—all of them written in April:[2]

When I observe that my head begins to rear up on its hind legs.—The poet must have what the Hypoboreans expected in their heaven—a swine they could always carve a piece from, and it would always grow out new again.

One blows one's brains out, bing, bang, bover, so the story is over, and snip, snap, snother, now can begin another.

War against the Philistines! [He quotes Eichendorf:] 'I believe that I am the double of all human follies.'

One who went and thought of committing suicide—at the same moment a stone fell down and killed him, and he ended with the word, 'God be praised!'

There can be no doubt that S. K. seriously thought of suicide at this time, and perhaps more seriously (as we shall see) a month or so later. Nearly a year later he was surely reflecting upon his own case when he remarked that it is foolish to talk about suicide being cowardly, 'for only when one has had the courage to commit suicide can one tell whether it was cowardly to have committed it'.[1] In the Second Part of *Either/Or* (1843) he again had himself in mind when he (or rather Judge William) recounted the story of poor young Ludwig Blackfeldt. For we have already been apprised that the name Ludwig always has some relation to S. K., and the letter in which this young man notified his brother of his demise is couched in the most characteristic Kierkegaardian style. S. K. was justified in boasting that the paper he wrote on had a distinctive water-mark—no one could fail to recognize his writing, even if it was plagiarized. One of the phrases in this letter might have been addressed to his brother Peter—one who was so near to him and yet so far. July is here indicated as the time of the suicide. This may be exact, but we have no other data which would indicate a time later than June for S. K.'s temptation to do away with himself. It is worth while quoting this letter here, because it so perfectly reflects the mixture of flippancy and profundity which characterized S. K.'s youth.[2]

> Honourable Mr. Chancellor!
>
> I write to you because in a way you are the nearest to me—in another way you are not nearer than other men. When you receive these lines I shall be no more. If any one should ask you about the reasons, you can say that once upon a time there was a princess named Morning Glory, or something else like that; for so would I myself answer if I had the pleasure of surviving myself. Should some one ask you about the occasion, you can say it was on the occasion of the great conflagration. Should some one ask you about the time, you can say that it was in the month of July so memorable to me. Should no one ask you anything of the sort, you can answer nothing.
>
> I am far from considering suicide a praiseworthy thing. It is not out of vanity I have determined upon it. I believe in the rightness of the thesis that no one can endure to look upon the infinite. That was once proved to me in an intellectual respect, and the expression of that is ignorance [i.e. the Socratic

ignorance]. Ignorance, that is to say, is the negative expression for infinite knowledge. And suicide is the negative expression for infinite freedom. It is a form of the infinite freedom, but the negative form. Lucky is he who finds the positive.

With the highest regards,
Yours respectfully.

Now we return to the entries of April 1836:[1]

> Death and hell! I can abstract my thought from everything, but not from myself: I cannot forget myself even when I am asleep.

Then come the two entries quoted above about wit's omnipresence, &c. And finally two which have to do with a notorious reprobate, Jürgen Jürgensen, who was an old man at forty-five:

> What can explain the inclination of people who in one respect or another are dilapidated, to rush out into the world instead of shunning it? For example, J. Jürgensen says that when he is drunk he feels an almost irresistible urge to go amongst people, to go especially where there are many.
>
> Conversation with J. Jürgensen, April 18, 1836:
>
> He was drunk, as one could remark especially by observing the corners of his lips. He expressed the opinion that poetry is really something quite secondary, an excrescence, and extolled the philosophical; he extolled memory, envied me my youth, talked about the fading leaf, about the howling wind, tempest. 'The one half of life is for living, the other half for repenting, and I am rapidly entering the last.' 'In youth one can do lots of mad things, and very well do them over again.'—'I have led a very stirring life, stood in relationship to everybody that now amounts to anything, I am chummy with all the men of talent. Ask me now about them.'

I cannot agree with Heiberg that this conversation was of a sort that might be seductive to S. K. and might have led him into vice. But it clearly enough punctuated the low point in his career. It is evident from all these entries that he was riding for a fall.

But if the fall occurred in May, when was the 'awakening'? The answer to this question is very intricate. It includes incidentally the cunning discovery of certain proofs of an intimacy between Hertz and S. K. Here is an example. There is an entry in Hertz's Diary for November 3, 1836: 'Met K— at the Student Association, who later was in my room.' In S. K.'s Journal there is this brief entry for the same date: 'One wrote on flying leaves.' Hertz's study-book for 1836 contains between the pages diminutive sheets of paper ('flying leaves') on which clever and satirical epigrams are scribbled in pencil, some of them in S. K.'s handwriting.

But the important entry in Hertz's Diary is one of June 4: 'In the afternoon at the Heibergs' and bade them farewell before their departure for Paris. There S. K., Paul Møller, &c.' (Note that precisely S. K. and Paul Møller are singled out for mention in such a company of wits as was likely assembled on that occasion —and that young Kierkegaard is mentioned first, as if he were the most important member of the party.) Brandt associates this with a passage in the comic play which S. K. prepared for the Student Association (cf. p. 92). There, too, an afternoon party is implied, where S. K. and Hertz (i.e. Willibald and Echo) had been together, from which S. K. had departed incontinently and on returning to his room was about to kill himself when Echo interrupted him.

Brandt would place at this point (that is, after the Heibergs' party) an undated entry which is now printed in the midst of the series I have just quoted. He is quite at liberty to do so, for Heiberg, the editor of the *Papers*, subsequently concluded that it ought to have been placed in May or June—therefore why not the 4th of June?[1]

> I have just come from a party of which I was the soul: witticisms flowed from my mouth, all laughed and admired me—but I went (here in fact the dashes should be as long as the radius of the earth's orbit) — away and wanted to shoot myself.

But what prompted S. K. to leave such a party in haste? And what in the world could have happened there to prompt him to suicide? Brandt answers, 'The "awakening".' He supposes that it was then, at the moment when S. K. was in his wittiest, wildest, and most nihilistic mood, that Paul Møller sounded 'the mighty trumpet': 'You are so through and through polemicalized that it is perfectly frightful!'

It is certain that, on one occasion or another, these words were actually addressed to S. K. by Paul Møller. S. K. remembered them to the end of his life, as we learn from an entry of the year 1854,[1] where he associates them with the message which Paul Møller on his death-bed charged Professor Sibbern to deliver to him: 'Say to little Kierkegaard that he take care not to lay out too big a plan of study, for this has done me much harm.' It is true, he says in this passage that Møller had made this reproach to him 'often', and that it was 'his constant expression while he lived'. But he must once have said it for the first time, and I can well imagine that when it was uttered in the nick of time, with a voice expressive of abhorrence, by a man whom he so much admired and who understood him so deeply, it must have sounded like a trumpet-call to S. K. And all the more because it was aimed so accurately at the vital seat of his daimonia, his defiance of God and man.

Certain it is that S. K.'s disposition was polemical through and through. So it was in his childhood, and so it remained to the end. His polemical talent was never displayed on so grandiose a scale as in his attack upon established Christianity. His awakening did not change his nature in this respect—nor did his subsequent religious conversion. What it did was to purge the daimonia from his polemic.

And perhaps not even this effect was accomplished at once. The first effect, as we have seen, was the desire to shoot himself. It was characteristic of S. K.'s nature that no event (not even a trumpet-call) affected him so profoundly at first as after a long interval of reflection. Perhaps he was awakening to the trumpet-call on November 12 (four months later), when he made the brief entry:[2] 'It is highly important in life to be attentive when one's cue comes.' Then it was merely a 'cue'—he had not yet learnt to think of it as 'the mighty trumpet of my awakening', for in fact he was not yet fully awake. I have no doubt that the trumpet sounded much louder to him after Paul Møller's death—just as his father first acquired full authority over him when his voice came from beyond the tomb.

Paul Møller died on March 13, 1838. Not until the first day

of the following month is there a reference in S. K.'s Journal to this loss:[1]

> Such a long period has again passed in which I have not been able to collect myself in the least—I will now try to make a new start.
>
> Paul Møller is dead.

In fact, S. K. had written nothing in his Journal since the end of December, and one of the last entries (quoted on p. 156) reflects his desolate mood: there is more pathos in the second entry about Paul Møller, which was written on April 2:[2]

> I was there to hear Nielsen declaim [Paul Møller's] 'Joy over Denmark'; but I was so strangely moved by the word: 'Remember ye the far travelled man.' Yes, now he is far travelled—but I at least shall still remember him.

We have seen how tenaciously he remembered.

V. THE ETHICAL STAGE

1836–8

It is out of deference for S. K.'s own nomenclature, his sharp distinction of the three stages, that I have adopted this title (The Ethical Stage) to describe the present chapter, which deals with a period stretching from the afternoon of June 4, 1836, to 10.30 a.m. on May 19, 1838—that is, from his 'awakening' to his conversion with the experience of 'an indescribable joy'. Where else could we look for the ethical stage? S. K. instructs us that it lies between the aesthetical and the religious—therefore this must be the place. And what have we a right to expect of S. K. in his ethical stage? Surely no more than that he was trying to be good. It must be confessed that this conclusion has more truth than evidence on its side, so far as the testimony of the Journal is concerned. During this period the entries in the Journal are not strikingly different from those that went before. The fact is that S. K. had not yet acquired the habit of making the Journal the confidant of his deepest resolutions and of the long and laborious reflections which led up to them. This was characteristic of his last years, and this it is that makes the Journal so voluminous. It did not begin to be voluminous until the year 1847. Every year following that date he deposited in the Journal an amount of material one and a half times greater than all the entries that are made during the ten years he was at the university. During the period we are now concerned with, the entries are for the most part of an objective sort, registering thoughts that occurred to the author or reflections prompted by books he happened to be reading.

It is interesting to observe that this greatest of all journal-writers had no innate disposition for that sort of thing. Although he headed his Journal for the year 1838 with the motto *Nulla dies sine linea*, he seems to have had no serious intention of living up to it. He totally lacked the interest in current happenings and events which commonly prompts one to keep a diary. It might be said, without too much exaggeration, that there were only three external events in S. K.'s life which deeply moved him: his father's death, his engagement to Regina with its rupture, and the attack of the *Corsair*. There are great gaps in the Journal, especially in the early period, and many entries were made on loose sheets. The greater part of the entries are undated.

But here is one which in the margin is very precisely dated, and evidently with a mock gravity: 'Resolution of July 13, 1837, given in our study-chamber at 6 o'clock p.m.'[1]

> I have often wondered how it comes about that I feel so great a distaste for setting down single observations. . . . The reason evidently was that in every individual case I thought of the eventual possibility of publication, which perhaps required a more elaborate development than I felt like troubling about, and under the exhausting pressure of such an abstract possibility, the aroma of fancy and mood evaporated. . . . It would be better to let the thoughts come forth fresh with the umbilical cord attached, and to forget so far as possible every reference to their possible utilization, . . . unbosoming myself as in a letter to an intimate friend, gaining thereby the possibility of knowledge of myself at a later moment, as well as readiness in writing, articulation in written expression, which I have to a degree in speaking, . . . and finally also the advantage, which Hamann suggests in another connexion, that there are conceits one hits upon only once in a lifetime. Such practice behind the scenes is certainly necessary for every man who is not so gifted that his development is in a way public.
>
> . . . The seeming wealth of conceits and ideas which one feels in the abstract possibility is just as uncomfortable and occasions the same unrest as cows suffer from when they are not milked at the right time. One had best, therefore, if the outward circumstances do not come to one's aid, do like the cows—milk oneself.

It must be confessed that the Journals afford no evidence that this resolution was taken seriously, and it is certain that it was not by 'practice behind the scenes' that S. K. developed his remarkable style as a writer. We have had occasion to notice in many other entries that the thought of becoming a writer was constantly in the back of his mind, and it was at about this time he launched his newspaper campaign and wrote his criticism of Andersen. But when he stepped to the front of the stage with his first great works, after the depths had been stirred by the separation from

Regina, both matter and form were unpremeditated. It was the inexplicable welling up of genius. From that time on, his development (to use his own expression) was 'public'. Though he recognized that the best practice was writing to a familiar friend, he wrote few letters, and none of them were confidential, except a few addressed to his friend Emil Boesen. He had no other friend. And the love-letters he addressed to Regina were anything but confidential, because the obstacle to marriage consisted precisely in the fact that he could not reveal himself to her. But in the midst of the period we are now concerned with he expressed pathetically his need of a friend. About the end of 1837 he had been out in the country and was attracted by the qualities of the simple peasantry. On returning to 'our study-chamber' he jotted this down:[1]

> Would that out there I had one I could communicate myself to—one of the few, to whom now more than ever I could tightly attach myself, and be rid of these philistines and cadets. . . .

Perhaps it was at this time he attached himself to Boesen. This was his sole friendship, but with his usual tenacity he clung to it 'tightly' to the end of his life.

S. K. insists so much upon the necessity of making a 'leap' from the aesthetical to the ethical stage that we may be prompted to suppose that his own moral reformation was accomplished in an instant. But this was very far from being his experience. The resolution itself, the free act, the decisive choice in the face of an either/or, is indeed accomplished in an instant. But the 'instant', according to S.K., is not an infinitesimal fraction of time but a fraction of eternity. And the individual who in that 'acceptable time' has made his choice is not thereupon translated into eternity, but is still subject to the vicissitudes of ordinary clock time and obliged to work out his salvation with fear and trembling.

Near the end of 1837 there is an entry which seems at first sight to belong to the religious stage, inasmuch as it uses a specifically Christian terminology:[2]

> This is the way I think of the relationship between vicarious satisfaction and man's own atonement for his sins. On the one hand, it is very true that sinners are forgiven by reason of Christ's death; but, on the other hand, one is not by magic

plucked out of one's old situation, the 'body of sin' about which St. Paul speaks (Rom. 7: 25). He must go backward the same way he went forth, while the conviction that his sins are forgiven holds him erect, gives him courage, and prevents despair—like one who with a deep sense of his sin gives himself up to the judge and then encounters intrepidly the execution of the sentence of death pronounced upon him as an evildoer, feeling that so it must be, yet supported by the conviction that the case will eventually be carried before another and a kinder Judge. He treads the perilous path (which may be thorny in spite of the conviction of the forgiveness of sins, which one is so prone to forget) and he will not tempt God or demand a miracle.

When we inspect this passage closely we perceive that it belongs properly to the ethical stage. It is evident that during this period resignation was the highest experience S. K. could reach on his way to faith.

It is plain from the Journal that into S. K.'s ethical stage a great deal of the aesthetical was carried over. One of the entries made in the ethical stage appeared later among the *Diapsalmata* ('I don't care', &c., on p. 102) as an illustration of the aesthetical point of view, and several of the *Diapsalmata* were plucked from the Journals of the religious period. This is not an inconsequence on S. K.'s part. He represents that the aesthetical is not discarded when one enters the ethical stage, but is 'dethroned'.

It is evident that S. K.'s resolution to reform did not include a purpose to return to the study of theology, which was ostensibly his reason for being at the university. That was definitely put aside, except for a course of lectures by Martensen, which he attended out of a sense of duty. He devoted himself with all the more zeal to the study of philosophy—and the subject of aesthetics philosophically conceived. It was a matter of course that a young man so philosophically inclined would take an interest in religion. Historically, religion is one of the principal factors in human life, and to ignore it, as our American universities do, is to close in the face of inquiring youth the book of history, if not the book of sociology. S. K. in his youth was profoundly interested in the philosophy of religion—that is to say, in religion in general and in all sorts of religions. Therefore at a later time he was able to say many searching things about this subject, and, what is of more importance, he knew how to distinguish all this from Christianity.

Many of the entries I am about to quote from the Journal indicate an 'interest in religion', and in the Christian religion particularly. But for the most part, and until the end of this period, they express rather an interest than a concern. They are not therefore to be regarded as an anticipation of the definite religious stage, but rather as a vestige of the aesthetical. For 'interest is an aesthetical category', as S. K. rightly perceived.

I quote here a long catena of entries in the Journal and let them speak for themselves. They run from June 1836 to (and not including) the date of his religious conversion, May 19, 1838. I have set down all the passages which clearly reveal his mood during this period, and I have put them as nearly as possible in chronological order, noting the dates when any are indicated in the Journal. The fact that many of these entries are proofs of his despair should not surprise the reader; for S. K. insists in the Second Part of *Either/Or* that 'no one can despair without willing to despair', and that the first act of reformation is 'the choice to despair'. That again is a choice which, though it is made in an 'instant', must be carried out in time—and with S. K. it took a very long time.

We have to remember here that during the whole of this ('ethical') period S. K. remained unreconciled with his father. For that reason he was unreconciled to Christianity, his father's religion. It was about the middle of this period (on September 1, 1837) that he definitely removed from his father's home and was put on an allowance. It was at the same time, however, that he gave the most ostensible proof of reformation by undertaking to provide in part for his own livelihood by teaching Latin at the School of Civic Virtue in which he had been a pupil. He taught there during the year 1837–8. This assures us at least that he was no longer leading a dissolute life. In the Journal there is no express reference to this activity, but his interest in the Latin grammar is attested by numerous entries which remark upon the analogy between the parts of speech, &c., and the situation of individuals in society. Among the entries I quote below there are two which apply the grammatical analogy to his own case.

Reformation goes slowly. One must, as Franz Baader rightly remarks, go the same way backward that one went forward. One easily becomes impatient; when it cannot be brought to pass at once, one can just as well let it be, or begin to-morrow and enjoy to-day; that is temptation.—Is not this the meaning of the saying: to take the kingdom of God by violence—?

And therefore it is said that we shall labour for our salvation with fear and trembling, just for the reason that it is not finished and complete, but a relapse is possible.—And it is surely in part this disquietude which prompts people to seek with such zeal to become martyrs, in order to make the test as short as possible, and as strong as possible momentarily—a test which is always easier to endure successfully than one which is long drawn out.[1]

It is dangerous to separate oneself too much, to withdraw oneself from the ship of society.[2]

Do you not need the leading-strings of the community; can you get along without the support of the go-cart your contemporaries give you?[3]

This was a timely and wholesome reflection for young Kierkegaard, who had not only broken off relations with his evil companions but with society in general, and had set himself against the whole world. And it is important for us to notice it because S. K.'s later insistence upon the category of 'that single individual' (*hiin Enkelte*) has caused some to suppose mistakenly that his ideal was 'individuality' in the sense of the isolation of the individual, whereas he required that the individual should become himself in order to be profitably integrated into society, which is strong only as it is composed of real individuals.

But this was a period of frequent relapses:[4]

Strange apprehension, every time after I have drunk too much, on awaking in the morning, was ultimately verified. [Apprehension of insanity?]

Twice he registers the strange statement:[5]

One who went crazy every time he was convinced that the world goes round. [Was that a reflection upon the situation of the idealistic philosopher when obliged to face facts?]

Strange that people are so angry with the Jesuits. In a certain sense every one who is enthusiastic about an idea and intent solely upon realizing that—is a Jesuit.[6]

On July 20 he remarks upon the tragedy of repeating an identical experience—which also has a comical side because it makes life seem like organ-grinder's music.

Dec. 2.[1] [In the form of a letter—very disconsolate—and far too long to quote here, except for the following scraps:] I will talk with the world no more, absolutely. I have read of one who lay on his bed fifty years and never spoke to any man. . . . No, I will not go out of the world—I will go into a mad-house, and I will see if the profundity of madness will not unveil to me life's riddle. . . .—Do you not believe I can get into it? . . .

I want . . . No, I don't want anything. Amen.

There is a way we all must go—over the Bridge of Sighs into eternity.[2]

It is these little teasing things which so embitter life. I can joyfully labour against the storm till the blood is ready to spurt out of me; but the wind which blows a grain of dust into my eye can make me so angry that I stamp my feet.

These little teasing things—as if when one would accomplish a great work, a great undertaking, decisive for his life and for that of others—and just then a gad-fly should settle upon his nose.[3]

The one thought displaces the other; so soon as one is thought and I start to write it down, there is a new one—hold it! grasp it tight!—madness!—insanity![4]

I talk preferably with old women who indulge in family gossip, next with the insane, and last of all with very sensible people.[5]

This was not mere petulance. S. K. often expressed his preference for conversing with the common people and with children, remarking that to talk with Heiberg and other men of intellect was no recreation.

S. K. begins his entries afresh about the end of January 1837, entitling them 'Miscellanies' (*Blandinger*). We are surprised to see that the first entry is a long plan for a sermon, but we find that it is addressed to himself. Already in the earlier volume there is an entry dated January 17,[6] expressing the hope that his momentary comfort and satisfaction may not prove ephemeral like Jonah's gourd, but 'will give place to a much deeper repose which will assure that though the surface may be painfully troubled the most inward parts will not be moved'. There follows a long and serious entry[1] which begins thus: 'For the moment one is distressed about nothing so much as the total bankruptcy towards which the whole of Europe seems to be heading, and with this one forgets the far more serious danger in a spiritual respect, which is at the door and seemingly inescapable—a confusion of tongues far more dangerous than that Babylonian (symbolical) one, &c.' A note[2] to the above shows that this Protestant youth has been reading the great Catholic author Görres with intimate satisfaction. It ends with a characteristic Kierkegaardian saying: 'And so in the end the theatre will become reality, and reality comedy.'

An entry (which still seems to belong to January) shows a growing suspicion of philosophers:[3] 'Philosophy sheds a skin with every step it takes, and the stupid followers crawl into it.' Then there is one[4] about the significance of 'loving one another in Christ', i.e. in a third person—a thought which later developed fruitfully in one of his sermons. Then comes a very appreciative reflection about Christianity:[5]

> Christ exercises a very tranquillizing power in a certain respect, by the fact, namely, that He asserts the highest degree of relativity, by setting up an idea, an ideal, which is so great that everything else beside it is lost sight of (the romantic, the humorous side of Christianity). Hence it is always much more agreeable to talk with a Christian, since he has a standard which is definite; he is in possession of an abundance in comparison with which the endless difference in talents, in position, &c., is as nothing. Hence it is that firmness, if it does not degenerate into pride, is so respectable.

Then, between May 8 and 16, there are two most notable entries, which must have been occasioned by his first sight of Regina Olsen, who was then but 14 years of age. On his part it was love at first sight; and Regina when she was an old woman recalled how deeply she had been interested on that occasion by the brilliant conversation of this young man. He met her accidentally when he was visiting the Rørdams, the family of a deceased clergyman who lived at Frederiksberg (a suburb of Copenhagen) which included a daughter, Bolette, in whom S. K. seems to have had a great interest, but only as an intellectual friendship. It appears from these entries that this experience of falling in love was in strident contradiction to a purpose he had formed. We must suppose that already, because of his sin, he had resolved that he must lead the life of a penitent, which in his view excluded all notion of marriage—and so precluded him from 'realizing the universal human'. In this sense, therefore, he recognized that even in 'the ethical stage' he was incapacitated from leading the normal ethical life, he was 'outside the ethical', he was 'the exceptional man—in a bad sense'. (I here use the terms S. K. has made familiar to us in *Either/Or*.)

> O God, but how easily one forgets such a resolution! I have for some time been turned back again to the world, deposed from ruling in my own inmost seat. Ah! but what does it help that man if he gained the whole world but suffered damage to his soul! To-day also (May 8) I have tried to will to forget myself, yet not with loud noise—that substitute does not help—but by going out to the Rørdams' and talking to Bolette, and compelling the devil of witticism to remain (if possible) at home, the angel with the flaming sword as well I have deserved!—who stations himself between me and every innocent maiden's heart—then Thou didst overtake me, O God. I thank Thee that Thou didst not let me lose my senses at once—I have never dreaded that so much. I thank Thee that Thou hast once again bowed down Thine ear to me.[1]
>
> To-day again the same scene—I went nevertheless out to the Rørdams'—merciful God, why should the inclination awaken just now! Oh, how I feel that I am alone—Oh, a curse upon that proud satisfaction at standing alone—all will now despise me—Oh, but Thou, my God, take not Thy hand from me, let me live and improve.[2]

About two months later he was again at the Rørdams', as we learn from a loose leaf[3] dated with unaccustomed precision: 'Sunday the 9th of July in Frederiksberg Garden after a visit to the Rørdams'.'

> Like a lonely fir-tree, egoistically separate and pointing toward the height, I stand, casting no shadow, and only the wood-dove builds its nest in my branches.

These passages belong, of course, to the chapter about Regina;

but they cannot be omitted here, because nothing else in the Journal throws so searching a light upon S. K.'s condition at this time.

The next entry (presumably in May) strikes a note which at a later time was characteristic of his theology. It is the either/or applied to divinity.[1]

> An observation for theologians: *King Lear*, Act IV, Scene 6: ' "Aye" and "no" too was no good divinity.'
>
> June 2. The recognition of the negative side of the Reformation and the *possibility* of a return to the Mother Church of the parties who left it (without their being required to go back as prodigal sons) is indeed rather timidly indicated by the fact that they have not had the courage to do what the Catholics did to them—to declare them heretics.[2]

Three very serious entries follow about Christ's atonement for sin.[3] It seems as if we are leaving the ethical stage! And then this:[4]

> One must retrace backward the same path one has gone out by, just as the enchantment [in a certain fairy-tale] is broken only when one succeeds in playing backwards without a single mistake [the same piece of music by which one was enchanted].
>
> Nov. 29.[5] Monotheism always lies hid in polytheism—without being, as with the Greeks ('the unknown God'), an abstract possibility hovering over it.

Here he has anticipated the most modern discovery of 'the science of religion'! There follow (on July 14) four reflections on religious themes.[6] And on the same date:[7]

> So I have united the tragic and the comic: I utter witticisms, people laugh—I weep. [And later we have:[8]] I am a Janus Bifrons; with the one countenance I laugh, with the other I weep.
>
> And this is indeed the way Christianity has always gone through the world, between two thieves (for such are we all), of which only one was penitent and said that he suffered deserved punishment.[9]
>
> [About 'the humorous trait' in Christ's utterances]—with a polemical tinge . . . but in Christ's mouth they are conciliatory.[10]
>
> It is so impossible that the world could continue to exist

without God, that if God could *forget* it, it instantly would dissolve.[1]

Sept. 29. There are men who in life stand like interjections in the discourse, without having any influence upon the sentence—that is, hermits in life, which at the most govern one case, e.g. *O! me miserum.*[2]

Oct. 7. My life unfortunately is all too much in the conditional mood; would to God I had some indicative power.[3]

Oct. 7. How terrible it is when all history vanishes before a morbid brooding over one's own sorry history! Who points out a *via media* between this consumption of oneself by reflections which imply that one is the only man that ever has been or will be—and a sorry comfort in a universal human *commune naufragium?* Yet it is this which properly a doctrine about the Church ought to supply.[4]

Nov. 6. The a priori of faith which hovers over the a posteriori of actions is so beautifully expressed in the words: 'I know that nothing in the world . . . principalities &c. shall separate me from Jesus Christ our Lord.' Where his faith sets him upon a rock lifted up above all that is empirical, whereas on the other hand it is impossible that he can have lived through the whole empirical experience here spoken of.[5]

Dec. 8. I have so often reflected in thanking God for something, whether it was rather the fear of losing it that prompted the prayer, or—that it was done with the religious certitude which had overcome the world.[6]

Dec. 8. I think that I, if ever I become a serious Christian, will be ashamed most for the fact that I did not become so sooner, that I have desired first to try everything else.[7]

It must be terrible at the Day of Judgement when all souls come to life again—to stand there entirely *alone*, solitary and unknown to all.[8]

But before we go further I would refer back to an entry of January 22, 1837:[9]

It is quite remarkable that Christ was exactly 33 years old—which number of years, according to the usual reckoning, designates the period of a generation, so that here also there is something normative, inasmuch as what exceeds this number is fortuitous.

This reckoning gave young Kierkegaard an expectation of only nine more years of life. Apart from his father's gloomy foreboding that he was condemned to outlive all his children (five of whom were already dead), S. K., in view of his frail constitution, had sound enough reason to expect that he would not live beyond the average term of life. Consequently he planned his life (and disposed of his fortune) as a man who had not long to live. In 1848 he was astonished at surviving his 35th birthday. At that time he said of himself, in view of the prodigious labours accomplished during that year, 'I have worked more than ever like a dying man.' His life will appear more comprehensible to us if we realize thus early in the story that he worked like a dying man who did not expect to wear for many years 'the penitent's garb'. He lived, however, nine years longer than the 'norm', and was already an old man at 42.

There are several loose sheets which help to fill the gap in the Journal before Paul Møller's death.

> Jan. 1 [1838].[1] Irony is an abnormal development, which, like the abnormality of the Strassburg goose, ends by killing the individual.

The fight against his mordant wit and his sarcastic irony was a principal part of his ethical development at this time. Hence at this time he was inclined to speak disparagingly not only of irony but of humour.

> Feb. 2. [Another loose sheet.][2] When sometimes there is such uproar in my head, then it is as if the cranium were heaved up, and it is as when kobalds heave a mountain up a little and then hold balls and festivities in it. [In the margin is written:] God forbid!
>
> In these days I have read Görres' *Athanasius*, not only with the eyes, but with my whole bodily frame—with the heart's very depths.[3]
>
> The very reverend avenue of the Church Fathers in the shade of which I still can sometimes find repose.[4]
>
> That God could create free beings apart from Himself is the cross which the philosophers cannot bear but remain hanging upon.[5]
>
> If Christ shall come to dwell in me, it must occur as in the

title of the Gospel for to-day in the almanac: Christ enters through closed doors.[1]

Probably this was written not quite a month before S.K.'s conversion, for he refers to the Gospel for the Second Sunday after Easter (April 22nd in that year). It hardly seems to presage it. And yet it by no means implies that he had hardened his heart and shut the doors. On September 10, 1836, he wrote:[2]

> With relation to a Christian's view of paganism cf. Hamann, 1 D, pp. 406, 418 f., especially 419: 'No, if God Himself would speak to him, He is obliged to dispatch ahead the *authoritative word* and bring it to pass: Awake, thou that sleepest.'

We shall see that it was an authoritative challenge which aroused the slumbering S. K. So he himself understood it, and did not seek for any psychological explanation. And for my part I can discover in the Journal nothing that presaged it.

But here is an entry[3] of July 8, 1837, which I omitted, and which might be regarded as an indication of an approach to Christianity:

> The ancient dogmatic terminology of the Church is like an enchanted castle where the most beautiful princes and princesses repose in a profound slumber—they need only be awakened [quickened] to stand up in their full glory.

I confess that to me this does not suggest an approaching conversion—although it is true that in the end S. K. did potently contribute to the 'quickening' of the dead formulas of theology. But before this he had to be quickened himself. Nor does this next, which is also the very last entry before his conversion (written on April 6, 1838), seem to presage any such event:

> There are on the whole few men who are able to bear the *Protestant* view of life, and these, if it is to be truly strengthening for the *common man*, must either constitute a smaller society (separatism, conventicle, &c.), or approach Catholicism, in both cases for the sake of developing the social element, the common bearing of life's burden, which only the most greatly gifted individuals can get along without. Christ indeed died for all, for me as well; but this 'for me' must still be construed to mean that He has died for me only inasmuch as I belong to the many.[4]

Taken simply as a repudiation of one-sided individualism, this is a notion implied in the very idea of the Church. On the other hand, it is a travesty of Catholicism to make 'the many' the premiss and 'for me' a deduction. This cool and objective reflection (which must seem very sensible to any one who has not encountered the personal God speaking to him personally) savours more of Hegelianism than of Christianity, and though it might be taken to indicate a theoretical approach to Catholicism, it clearly does not presage a re-approach to Protestantism, and least of all a personal conversion. Why is it that S. K., in spite of his sympathy for many of the characteristic institutions of the Roman Church, never 'approached' Catholicism more closely than at this moment? This has to do with the fact that almost before a month was up something occurred—he got a vivid apprehension of what it means to receive and appropriate God's grace as 'for me'; and from that moment on, nothing is more characteristic of S. K. than the constant comfort and disturbance of feeling himself to be 'the single individual before God'.

In conclusion, I revert to an earlier point in the Journal in order to trace the successive steps which resulted in a revolutionary change in S. K.'s mental attitude, constituting at least a negative preparation for conversion. As a starting-point I refer back to the entry of October 1835 (quoted in part on p. 112) which recognized that 'Christianity and philosophy cannot be united' and betrayed an inclination to sacrifice Christianity to philosophy. Yet even at that moment, when he was about to take the 'leap' into sin, it might seem that he was intellectually prepared for conversion by the amazing clearness with which he envisaged the situation:[1]

> Indeed, viewed from this standpoint, philosophy will not serve as a transition to Christianity, for it must necessarily stop with this negative result, and the whole conception of the urge for redemption must necessarily reach man from an entirely different side, that is to say, be first felt and then comprehended. . . . The philosopher can very well attain conceptions of man's sin, but from this it does not follow that he recognizes man's need of redemption, least of all a redemption which (in correspondence with the universal sinfulness of creation) must be wrought by God, but rather a relative redemption (i.e. the thought that a man redeems himself).

We are to learn in the next chapter that S. K. 'first felt and then comprehended'; but at this time he was disposed to think that 'one must not be too hasty about regeneration, lest it happen as to the magician Virgilius, who, to renew his youth, had himself put to death (chopped to bits and boiled in a cauldron), and then, because of the indiscretion of him who had charge of the cauldron, this was opened too early, and Virgilius, who had only become a child, vanished with a wail'.[1]

In the course of the following year S. K. gradually became less and less confident of finding in philosophy 'the true Archimedian point'. As I have said, this was important as a negative preparation for salvation. He notices that 'Fichte cast the whole empirical ballast overboard and capsized';[2] that 'Schleiermacher is Stoicism reborn in Christianity';[3] that 'what Schleiermacher calls "religion" and the Hegelian dogmaticians call "faith" is at bottom nothing else but the first immediate condition for everything—the vital fluid, in a spiritual sense the atmosphere which we all breathe—and which therefore cannot properly be described by these words'.[4] 'Naturally, one can do with Hegel's logical trinity what one can do with everything—namely, utter it, with application to the simplest object, where it is true indeed but none the less ridiculous. Thus, if one would apply it to shoes, point out the position of immediacy, then the dialectical (that they begin to split), then, third, the unity.'[5]

Undoubtedly the factor which most profoundly influenced this change of mind was Hamann. I am inclined to say that he is the only author by whom S. K. was profoundly influenced. Johan Georg Hamann died before the end of the eighteenth century, but in Germany he was one of the most decisive influences of the nineteenth. He was the better fitted to lead S. K. out of his doubt and despair in that he had gone through a like experience. And he was the more congenial to our hero because he was not only serious but amusing. He was as witty and ironical as S. K. Indeed, at this time, when S. K. was fighting against his own demon of wit and irony, he was sometimes aghast at Hamann. Twice[6] he exclaimed at the 'blasphemy' of Hamann's remark that he 'would rather hear wisdom from Balaam's ass or from a philosopher against his will than from an angel or an Apostle'. In later years S. K. made this remark his own. However much Hamann surprised him, he hailed him reverently as

'Emperor!' the very first time he made mention of him in the Journal.[1] He notes that his style is stamped with an inimitable character which would prompt one to exclaim, wherever he might see a plagiarism of it, 'Give unto Caesar that which is Caesar's.' He recognized him as 'the greatest humorist in Christendom—which is the same as to say, the greatest humorist in that life-view which is the most humorous life-view in world-history—hence the greatest humorist in the world'.[2] Hamann's humour made palatable to S. K. the serious truth he most needed to hear at this time. This, that he quoted from him on September 12, 1836,[3] became ultimately his own favourite paradox: 'Is it not an old idea you have often heard from me: *incredibile sed verum*? Lies and novels must be plausible, also hypotheses and fables; but not the truths and fundamental propositions of our faith.'

On the very day he discovered Hamann and celebrated this discovery at the proper place in his Journal on the date September 10, 1836, he turned back to the two entries of nearly a year before (October 17 and 19, 1835) in which he had decreed that Christianity was not compatible with philosophy and had described superciliously how Christianity must look to a pagan, and now he inscribes at that point a brief note about Hamann which suggests how paganism must appear to a Christian. I owe it to Heiberg that my attention was directed to this entry and its ironical juxtaposition with S. K.'s earlier dictum. For this entry does not seem important, until one takes the pains to read in Hamann's works the passage by which S. K. was so much struck and to which he refers expressly, mentioning the page-numbers.

We get a clear idea of the revolution which was about to occur in S. K.'s thought when we read the statement of David Hume upon which Hamann comments, and then the whole of a sentence of Hamann from which S. K. quotes only a part. Hamann quotes from the chapter on miracles in Hume's famous *Inquiry concerning the Human Understanding*:

> So that upon the whole we may conclude, that the *Christian Religion* not only was at first attended with miracles, but even to this day cannot be believed by any reasonable person without one. Mere reason is not sufficient to convince us of its veracity: and whoever is moved by *Faith* to assent to it, is conscious of a continued miracle in his own person, which subverts all the

principles of his understanding, and gives him a determination to believe what is most contrary to custom and experience.

S. K. was greatly struck by Hamann's comment:

> Hume may have said this with a scornful and critical air, yet all the same, this is orthodoxy and a witness to the truth from the mouth of an enemy and persecutor—all his doubts are proofs of his proposition.

I quote almost in full the other passage from Hamann from which S. K. quotes only the last sentence:

> A man who lives in God stands therefore in the same relation to the 'natural man' that a waking man does to one who is snoring in profound slumber—to a dreamer—a sleep-walker. . . . A dreamer may have images more vivid than a man who is awake, may see more, hear and think more than he, may be conscious of himself, dream with more orderliness than a waking man thinks, may be the creator of new objects, of great events. Everything is true for him, and yet everything is illusion. . . . The question is whether it might in any way be possible for a waking man to convince a sleeper (so long as he sleeps) of the fact that he is asleep. No—if even God himself would speak to him, He is obliged to dispatch ahead the authoritative word and bring it to pass: Awake, thou that sleepest!

From this time S. K. was only waiting for the 'authoritative word'. But we can trace in the Journal the progress he was able to make under the influence of Hamann. We find a half-way approach to his new position in an entry dated August 1, 1838:[1]

> *About the relationship between Christianity and philosophy.*
>
> *Motto*: [It is a doggerel rhyme in Jutland peasant dialect which I venture to translate as follows:]
>
> If a body meet a body
> Carrying a spade,
> And if a body bears a rake,
> Need either be afraid?

This obviously means that neither Christianity nor philosophy has anything to fear from the other. In spite of the triviality of its expression, this entry had immense significance for S. K. We can measure its importance by the fact that he repeated it (without substantial change) on a loose sheet (undated) and that the next following sixteen entries, as the editor of the Journal has arranged them, are all comments upon it.[1] One of these comments is: 'And they cast lots for his *seamless* vesture.' Does this mean that the truth is *one* and cannot be divided among rivals? Another entry[2] is more important. It implies clearly enough and decisively that Christianity is not and will not be dependent upon philosophy. Hence it is an anticipation of the slogan of Johannes Climacus: 'Away from speculation!'

Motto: [in Latin]
'Cursed be he who keeps swine and teaches his son Greek wisdom.' A Jewish edict of the year 60 B.C.

Christianity will have no dealing with the philosophies, even if they are willing to divide with it the spoils; it cannot endure that the king of Sodom should say, I have made Abraham rich.

He could get no farther until he heard the authoritative word: 'Awake, thou that sleepest!'

VI. THE PRODIGAL'S RETURN

1838

I TAKE up here again the catena of entries in the Journal at the point where we left off at the end of the previous chapter—except that (for reasons which will presently appear) an important entry for the month of May is for the moment omitted, although it is the only one for that month. It may be remembered that the last entry quoted was of April 6. Here I quote (without any omissions) ten consecutive entries, the first being the only entry in June, which will seem a trivial one, the rest dating from July 7–18, 1838.[1]

Fixed ideas are like a cramp, for example, in the foot—the best remedy is to tread upon it. June 6.

It takes a long while for a man to get accustomed, to become at home (to know where everything has its place) in the divine economy, one gropes among a multiplicity of moods, does not know even how one ought to pray; Christ does not come to a definite configuration in us—one does not know what the comfort of the Holy Ghost means. July 7.

How I thank Thee, Father in heaven, that Thou hast preserved to me here on earth, for a time like the present when I stand so greatly in need of it, an earthly father, who, as I hope, shall by Thy help find more joy in being for a second time my father than he had the first time. July 9.

I will strive to come into a far more inward relationship to Christianity; for until now I have in a way been always standing outside it, have contended for its truth; in a purely outward way I have borne Christ's cross, like Simon of Cyrene (Lk. 23: 26). July 9.

I hope that with respect to my contentment with the conditions of life *here at home* it may be with me as with a man I once read about, who likewise was tired of his home and would ride away from it; when he had gone a little way the horse stumbled and he fell off, and as he picked himself up he chanced to see his home, which now seemed so fair to him that he at once mounted and rode home and stayed at home. If only one gets the right view of it. July 10.[2]

It would be splendid tragical material—the youth who during the persecution of Marcus Aurelius was filled with enthusiasm for the courage of a Polycarp and other such men in their hour of death and so desired to be a martyr, but when they described to him the horrible tortures he became afraid of them and . . . cursed Christianity as the pagans required. —One sees from this that the same thing occurs in Christianity as in worldly life: that one must first become full-grown in the sight of God and man, and although we in our time are not exposed to such great temptations which in so terrible a way bring the whole to naught, yet would-be theologians, for example, must be on their guard lest by beginning too soon to preach they rather chatter themselves into Christianity than live themselves into it and find themselves at home there. July 11.

How close and essential the relationship is between knowing oneself and believing that one is known, can be perceived in the fact that near-sighted persons do not believe at all that others at a greater distance can see them. So the near-sighted sinner does not believe at all that God espies his erring way, whereas the pious Christian, when he is known of God, then knows also his own frailty with a clarity which is possible only by participation in the clairvoyance of the Spirit which searcheth the reins. July 11.

With my longing thoughts the case is in many ways similar to Nebuchadnezzar, who required the wise men not only to interpret his dreams, but to tell him what he had dreamt.

God created out of *nothing*—Wonderful! you say. Yes, indeed, but He does what is far more wonderful—he creates saints (the communion of saints) out of sinners.

Hereby one knows that one has become a Christian: he encounters one like Rebecca—'I will not only give you to drink, but also your camels.' July 18.

These entries are in themselves of no great importance, they are not so interesting as many we have already quoted, their significance lies in the fact that when we compare them with all that went before there seems to be a whole world of difference. For here we encounter a young man who not only shows deep sympathy with Christianity but is earnestly endeavouring to be a

Christian. In the meantime something must have happened. The prodigal has come home. The prayer of July 9 (the first inscribed in S.K.'s Journal) shows that he had returned to his 'earthly father', with a devotion we cannot easily account for. But it appears no less evident that he had returned to the 'Father in heaven'. And inasmuch as he had not yet left his lodgings[1] and never did return to live in his earthly father's home, we must understand that when he underscores '*life here at home*' he is expressing his 'contentment' with the return to Christianity.

What happened in the meantime is revealed (in part) by the one entry in the Journal we omitted, the first of the series:[2]

> There is *an indescribable joy* which glows through us as unaccountably as the Apostle's outburst is unexpected: 'Rejoice, and again I say, Rejoice.'—Not a joy over this or that, but full jubilation, 'with hearts and souls and voices': 'I rejoice over my joy, of, in, by, at, on, through, with my joy'—a heavenly refrain, which cuts short as it were our ordinary song; a joy which cools and refreshes like a breeze, a gust of the trade-wind which blows from the Grove of Mamre to the eternal mansions.
>
> May 19, 10.30 a.m.
>
> [The Saturday before the 5th Sunday after Easter.]

This reads like the record of a characteristic mystical experience of a definitely ecstatic sort, like St. Paul's experience when he was 'caught up into paradise and heard unspeakable words which it is not lawful for a man to utter' (2 Cor. 12: 4). And yet S. K. frequently and emphatically affirmed that he enjoyed no mystical experiences, 'no direct relationship with God'. In the Second Part of *Either/Or* he allows the judge to argue at length against a mystical conception of religion, and over his own name he frequently repudiated it. Such utterances are congenial to Barth and his school, and they are not to be blamed for making the most of them. But, on the other hand, S. K. is often described as a mystic by persons who carelessly confound mysticism with religion in general, or at least regard it as the most sublime experience of religion, and therefore take it for granted that a man so profoundly religious as S. K. must have been a mystic. But no well-informed writer has gone so far as to affirm that S. K.

actually was a mystic, in defiance of his own assertion to the contrary. Przywara ventures merely to point out expressions which suggest an experience akin to that of the characteristic Catholic mystics, especially St. John of the Cross. It can be said with much plausibility that S. K.'s early strictures upon mysticism were prompted by the fact that he first became acquainted with mystics like Jacob Böhme, whose experiences had little or nothing to do with the specific character of the Christian faith, and that when he got to know the Catholic mystics he rather liked them. Perhaps he did, yet it must be recognized that his was an 'antipathetic sympathy'. He spent some time reading Görres' *Mystik* and other works describing the experiences of Catholic mystics. But of Görres' book he says:[1] 'I admit that I never have had the courage to read it straight through, for there is in it such an anguish of dread . . . there is an element so fearfully demoniac that . . . he must be used with caution.'

Controversy about the question whether S. K. was a mystic or not may be nothing more than logomachy. If all religious experience can properly be described as mystical in one degree or another, S. K. was undoubtedly a mystic, and he would not have hesitated to admit it. For it is easy to perceive that his motive for opposing mysticism was sympathy with the common man. He zealously maintained the proposition that 'every man, absolutely every man' is exactly in the same position before God, equally capable of appropriating the promises of the Gospel, whether he has or has not a mystical temperament, or, as we say more commonly, 'a religious disposition'. If it is allowable to bestow the name of mystic upon a man who did not stress the immanence of God but rather the transcendence, who did not think of God as the power within him making for righteousness but as the power confronting him and exacting obedience, who did not receive from God direct illumination and guidance but experienced only a divine governance which shaped his ends by overruling them, who did not seek edification through the practice of meditation and contemplation but through the dialectical exercise of reflection, who did not dwell upon the importance of religious feeling and experience but rather upon the necessity of translating faith into action—then I can raise no objection if any one prefers to call S. K. a mystic. But I cannot comprehend why the experience of hearing the Deity speak within the depths of one's own soul, with a voice hardly distinguishable from the consciousness or subconsciousness of the individual, should be thought a more real or momentous experience than that of standing 'before God' (to use S. K.'s significant expression) and hearing Him, as the absolutely other Thou, speak the 'authoritative word, "Arise, thou that sleepest!"' This is the phrase S. K. used to describe his experience. It is perfectly evident that it was in this way the men of the Bible, in the New Testament as well as the Old, apprehended the voice of God.

Unquestionably the word 'mystic' is ordinarily used to describe the *élite* of the religious class. S. K. would admit no such invidious distinction—and least of all was he disposed to claim it for himself. This, I suppose, is the reason why he denied so roundly—so much more absolutely, perhaps, than the situation justified—that he possessed any credentials to religious aristocracy. And yet, because of his unusual experience, his sense of an extraordinary task which he was called upon to perform for the sake of Christianity, and his apprehension that divine providence was constantly ruling and overruling him, he could not but be anxiously preoccupied by the question whether his relationship to God was a direct one, like that of a prophet or an apostle, or whether it was merely dialectical. It was this preoccupation with his own problem which prompted him to ponder so long and so profoundly the case of Adler, a Danish pastor who had lately been deprived for pretending that his books were written by direct inspiration. This case prompted S. K. to be cautious in judging his own situation. He recognized that he was faced by a temptation, and he resolutely opposed it[1] with the assertion that 'with me everything is dialectical'. Perhaps he would not have rejected the other alternative so decisively if he had not conceived of it as a temptation.

He evidently had in mind his own experience of conversion when, in *The Point of View*, in a passage dealing with his relationship to Regina, which he here speaks of as a 'fact' which deepened his apprehension of Christianity, he unexpectedly breaks out with this:[2] 'I beg the reader not to think of revelations or anything of the sort, for with me everything is dialectical.' His experience of conversion was never referred to explicitly in any public document. He confided it only to his Journal, in the brief entry we have read. And although he used there exuberant terms in his effort to describe the 'indescribable joy', he was not so extravagant in his expressions as Luther was in recounting his own conversion: 'Whereupon I straightway felt that I was reborn and entering the open gates of paradise.' We know, however, that this experience of Luther's was not mystical in the sense commonly attached to that word, but was a dialectical consequence of reading an intelligible word of Holy Scripture, in Rom. 1: 17, and apprehending suddenly that God's gracious acquittal of man's sin 'is the power of God unto salvation . . . a righteousness of God by faith unto faith'. By this experience Luther was transported into 'paradise' (like St. Paul), whereas S. K., with greater moderation, spoke only of 'the Grove of Mamre'. This reference, however, to Gen. 18: 1 has a significance we should not overlook. It decribes Abraham's momentous experience: 'the Lord appeared unto him by the oaks of Mamre, as he sat in the tent door in the heat of the day.' Something at least as momentous as a mystical experience happened to S. K. at half past ten on the morning of May 19. Did Christ 'enter in through closed doors'?—according to the expression S. K. applied to himself some years earlier. Or must we not say, in view of the passages quoted from the Journal, that young Kierkegaard had at least so far prepared himself for the visit that he had gone out to sit in the door of his tent?

He did not confide to his Journal *what* happened, but only the joy that resulted. The observable change in him consisted in the fact that (to use his own expression in an entry quoted above) he got 'a right view of the home'. With that everything was changed for him. He learnt then (in a deeper sense than he had apprehended it before) that 'Christianity is a radical cure'. How radical it was in his case we learn from the following passage in *The Point of View*:[1]

> I was so profoundly shaken that I understood perfectly well I could not succeed in striking the tranquil and safe *via media* in which most men pass their lives. I must either cast myself into despair and sensuality or choose religion absolutely as the only thing—either this world on a scale that would be dreadful, or the cloister. That it was the latter I would and must choose was already substantially decided: the eccentricity of the first

movement was only an expression of the intensity of the second, so that I understood how impossible it was for me to be religious only up to a certain point.

That this was a profound and genuine religious conversion we learn from the sequel, but to the mere 'experience' connected with it, the fringe of feeling which accompanied it and which he attempted to register in his Journal, he attached no more importance than the wiser mystics have commonly done. Some of them have treated lightly those features of their experience which the observer might think most worthy of attention and admiration. But S. K. as a profound psychologist learnt to regard so lightly his 'experience', viewed merely as a phenomenal experience, that he could find pleasure in parodying it, as he does in a description of the culminating aesthetical experience of Constantine Constantius which we find in *The Repetition*. He attributed to Constantine an experience as precisely dated as his own, but far more sublime, so far as feeling is concerned, and expressed in language far more exuberant—which, however, because it was only an aesthetical experience, lasted but a few hours and departed more suddenly than it came, leaving no trace. That S. K. had in mind his own experience of conversion is made more evident by the fact that in the immediate context Constantine is permitted to trivialize the deeply pathetic entry in the Journal about seeing his 'home' in a new light. In order to understand this passage it must be understood that Constantine was a purely aesthetical individual, untouched by religion. Commentators characterize him as hard-headed. They might also say hard-hearted. But without meaning anything different they might also say soft-hearted. On the hard heart no impression can be made; on the soft heart, no permanent impression—so it amounts to the same thing in the end. It is the aesthetical softness of Constantine that most impresses me. Constantine, it is said, represents S. K. This is true in a sense. But so also did the young man with the love-affair whom Constantine was studying. The difference between these two characters was, as S. K. explains, that Constantine was without religion, and so could not attain an experience of 'repetition', whereas the young man had some religion and so got farther. Constantine Constantius, like many of the other pseudonyms, was S. K.'s parody upon himself, representing not what he was at any time (even in his aesthetic stage) but a possibility he discerned in himself. Here is the passage:[1]

> Once I was very close to it [i.e. the experience of perfect contentment]. I got up in the morning feeling uncommonly well. This sense of well-being increased out of proportion to all analogy during the forenoon. Precisely at one o'clock I was at the highest peak and surmised the dizzy maximum which is not indicated on any scale of well-being, not even on the poetical thermometer. The body had lost all its earthly heaviness, it was as though I had no body, just for the reason that every function enjoyed its completest satisfaction, every nerve tingled with delight on its own account and on account of the whole, while every pulsation, as a disquietude in the organism, only suggested and reported the sensuous delight of the instant. My gait became a glide, not like the flight of a bird that cleaves the air and leaves the earth behind, but like the billows of the wind over a field of grain, like the yearning bliss of the cradling waves of the sea, like the dreamy gliding of the clouds. My very being was transparent, like the depths of the sea, like the self-contented silence of the night, like the quiet monologue of midday. Every mood of my soul composed itself to rest with melodious resonance. Every thought proffered itself freely, every thought proffered itself with festal gladness and solemnity, the silliest conceit not less than the richest idea. Every impression was surmised before it arrived and was awakened within me. The whole of existence seemed to be as it were in love with me, and everything vibrated in preordained *rapport* with my being. In me all was ominous, and everything was enigmatically transfigured in my microcosmic bliss, which was able to transfigure into its own likeness all, even the observations most disagreeable and most tiresome, even disgusting sights and the most fatal collisions. When precisely at one o'clock I was at the highest peak, where I surmised the ultimate attainment, something suddenly began to chafe one of my eyes, whether it was an eye-lash, a mote, a bit of dust, I do not know; but this I know, that in that selfsame instant I toppled down almost into the abyss of despair—a thing which every one will understand who has been so high up as I was, and when he was at that point has been engaged

with the fundamental question how nearly absolute contentment can be attained.

How well Ariosto has described this little tragedy of Constantine's:

Chi sale tropp' in alto
Casca sovente
Precipitevolissimevolmente.

I have no doubt that an aesthetic experience of this sort might be reproduced by the use of a drug. I remember that William James took a sly delight in the discovery that by the use of hashish he could reproduce the Hegelian ecstasies of his friend Josiah Roice. This discovery suggests that one ought to be wary of attaching too much importance to religious experience in any of its 'varieties'.

If there is some one who thinks it instructive to dwell longer upon the phenomena of S. K.'s conversion as they are observable on the psychological level, I refer him diffidently to Hjalmar Helweg's psychiatric-psychological study of S. K.,[1] where the learned author takes account of the disposition of various members of the family not only to 'depressive' symptoms but to a swift transition to a state of 'exaltation', which is supposed to explain the possibility of the experience of sudden conversion.

It needs to be remarked that only in this one place in his Journal did S. K. confide *to himself*, *ad se ipsum*, the experience of his conversion. Never again did he refer to it. He observed the completest silence—for a reason which he himself gave during the last year of his life:[2]

> [A maiden who is truly in love will not speak to any one about her deep experience.] So also does God love silence. He will not have this prating to other men about a man's God-relationship. It is done perhaps out of vanity—and that is displeasing to God. Or it is cowardice and lack of faith, because a man does not really trust, because he is apprehensive lest perhaps some time, if I may say so, he might get into trouble and that sort of thing—all of which is displeasing to God. Will one say that when one man is more advanced than another, it is a proper expression of kindness of heart to let another participate in his relationship to God—this again is objectionable to God, for this is conceit. What conceit! says God. Have I not

had it proclaimed that every man, absolutely every man, can turn to me? So then that other man can do it too.

It may be thought strange that in this passage S. K. takes no account at all of that reason for talking about one's God-relationship which many people to-day (especially very young people) regard as a compelling reason to cast aside all modesty for the sake of proving to others the existence of God by the story of their own conversion. That is a reason which S. K. evidently overlooked. For if he had thought of that as a possibility, he would not have said of the attempt to prove the existence of God *by rational argument* that it is 'the greatest affront one can offer to God'. It would surely be a greater affront were we to set out to prove God's existence by the evidence of our own sanctification.

He does, however, in this passage contemplate one reason which still works potently to-day, though it is always concealed —that is 'lack of faith'. At this very moment I am struck by reading in a recent book by Karl Heim[1] the same thought more discursively expressed:

> So soon as I act in reliance upon such an object [i.e. either a self-chosen or a 'given' object of faith] I observe at once that there are two possibilities present. Either I must establish the validity of this value and retain it in circulation by my very act of trust; or else this value exists quite independent of all human trustfulness, as the sustaining possibility of the trust I repose in it. Luther expresses this opposition when he says, That upon which I rely is either God or an idol. That in which I trust is either a self-chosen object of faith (which according to Luther is the case with all pagans), or I have found the ground which, entirely independent of all my choosing and making, holds my anchor eternally.
>
> So then there are two sorts of trust, both of which can be religiously expressed, and yet each has a precisely opposite character. In the first case the object of trust will be validated by the fact that a band of trusting persons exists by whose devotion the content of the trust is upheld. In the other case the value of the object of trust is independent of all human actions and states of mind. Hence the object of trust retains its validity when from the flame of our enthusiasm and devotion only a pile of ashes remains. The object of trust retains even then its

glamour when we ourselves are incapable any more of an act of trust. In both cases we can speak of an act of trust, and yet in each case the trust has an opposite sign in front of it. In the first case the trust costs effort, endurance, vigour, and glow in the soul. One can recognize the men who live in this trust by the pathos with which they speak of that which to them is the holiest, by the 'chest-tone' of conviction which betrays a cramp-like condition of the soul. In the second case the trust is of an entirely contrary kind, an effortless repose, a sense of being borne up on eagle's wings, of being sustained by the everlasting arms.

If Karl Heim had not been profoundly influenced by S.K., I hardly could have found in him so good a commentator. He is thinking here of the 'German Christians' who trust in 'the myth of the blood'. But I am compelled to think of things nearer home, and I am inclined to say: May the Unknown God remain unknown, rather than be known as an object of trust that is patronized by a clique (though it were as big as the whole Church), demonstrated by man's very questionable experience of sanctification, floated and kept afloat by teams of attractive young persons.

At a later period S. K. found himself inhibited from publishing his confession, *The Point of View*, by reason of a doubt 'whether a man has a right to let people know how good he is'.

The immediate effect of S. K.'s conversion is registered in the apparently trivial entry of June 6, 1838 (p. 168), which speaks about a 'cramp in the foot'. It is notorious that the best remedy for a cramp in the foot is, as he says here, 'to tread on it'. But in reality it was a very different sort of cramp S. K. suffered from: it was dread of receiving the Body and Blood of the Lord. We discover the pathos of this entry when we learn, from the parochial register of the cathedral church of Our Lady, that on that same date (which was Friday after Whit-Sunday) S. K. came alone to receive the Holy Communion from the resident chaplain E. V. Kalthoff. (His conversion occurred on the Saturday before the 5th Sunday after Easter.) It seems likely that this was the first time he had been to church since the autumn of 1835. On the first Sunday after Easter he had got no nearer than to read the title of the Gospel in the almanac (see p. 162). Now he went *alone* (in spite of his late philosophical reflections about the importance of the 'social bond')—evidently because he had learnt in the meantime that the primary experience of Christianity is that Christ died 'for me'—and with that he was well able to 'bear the Protestant view of life'. If, as Heiberg argues from an entry of April 1,[1] he had been to church on that day (which was Passion Sunday), the reflection he registers shows that he was not greatly edified.

No wonder that S. K., after the life he had been leading, felt a dread of receiving the Holy Communion. Catholic spiritual directors have had much experience of that sort of dread, and S. K. was sufficiently informed about it by his reading in Görres' *Mystik*—which, as he remarks, is so full of 'dread' that he must warn his readers to be cautious in using it. In *The Concept of Dread*[2] he says, about the 'dread of coming to the altar', that it may be a daimonia, and only in the concrete instance can one discern whether it is this or a trial of faith, by observing that 'he who is subjected to this dread as a religious trial resolves to approach what the trial would hold him away from'. Görres, he remarks, does not know how to make this distinction. It is a clear instance of 'dread in the face of the good'. S. K. overcame this cramp by treading upon it.[3]

But now we must follow another clue suggested by the Journal, which will bring us to a much deeper understanding of S. K.'s conversion. He himself thought of it in terms of the parable of the Prodigal Son, which indeed applied to his case so exactly that it was more than a mere parable, it was a precise description of his return to his earthly father, and that in turn was a parable of his return to God. This means that his father's loving reception of him was a parable of the divine forgiveness—it made the divine love clear, it made it credible. We have misnamed this parable in calling it after the bad boy who was the romantic figure in the story. It should be called the parable of the Loving Father, and so it is to be understood here. In this case the analogy was so perfect that it extended even to the subordinate figure of the elder brother—as Søren reflected, with a wry face. Perhaps it was on account of the good brother Peter that he did not literally return to live under the paternal roof. With his brother he was never on good terms. He had long been living independently in his own quarters, and he continued to do so. Nevertheless he thought of his conversion as a home-coming in a figurative sense. In 1849 he jotted down in the Journal a plan for 'a simple romance' about a father and two sons, in which the following passage occurs:[1]

> 'He came to himself'—behold, now the foreign tour has come to an end. Properly speaking, it did not end with his coming home, but with his coming to himself.

The home-coming, as we have seen in the entries above cited, meant essentially his return to God in Christ, but it also involved a return to his earthly father. It might seem natural to suppose that the reconciliation with his father was a consequence of the greater reconciliation with God, a natural and necessary expression of moral obedience. But this is hardly the impression we get from the entries quoted above, and in *The Concept of Dread* S. K. exactly reverses the sequence which seems so natural to us: 'He repents himself back into himself, back into the family, back into the race, until he finds himself in God' (see p. 158). I have no doubt that this reveals the true order. It appears that, in precisest correspondence with the parable, the earthly father, while the prodigal son was yet afar off, 'saw him and ran and fell on his neck and kissed him heartily'.

The reader can hardly fail to be struck by the fact that the expressions Søren uses in his prayer of thanksgiving for such a father (p. 168) indicate something more than a dutiful sense of filial propriety. We may note by the way that this entry is significant also for the reason that it is the first *prayer* we encounter in the Journal—the first of many. I recall the phrases in this prayer which indicate that the father, so far from being merely the passive object of the son's new-found affection, must have deserved this affection by taking an active part in bringing Søren back to himself, back to the family, and back to God. It is thanksgiving to God for preserving here on earth a father who was able to help him so greatly 'in a time like the present when I stand so greatly in need'. It would seem as though his father must have done something extraordinary and momentous to justify the son in regarding him as 'for a second time my father'—almost as if he had begotten him again.

This impression is abundantly confirmed by the terms of the entry of August 11 recording his father's death, which occurred just a month later than the prayer of thanksgiving for his preservation:[2]

My father died on Thursday, the 8th, at 2 o'clock in the night. I had so heartily wished that he might live a few years longer, and I regard his death as the last sacrifice his love for me occasioned; for not only has he died from me, but *died for* me, in order that, if possible, something may be made of me still. Of all that I have inherited from him the dearest is his remembrance, the transfigured picture—not transfigured by poetic fancy (for of that there is no need), but transfigured by the many individual traits I now begin to take account of—the dearest thing to me, and I will take care to keep it most secret from the world; for I am well aware there is only *one* person (E. Boesen) I can truly talk to about him. He was a 'faithful friend'.

The name of E. Boesen was added later to indicate the '*one*' to whom he could speak freely about his father. We do not know when this friendship began, but the acquaintance must have been an early one, for Counsellor Boesen, the father of Emil, was an intimate in the Kierkegaard home; at all events this friendship (Søren's only friendship) lasted to the end of his life. And at this time he did in fact unbosom his grief in a letter to Boesen. Incidentally this letter refers to the motto these young men had adopted and to which they frequently referred: 'The church in the distance.' It was a line from a descriptive poem, but to them it meant the ideal Church of their aspiration. Not a bad motto for theological students. Perhaps Boesen was still inspired by it when he attained ecclesiastical dignity as Dean of Aarhus. Certainly it was S. K.'s motto to the end of his life—and never more so than at the very end, when he launched his formidable attack upon the established Church.

But, apart from this letter to Boesen, S. K. took amazing pains to 'keep this dearest thing most secret from the world'. His niece Henriette Lund[1] recounts that she learnt to understand only later, when his *Papers* were published, how deeply he had felt this loss. 'He continued apparently in his old way of life, forgathered in cafés as usual, and promenaded the streets with his customary animation.' This extraordinary ability to hide his feelings is only less amazing than his desire to do so. He himself recognized this desire as a form of daimonia.

But we have not yet touched upon the chief interest of this

entry concerning his father's death. It is obvious that it not only confirms our previous impression but suggests something very much deeper than we surmised. Again I call attention to the most significant phrases. 'I regard his death as the last sacrifice his love for me occasioned, for not only has he died from me, but *died for* me.... He was a "faithful friend".' These are very strong expressions—'a sacrifice' and a sacrifice '*for* me'. What is it his father could have done to merit description in such specifically religious terms? It seems to have been something which cost him so great an effort that Søren can plausibly ascribe to it his death—which in fact followed soon after. We must remember that this stalwart man died in his eighty-second year, when he was already enfeebled by age. At that time an extraordinary effort might well have hastened his death. Knowing his condition, Søren could not conceive that he might live more than 'a few years longer'. Whatever the old man did he must have done before the date of the 'indescribable joy' (May 19), for S. K. plainly ascribes his conversion to his father's intervention. May 5 was Søren's birthday, and this year it was an occasion of special solemnity, because on completing his 25th year he attained his legal majority according to Danish law. It is not a remote presumption that his father may have taken that occasion to intervene decisively in his son's life. What he said or did we can never know with certainty. But one thing I do know, that the greatest and most costly sacrifice this close-mouthed old man could have made to save his son was to open his heart to him completely. I am inclined to think that nothing else could have saved the youth. Søren, who had never opened his heart to any one, and could not do it to save his own soul, was capable of understanding that this prodigious effort was capable of costing the old man his life. For my part, I firmly believe that his father mustered up sufficient strength and courage to make this heroic sacrifice. It all seems very plain to me now. But I owe the suggestion of it to the studies of Professor Hirsch.[1] A man so shrewd as Michael Pedersen Kierkegaard, after he had been obliged for so many years to ponder sadly the loss of his Benjamin, could hardly fail to suspect that the son's wildness, which showed itself expressly as hostility to him, was prompted by a presentiment that all was not as it should be with his austere and godly father. And it is certain that his father's confession must have made a momentous impression on Søren. He has himself remarked that the crude fact is not nearly so dreadful as the presentiment of it. And if, at the same time that he learnt from his father's lips precisely what his sin and weakness was, he got also a just impression of his constant struggle and contrite repentance, if it dawned upon him then that the 'crazy bringing-up' he so bitterly resented was prompted by love, with the intent of shielding the son from the very sins the father so desperately bewailed in himself, then I can understand perfectly well how it was that so great a change was suddenly wrought in the son that for ever after his devotion to his father knew no limits and his veneration no bounds. And I cannot understand how anything else could have had this effect.

But such a reconciliation to his father meant that the barrier was broken down which separated him from God. For his defiance of God was primarily defiance of his father. Indeed, his father's sacrifice meant much more to him than this, it was performed *for* him in a more positive sense: the father who had proved himself such a 'faithful friend' helped him to understand what 'the divine father-love' is. This Søren says expressly in an entry during the tour he made in Jutland in the summer of 1840, after he had contented the dying wish of his father by passing his theological examination (cf. pp. 202 ff.). There is a tone of gentle sadness in the entries of this tour, for of course he was preoccupied with memories of his father when he was visiting for the first time the country where he was born. The following was written before he had reached his father's birth-place:[1]

> I sit here all alone (I have often been just as much alone but I never was so conscious of it), and I count the hours until I shall see Sæding. I can never remember any change in my father, and now I shall see the places where as a poor boy he tended sheep, the places which I have often felt a homesickness for on the basis of his descriptions. If I should now fall ill and be buried in Sæding churchyard! Strange thought. His last wish for me is fulfilled—might it really be that my whole earthly existence is to be concluded with that? In God's name! The task before me surely would not be so trivial in proportion to what I owe him. I learnt from him what father-love is, and thereby I got a conception of the divine father-love, the one unshakable thing in life, the true Archimedian point.

I must find room here for a passage which looks back from a remoter distance upon his father's death. It is a well-known passage from *The Point of View*:[1]

> So my father died. The powerful religious impressions of childhood, in a softened and idealized form, acquired new influence over me. Now, moreover, I had become so much older that I fitted better to my upbringing, the misfortune of which consisted just in the fact that it turns out to be an advantage to me only now when I am forty years old.

It is clear that his father brought Søren to God. But here we must be cautious, for here is a point where S. K. has discriminated more sharply than any man has ever done.[2] One man can help another only up to a certain point. Socrates may prompt a man to 'remember', he may help, like a midwife, to deliver a thought, but he cannot beget. God is the teacher. And so, in the matter of becoming a Christian, one man may do another an immense service by making him 'attentive', by ensuring that at least he is aware of God. But it is for the individual to judge—and he may reach a conclusion the exact opposite to that which the pedagogue would wish. Before the last step even the dearest friend must stand back and leave the individual to make his own solemn choice before God. Perhaps S. K. insists upon this not so much out of respect for God's sovereignty as out of zeal to vindicate man's freedom of choice. In his own case, his father had done everything that was humanly possible to break down the barriers (the 'closed doors') which hindered Christ from entering in—and no man can do more.

Consequently, Søren's union with his father became as close as it could possibly be—and it was realized more feelingly after the old man's death than before it. He was united to him not only by gratitude and admiration, but by the consciousness of a common guilt—which is the deepest, as well as the most universal, bond between man and man, the 'touch (*tache*) of nature' which 'makes the whole world kin'—so deeply united that 'he repents his father's fault'. This thought is so unusual that S. K.'s own experience must have suggested it to Judge William:[3]

> And if it was a fault of the father which descended to the son as a part of his inheritance, he will repent of that together with his own guilt. . . . The pious Jew felt his father's fault

resting upon him, and yet he did not feel it nearly so deeply as the Christian; for the pious Jew could not repent it, because he could not choose himself absolutely. The guilt of his forefathers weighed upon him, brooded over him, he sank under this weight, he sighed, but he could not lift it up. That only he can do who absolutely chooses himself. The greater the freedom, the greater the guilt, and it is the secret of salvation; and if it is not cowardliness, it is at least pusillanimity not to be willing to repent the forefathers' guilt; if it is not paltriness, it is at least small-mindedness and lack of magnanimity.

Now we are in a position to understand the pathos of the motto S. K. chose as the expression for the moment when he attained his majority. I am referring here again to that gilt-edged document which was our guide in the study of S. K.'s childhood and youth (pp. 58 f., 68, 72). We have seen good reason to believe that this undated paper was not written earlier than an entry of September 9, 1839.[1] We must understand, therefore, that it looks back from a distance of more than a year to his twenty-fifth birthday and his father's death. It is clear from the text that he was then in the midst of his long preparation for the theological examination, which he had undertaken out of deference to his dead father's wish. We learn more clearly from other passages how distasteful this task was to him. He called it 'the long parenthesis'. And we can understand how irksome it must have been to a youth, who already was acclaimed as a promising author, to submit himself again to the discipline of the school and lay aside the studies which had engrossed him for so many years. In the long prose entry appended to the motto, he describes the strife between his 'reflective self' and his conscientious 'practical self', which he had now learnt to regard as his 'proper self', the self he had chosen. This is all clear enough. But the quotation from Shakespeare, which he adopts as the motto for the period following his majority, would not seem relevant to us had we not lingered so long upon the deep reconciliation with his father which followed upon a period of estrangement and misunderstanding. Though his father had been dead a year, we must not think it strange that Søren felt united with him in frank companionship. He felt in fact more closely united with him now than when he was an earthly father. In 1848 he wrote:[2]

My father was the most loving father, and my yearning for him was and is most deep—whom never a day have I failed to remember in my prayers both morning and evening.

I quote the gilt-edged entry in full, as I did the other sheets which characterize the periods of childhood and youth. But here I supply (in brackets) four lines from Lear's speech which reveal the motive of S. K.'s interest in this passage. It is characteristic of him that he omitted these most essential lines because they too poignantly described his own father's humble confession of his sins to him. What he has quoted describes merely the terms of frank and affectionate confidence in which Cordelia and Lear (Søren and his father) were living in their prison, without revealing how it was regained.[1]

TWENTY-FIVE YEARS OF AGE

[*Lear*. No, no, no, no! Come, let's away to prison:
We two alone will sing like birds i' the cage:
When thou dost ask me blessing, I'll kneel down,
And ask of thee forgiveness.] So we'll live,
And pray, and sing, and tell old tales, and laugh
At golden butterflies, and hear poor rogues
Tell of court news; and we'll talk with them too,
Who loses and who wins, who's in, who's out;
As if we were God's spies: and we'll wear out,
In a walled prison, packs and sects of great ones,
Who ebb and flow by the moon.

What I have often suffered from was that while my proper self wished to forget all the doubt and care and unrest involved in attaining a world-view, my reflective self sought to impress this upon itself, as it were, and to conserve it, as a transitional factor, necessary in part, in part interesting, for fear I might have reached a conclusion illicitly, mendaciously.

So now, for example, when I have so arranged my life that it seems as if I were destined to be reading in perpetuity for examination, and that my life, however long it might last beyond my expectation, shall get no farther than the point where I myself arbitrarily broke off—as one sometimes sees weak-minded men who have forgotten the whole of their intervening life and remember only their childhood, or forget everything with the exception of a single moment of their life—that so I, with the thought of being a theological student, might some time be reminded of that happy period of possibilities (what one could call one's pre-existence) and my stoppage at that point, feeling very much as a child might feel to whom they have given brandy and thereby stunted his growth. When now my practical ego seeks to forget for the sake of getting to work, my reflective self would fain hold fast to it because it seems interesting, and would abstract itself from the control of my personal consciousness by raising itself to the power of a universal consciousness.

In 1847 S. K. made the following entries in his Journal which leave no doubt that he regarded his dissolute life and his defection from Christianity as due not essentially to doubt, but to despair and to rebellion against God:[1]

They would have us believe that the objections against Christianity come from doubt. This is always a misunderstanding. Objections against Christianity come from insubordination, unwillingness to obey, rebellion against all authority. Therefore they have hitherto been beating the air against the objectors, because they have fought intellectually with doubt, instead of fighting ethically with rebellion.

(Nov. 20.) . . . So it is not properly doubt but insubordination. In vain do they try to get the machinery into action, for the ground is bog or quicksand. 'We shall all get saved together, &c.' is about what the refrain comes to. When such is the case, what does all this about the comfort of religion mean?

To this chapter evidently belongs the story of 'Nebuchadnezzar' in the *Stages*, which I do not quote here or comment upon, except to say that it expresses the certain conviction of God's reality which was the paradoxical consequence of seven years spent by Nebuchadnezzar (namely S. K.) 'as a beast of the field, eating grass'.

I have already indicated that what S. K. would not do for a living father he did dutifully for a dead father. That is, he began soon after his father's death to study for his theological examination, which was ostensibly his reason for being at the university for the previous eight years. That was a surprise to all his acquaintances, who naturally enough expected that now, when he had inherited a considerable fortune and was entirely independent, he would do only what he pleased to do. He passed his examination *cum laude* on July 3, 1840, and immediately afterwards made the tour in Jutland to which we have referred. The period which S. K. himself regarded as 'the great parenthesis' was so void of adventure (even of spiritual adventure) that we can pass it over and hasten on to the next chapter, which deals with the amazing adventure of his first love, which was also to be his last.

KIERKEGAARD AS A YOUNG MAN

From a plaster relief by CARL AARSLEFF

PART THREE

EARLY MANHOOD

1838–1844

Such books are mirrors: when an ape peers into them, no apostle can be looking out.

LICHTENBERG.

(Used by Kierkegaard as motto for *The Banquet*.)

I. REGINA

1838–41

WHAT a love-story! Of course it has often been told, and the material is only too abundant. S. K. himself told it over and over again to himself—in innumerable entries which refer to 'her'—and he told it over and over again in his books. Regina, who, as the widow of another, survived by four years the nineteenth century, substantially confirmed the story of their love.

We are startled at hearing S. K. affirm that he will take 'her' with him down to history, yet that magniloquence has been fully justified by the event. If S. K. and Regina will not be mentioned in history along with Dante and Beatrice, Petrarch and Laura, or even Abélard and Héloïse, this pair deserves at least to rank higher in the minds of the romantic than Dean Swift and Stella.

The last step with reference to 'Her'.

Nov. 1849.

My will is unaltered that after my death the writings should be dedicated to her and to my deceased father. She shall belong to history.[1]

But all my fame—that is our will—shall be shared, shall belong to thee, 'our own dear little Regina'.[2]

My existence shall unconditionally accentuate her life, my work as an author can also be regarded as a monument to her honour and praise. I take her with me to history. And I who with all my melancholy had only the one wish, to enchant her —*there* it is not denied me; there I walk beside her; like a master of ceremonies I lead her in triumph and say, A little place, please, for her, for 'our own dear little Regina'.[3]

His reply to the refusal of the Schlegels to accept him on a friendly footing was the dedication of the *Two Discourses at the Foot of the Altar*, which were written in 1849 and published in 1851:[4]

To One Unnamed
whose name some day shall be named

is dedicated,
together with this little work,
the whole production of the author from the very beginning.

S. K. shrewdly realized that, if Regina had become his wife, the same glamour would not have attached to her in history.

> To take her along to history when she had become my wife—no, that is out of the question. She can perfectly well become Madame and Mrs., but she must be kept in the role of being no longer my lover, it must be contrived as a story of unhappy love, while to me she remains the loved one 'to whom I owe everything'—behold, thus shall history receive her; that I shall yet teach to history.[1]

This is an amazing love-story. It began idyllically with love at first sight—the first love, and for a girl who was only 14; three tormented years of waiting until she was approaching her 18th year ; then (1) a sudden and successful wooing; then (2) a lovers' quarrel, which was swiftly resolved (3) by her all-too-devoted attachment, while he perceives (4) that they must separate. He sends her back the ring; but (5) she fights like a lioness to retain him, beseeching him in the name of Christ and by the memory of his deceased father not to desert her, so that, to save her life and reason, the hero feels himself obliged to pretend that he is only a mean scoundrel who has been playing with her affections—and after two months of this cruel deceit (cruel most of all to himself) she lets him go.

The numbers inserted above indicate the five phases which S. K. distinguishes in the drama. But with this the story was by no means finished. S. K. fled to Berlin and there wrote a huge book (*Either/Or*, in two volumes, to say nothing of *Two Edifying Discourses*) with the intent of persuading Regina that he was indeed a wastrel. But a few months after these works were published Regina caught his eye in church and nodded to him in a friendly way—so he perceived that all his labour was in vain. Again he fled to Berlin and wrote three books (*Fear and Trembling*, *The Repetition*, and *Three Edifying Discourses*), in the hope of making it clear at least that, even if he were not a scoundrel, it was impossible for them to marry—or else (for here an either/or was obscurely presented to Regina), if she proved able to understand the situation, they might be happily reunited on the basis of 'the immediacy after reflection', through a deep religious experience of 'repetition' consequent upon an act of 'infinite resignation'.

At this point the strain of intense pathos was relieved by a touch of the comic. Just when the last chapter of *Repetition* had been concluded, and the hero had killed himself because he could not endure to think that his beloved was rendered desperate by his desertion—just at that moment S. K. learned that Regina was engaged to Fritz Schlegel. So the conclusion of the book had to be changed, the plan of it was marred, and its purpose was obscured. Regina had protested loudly that she could not survive the loss of him, or that, if she did not literally die, she would renounce the world and 'become a governess'—and in the space of only two years she had found consolation. This was just what S. K. had laboured to bring about, and yet the proof of his success was a severe blow to him. It took time for him to adjust himself to it. But in 1855, when Schlegel was sent as Governor to the Danish West Indies, S. K. was able to speak humorously of her as 'my dear little Governess'.

The story ended in pure pathos. S. K., who was ever faithful to his one love, made a heroic effort to establish an affectionate and brotherly relationship with the Schlegels after their marriage had been consolidated by six years and Regina's unrelenting father had died. Unfortunately, this offer was declined. Unfortunately for S. K. at least, for this seemed to be the one chance open to him for affectionate human intercourse. But it may be that Regina was fearful lest his personality might move her too deeply. Regina remained enshrined in his heart. And enshrined also in a 'rosewood pedestal' which was made according to his design in the form of a closet 'without shelves'—with pathetic but whimsical reference to the assurance she had once given him that, if only he would remain with her, she would be content to live with him in 'a little cupboard'. In the 'pedestal' (which means here a small console in the form of a cupboard) he treasured his own love-letters to her and hers to him; the letters he had written from Berlin to Emil Boesen immediately after his separation from Regina; the brief letters he wrote to Schlegel and Regina suggesting a *rapprochement* (and the much more lengthy drafts from which they were distilled); copies of all his pseudonymous works, which he had had printed on vellum paper for Regina; and a carefully weighed account of his engagement and its rupture, entitled 'My Relation to "Her"—Something Poetical', dated August 24, 1849 (i.e. after her refusal of his friendship), and adorned with the motto: *Infandum me jubes, Regina, renovare dolorem.*[1] All of these documents came ultimately into the hands of Regina, and though she burned her own letters, the other papers have been preserved and are the principal source of this story. S. K.'s last will and testament was enclosed in an envelope addressed to his brother:[2]

To Pastor Dr. Kierkegaard.
To open after my death.

Dear Brother!

It is naturally my will that my former fiancée, Madame Regina Schlegel, shall inherit unconditionally the little I can leave. If she will not herself receive it, the request is made whether in that case she will not dispose of it by distributing it to the poor.

What I wish to express is, that for me an engagement was and is just as binding as a marriage, and that therefore the property I leave devolves upon her quite as if I had been married to her.

As a matter of fact, of his considerable fortune S. K. had hardly enough left to defray the expenses of his burial. But without inquiring whether it might be little or much the Schlegels (who were then in the Virgin Islands, where they could not distribute the property to the poor of Denmark) agreed to refuse this bequest.[3]

Regina lived till 1904, surviving her husband by eight years. She lived to inherit the fame S. K. conferred upon her and was especially delighted by the interest his works excited in Germany. 'The French', she said, 'will never understand him.' In the early days she and Fritz Schlegel (even during the period of their engagement) had read aloud to one another S. K.'s 'aesthetical works', in which she could easily discover many references to their relationship, although 'they were embellished by his own rich imagination'. Her husband cherished 'no petty resentment'. She recalled that in the house of Inspector Ottensen, where a picture of S. K. hung on the wall beside one of Grundtvig, he responded to his host's declaration that it was to S. K. he owed exclusively his spiritual development by pointing to S. K.'s picture and saying, 'When Grundtvig's influence is long past, this one's will still be living.' Later she learned through the publication of the *Papers* how deeply S. K. had loved her and how much the separation had cost him. She learned to recognize that 'Kierkegaard's motive in this breach was the conception he had of his religious task; he did not dare to bind himself to anything upon earth lest it might check him in his calling; he must offer the best thing he possessed in order to work as God required him'. 'The pain he was obliged to inflict upon himself and me was unspeakably heavy and grievous and indeed left its mark for life: easy my life has not been, but happy.'[1] Without being in the least unfaithful to the man she had been married to for fifty years, Regina wished to make it known that she had always cherished for S. K. a—'spiritual affection'. Hence, after she had delivered (1895) to Henriette Lund, S. K.'s niece, the documents once contained in the rosewood pedestal, she recalled her the following year in order that she might hear the story from her own lips and preserve it for posterity. How anxious she was to defend S. K.'s memory from blame with respect to his treatment of her is shown by the fact that she repeated her tale in 1898–9 to Raphael Meyer, a friend of her youth, and again in 1902 to Miss Hanna Mourier, a friend of her old age. Immediately after Regina's death in 1904, both Meyer and Henriette Lund published their recollections of Regina's story together with the documents she had inherited.[2] The more circumstantial report of Miss Mourier remained unpublished till 1933, when it was printed as an appendix to Hjalmar Helweg's book.[3] It repeats the story in the form of a letter to Regina Schlegel ('You said . . . you felt . . .', &c.), incorporating her corrections and the attestation of her approval.

Besides these collected sources of information we have innumerable scattered entries in S. K.'s Journals. Unfortunately his many long and anxious reviews of the situation, which were for the most part written in 1849, begin (as he says)[4] at the wrong end, because what most deeply concerned him was his responsibility in breaking the engagement. The entries, which date from the time of his engagement and the year preceding it, are most of them brief and some of them symbolical, but in many respects they are more precious than the later ones. We find, besides this, an inestimable mass of material in the pseudonymous writings, which deal very largely with the experience of his love and its tragic consequences. If I make scanty use of this last source, it is not so much because of the difficulty of distinguishing between the real history and the imaginative embroidery, as because the material is too abundant to be dealt with in the compass of this book. It is deplorable that these works do not exist in English, so that I could refer the reader to the passages which most vividly recount S. K.'s own story. S. K. states very clearly[1] the rule which ought to be observed when using one's own experiences in telling a story: namely, that they ought to be so disguised that the personal reference would not be recognized. It may seem to us as if he had disregarded this rule, for the personal references are obvious to us now. But we must remember that for the most part they were not obvious to his contemporaries—except to Regina, and from her he had no desire to hide them.

In telling this story for the first time in English, I would tell it so far as possible in S. K.'s own words; but because he tells it piecemeal, and often 'wrong end foremost', with a few ejaculations of ecstasy and with many groans, it seemed to me necessary to orient the reader by recounting, as I have done, succinctly and prosaically, the principal phases of this history.

But before we go further I must say a word about 'Her'—if it is not already too late. Regina was the youngest daughter of State Councillor Olsen, a superior official in the Ministry of Finance, immediately under the famous Privy Councillor Collin, who was the benefactor of Hans Christian Andersen. As the youngest of a numerous flock she was much petted. S. K. obviously makes use of a phrase familiar to the home when he calls her repeatedly 'our own dear little Regina'. At the time of their engagement she was in her eighteenth year and he in his twenty-seventh.

In his account of 'My Relationship to "Her"' S. K. passes rapidly over the first part of the story:[2]

> I saw her first at the Rørdams'. There it was I saw her for the most part during the first period when I did not visit her family. (In a certain sense I have a responsibility with respect to Bollette Rørdam, apart from the fact that she made an impression on me, and perhaps I on her, though in all innocence and merely in an intellectual way.) [She was already engaged at that time to another theological student.]

How much more 'poetical' he could have made the story we can see from the passage in 'The Diary of the Seducer' where the hero, chancing to call at a certain house when the elders were out, throws a group of eight beautiful young girls into some embarrassment by appearing unexpectedly in their midst, but is able to enchant them by his discourse. This lively passage describes, perhaps, exactly what occurred at the Rørdams', except for the theme which the Seducer chose as a way of fascinating the group of girls: the various ways of breaking an engagement. This is a theme which was evidently meant for Regina in later years.[1]

This story is told also by Regina through the pen of Miss Mourier:

> You remember to have seen S. Kierkegaard for the first time when you were 14–16 years of age. You met him at the home of the widow Rørdam (mother of the well-known pastor Peter Rørdam) where you were invited to a party given for a girl of your own age (Thrine Dahl of Roskilde) who was there on a visit. Kierkegaard made a call on the family, and the liveliness of his mind made a strong impression upon you, which however you did not let any one observe. You remember that he talked incessantly, and that his conversation welled up and was in the highest degree captivating, but after the lapse of so many years you do not any longer remember the substance of it. You think that perhaps the passage in his Papers, 'My God, why should the inclination awaken just now! Oh, how I feel *that I am alone*', &c., refers to that meeting with you, when he also was for the first time impressed by you and you by him.

When we turn back to the entries of 1837 (see p. 158) to which Regina here refers, we cannot fail to observe ominous signs of the disaster in which this love-affair ended. We stumble upon phrases which seem perfectly incongruous with the normal experience of falling in love. In the first place we are astonished by the implication that even a friendly visit to the family of a deceased clergyman appeared to S. K. a breach of his solemn 'resolution', for which he must upbraid himself before God. It seems that his repentance of the riotous social life he had been leading exacted in the first instance complete isolation, even from innocent society. He felt that God had pursued him to the Rørdams' and there had 'overtaken' him with the tremendous experience he then encountered. This way of thinking about God is not abhorrent—unless Francis Thompson's 'Hound of

Heaven' is. A year earlier S. K. would have set this down to the account of 'life's irony'. At the end of his life he attributed it to the hand of 'Governance' (*Styrelsen*—providential guidance). We shall later become very familiar with his use of this word. In 1849 he wrote:[1]

> Ah! for in a way I did indeed seduce her, because I had not understood myself from the very beginning. That time Governance caught me thoroughly. If I had not wooed her, but with my coolness in surveying the relationship detachedly had made sure about her—that, in case I ought to marry, she was the one I ought to be united with—and so had begun from the very beginning to reflect whether I could marry—I had got out of the thing easier, for the conclusion would have been that I could not marry. But there Governance caught me, and I had to suffer in a frightful measure, just because in the strictest sense God entered into it, since there was an ethical obligation between her and me.

It may be that S. K. was right in his notion that he was 'uncommonly erotic'; but that is a very different thing from falling in love, and it is evident that he had never fallen in love before and had not the least notion what such a thing meant. He was so overwhelmed by the experience that he feared he was losing his senses and thanked God for preserving his sanity. Love has its fear and trembling as well as religion, it has its *tremendum* as well as its *fascinans*. The fascination soon drew S. K. out again to the Rørdams'—presumably very soon, for though the entry is not dated, it follows immediately upon the one just quoted, and an entry dated July 9 shows that he had seen her there again and was again overwhelmed with a sense of his loneliness, 'like a lonely fir-tree'. We have seen that in the first period he saw her chiefly there, and must have used his talent as a detective to learn when he might find her. It required no less sagacity to discover where, and at what hours, he might find her in the street and follow her unobserved.

But S. K.'s 'dread' (*Angst*) in the presence of Regina involved something more specific and more ominous than the usual *tremendum* of love. We who know the tragic ending cannot fail to see in his anxious presentiment an omen of disaster. In connexion with his engagement he constantly reminds us that he was 'a penitent', and he did not use that word lightly. He conceived that the role of a penitent excluded many of the normal satisfactions of life, and marriage in particular. This explains what he meant by the 'resolution'—'O God, how easily one forgets such a resolution!'—and the frantic exclamation: 'Merciful God, why should the inclination awaken just now?' He had no right to marry—and yet, 'Oh, how I feel that I am alone!' Marriage was plainly enough inconsistent with the role of the penitent—and yet at that moment he could not conceive of not marrying Regina. This he regarded not merely as a possibility but as an actuality. For what else can he mean when he says, 'All will now despise me'? We learn subsequently that he discovered a dire impediment to marriage in the fact that he could not reveal his secret, whereas Christian marriage—the implication of the marriage vow, as he understood it (for 'God is in it')—required complete openness and 'revelation'. Such was his thought on the second meeting with Regina. He must have thought then, as he often did afterwards, of making a public confession of his sin—with the consequence that 'All will now despise me'.

A year before this time (p. 139), when he had a sudden vivid remembrance of his sin, he compared it to 'a flash of lightning which intimates the approach of a great thunderstorm'. This storm broke over him the instant he beheld Regina. We can easily understand that he must have had a new and more poignant sense of his impurity when he fell in love with a beautiful and innocent child, and that intimacy with her after the engagement must have sharpened this sense, and also compelled him to realize how incompatible was his melancholy with her exuberant gladness of heart. In 1848 he wrote in his Journal:[1]

Extraordinary! In one of my first conversations with her, when I was most deeply moved and my being most profoundly stirred, I said to her that in every generation there were certain individuals who were destined to be sacrificed for the others. She hardly understood what I was talking about, and perhaps I hardly understood myself (in any case I understood it only of my inward sufferings), and least of all supposed that this should begin by overwhelming her. But just this spontaneous youthful happiness of hers, set alongside my terrible melancholy, and in such a relationship, must teach me to understand

> myself. For how melancholy I was I had never before surmised; I possessed no measure for conceiving how happy a human being can be.
>
> So I conceived of myself as sacrificed because I understood that my sufferings and torments made me inventive in ascertaining the truth.
>
> So has God gently led me on and on, and now I stand at the point where it becomes true also in an outward sense that there are men who are sacrificed for the others.

The significance of all this will be clearer when we have followed S. K. as far as the year 1848 and beyond it, when he attained a clear conviction that his call was to martyrdom. But even in 1840 he realized[1] that 'the existence of the poet' (the highest thing there is in the purely humane sphere) 'is an unconscious sacrifice' (cf. the first diapsalm on p. vi), and becomes *conscious* only in the religious experience, where the incongruity of the poet's fate as a channel between God and men is explained and illuminated.

But in spite of all these inhibitions and reflections, in spite of the fact that he had deliberately arranged for a solitary life, 'like a Greenlander alone in his kayak' (see p. 93), S. K. indulged his love. He says in the report we must so often quote:[2]

> Already before my father died I had decided upon her. He died. I read for the examination. During all this time I let her existence twine itself about mine.

But all this while he kept his own counsel. A very special delicacy is required of a man who is in love with a child; and in any case S. K. had very delicate scruples about courting, which he expressed in Quidam's Diary.[3]

> To-day a year ago I saw her at the house of her uncle where she and I were at the same party. With how much mystery I brood over my love, how secretly I imbibe love's nourishment! And why so mysteriously? Truly it is not because love stands in any need of the allurement of mystification. But, on the one hand, I am habituated to this *tentamen rigorosum* [severe test] from an earlier period, and more especially from the preparatory period [of my love—as illustrated in the preceding quotation]; and, on the other hand, it seems to me that I owe it to her. Surely it is inexcusable for a man to abuse the free intercourse

with the other sex which our relationship permits, by flirtation, as it is called. It is never possible to reckon in what way and in what degree this flirtation may have a disturbing influence upon a girl, or be disturbing to the man she will one day belong to. I know very well that a love-affair can overlook trifling occasions of disquietude; and yet, if I were in love with a girl, it would always pain me, it would affect me uncomfortably, to know that she had been the object of a flirt's attention. It would be far better had she been actually engaged or married, for a really serious impression of the erotic has not nearly so disturbing an effect as this nondescript sort, which just for this reason is called coquetry. I could wish that in this regard another might have consideration for me, and so I will be considerate of him, for I am very far from having the boldness to assume as a matter of course that she shall be mine. But either she is to become mine, or she is not to become mine—in either case my judgement remains the same. If she shall belong to another, then it is my wish that my thought, quickly killed, may flee back into my own mind and leave no least external trace.

According to Miss Mourier, Madame Schlegel did not remember at what time or on what occasion he had been introduced into her home. She remembered that he favoured her with gifts of nuts, but for the rest paid her no obvious attention. So that, although he had begun, a short time before he proposed, to lend her books and to take an interest in her piano practice, she was so unprepared for his sudden declaration that she was rendered speechless and could only show him to the door.

What was going on in his heart is plain enough to us from his Journal. On October 11, 1838, we have this:[1]

This period of love is surely the most interesting time, when after the total impression given by the first stroke of enchantment, at every encounter, every glance of the eye (even when the soul hastily hides itself as it were behind the eyelash), one brings something home, just as a bird in its busy season fetches one stick after another to its nest, and still constantly feels overwhelmed by the abundance of riches.

But especially from this outburst of February 2, 1839:[2]

Thou, my heart's liege lady, Regina, treasured in the deepest privacy of my breast, at the source of my most vital thought, there where the distance is equally great to heaven and to hell—unknown godhead! Oh, can I really believe the report of the poets that when one sees for the first time the beloved object he believes that he has seen her long before, that all love like all knowledge is recollection, that also love in the single individual has its prophecies, its types, its myths, its Old Testament? Everywhere, in the countenance of every girl, I see traits of thy beauty, but it seems to me as if I must have all girls in order as it were to extract from all their beauty the totality of *thine*; that I must circumnavigate the whole world in order to find that region which I lack and which yet is indicated by the deepest secret of my whole ego—and the next instant you are so near to me, so present, so mightily replenishing my mind, that I am transfigured for myself and feel that it is good to be here.

Thou blind god of love! Thou that seest in secret, wilt thou grant me to know openly? Shall I find here on earth what I seek, shall I experience the *conclusion* of all the eccentric premisses of my life, shall I *enclose* [conclude] thee in my arms, or—

Does the order read, Further?

Hast thou gone on before me, thou my yearning? dost thou beckon me from another world? Oh, I will cast everything from me so as to become light enough to follow thee.

In fact, S. K. was aware of an *order* which claimed to direct his life and which pointed ever further and higher. Even at the time of his vacation at Gilleleie, in the midst of reflections which resulted in the practical abandonment of Christianity, he earnestly desired to 'perceive just what the deity would have *me* do' (p. 109). When he made his visit to Jutland and reflected that he might die there and be buried in Sæding churchyard (p. 182), he exclaimed with dismay, 'In God's name! the task set before me surely cannot be so trifling!' He had a feeling that he was following a divine dispensation when he resolved to fulfil his father's wish and take the theological examination:[1]

I cannot but suppose it to be God's will that I should study for the examination, and that it is more pleasing to him that I do this than that by plunging into one or other inquiry I actually attain some clear apprehension or another; for obedience is dearer to Him than the fat of rams.

A plausible anecdote is told with relation to his unexpected resolution to take this examination. After his father's death some one said to him: 'Now, Kierkegaard, you can get out of studying for the examination, since you haven't your father any more to urge you on eternally.' His answer was: 'No, look you, my friend, now I cannot any longer hold the old man off with stuff and nonsense.'

Looking back from the year 1848, he says in his Journal:[1]

> And how strange it is that from my earliest time (that is to say, in my youth after my father's death) when I was independent and there was no question of seeking a settled occupation, when I went about in deep melancholy and regarded myself as the most miserable of all—how strange it is that even then I prayed every morning that God would give me strength for the work 'which Thou Thyself wilt assign me'. When I now think about that I wonder how in the world it occurred to me to pray in this way! And yet how true it has turned out to be that I have done a work which God himself assigned to me.

I might multiply indefinitely the proof that S. K.'s life was controlled by the thought of a special 'call'. He was led to think of this by his very misfortunes, by everything that made him unlike others, that made him an 'exception in a bad sense', yet prompted the hope that he might become 'exceptional in a good sense'. From this point on we shall not be able to understand S. K. at all unless we have in view this determining factor in his life. It was only the impetuosity of his love which caused him for a while to ignore it. He let her twine about his heart. This was one of the few occasions in his life when he did not exercise too much reflection (p. 84f.). Yet we must not suppose that he did not seriously weigh the step he was about to take. In his review of the story he says:[2]

> At one season I have prayed to God about her as for a gift, the very dearest; also in moments when I envisaged the possibility of realizing the marriage I have thanked God for her as for a gift; later I have been compelled to regard her as God's punishment upon me; but always I have carried her to God....

He speaks only of 'moments' when he could envisage the possibility of marriage. There were other moments when he was in despair. On one occasion he wrote in his Journal:[3]

> The only thing that comforts me is that I could lay myself

down to die and in the hour of death confess the love I do not dare to reveal so long as I live—a love which renders me in the same degree happy and unhappy.

The next entry reads:

Lord God, give me courage again to hope; merciful God, let hope again fructify my sterile and infertile mind.

Quidam, in the entry of his diary dated January 8, gives a vivid account of the way this season of waiting was spent [see p. 200f.]. Without doubt S. K. recounts here exactly his own experience, except that he abbreviates the period to one year, for a reason inherent in the plan of the diary.[1]

But now the fullness of time was approaching. Now for a full year since first I became enamoured of her I had abandoned myself secretly and clandestinely to my love. I have seen her in society, seen her in her home, I have followed her steps unobserved. This last was in a way the dearest to me, partly because it gratified love's secrecy, partly because it did not disturb me with the anxious fear that some one might observe it, which to her might be annoying, and which might drag me prematurely out of the school of preparatory exercise before I had made up my mind. This year of preparatory practice possesses a singular enchantment for me.

Through everything else I undertook was twined the silken cord of love....

How accomplished I became only he can conceive who understands what it means to undertake nothing, not even the least thing, except by force of reflection—which is as if one in order to walk had to use an artificial leg and could not take a single step without it, and at the same time desired to hide from people that it is an artificial leg. This is a thing that can only be done by force of reflection. A man has merely to think how much he does spontaneously, and then he will understand what it means not to do the least thing without calculation. Then he will know what a difference there is between coming into a merry circle and being joyous as a matter of course, and coming, on the other hand, out of the deepest gloom of melancholy, and yet precisely on the stroke of the clock indicated by the invitation, and with the sort of merriment required by the society and the environment. In case one is not in love, he must falter by the way.

Once a week she went to her singing-lesson. I knew where the singing-teacher lived. Far from making an effort to thrust myself into this circle, I wished only to see her while I remained in hiding. Now it chanced happily that in the same street there dwelt a pastrycook whose shop she passed as she went to and fro for her lessons. Here I had my post of observation. Here I sat and waited, here I saw her, myself unseen, here love's hidden growth waxed and developed before my eyes to my great contentment. It was a second-class coffee-house where I could be pretty sure not to be surprised. Nevertheless, some of my familiar friends took notice of it. I represented to them that the coffee was the best in the whole town, I even exhorted them with much pathos to try it. A few of them went there one day and tasted—naturally finding it very poor, as indeed it was. I disputed that with them hotly. The consequence was that when the question was raised by them among a number of companions, one said, 'Oh, that's nothing but his usual obstinacy. For a mere whim he has declared that the coffee is superb, and now to affirm that he is in the right he compels himself to drink the stuff. That's how he is—a good head, but the most contentious fellow—and the best way to revenge oneself upon him as upon Diogenes is not to answer him back, but to bother no more about him, and in this specific case to bother no more about his coffee-house.' Another was of the opinion that I had a strong disposition to fixed ideas, and he found it amusing that I could really think the coffee was good. At bottom they were all wrong, for to my taste too the coffee was bad. On the other hand they were not wrong in revenging themselves upon me by fulfilling my wish that they should leave me in peace with my pastrycook and his coffee. If I had not begged them to come, I could hardly have been so secure. I drank the coffee without giving much thought to it, but here it was I waited, here it was I approached with longing the experience of love and refreshed it with the sight of her, and from here I took much home with me when the sight had vanished. I never dared to seat myself near the window, but where I sat in the middle of the room my eye commanded the street and the opposite side-walk where she went, while passers-by could not see me. O blissful time, O lovely recollection, O sweet disquietude, O happy sight, when I embellished my hidden existence with the enchantment of love!

Such intrigue was highly characteristic of S. K. It may have been embarrassing to his friend Boesen when S. K. wrote to him from Berlin and required him to station himself in that same coffee-house to spy upon Regina and report how she was bearing the blow he had dealt her.

In the course of the Jutland journey he made the following entry:[1]

> Generally speaking my misfortune is that when I am pregnant with ideas I am enamoured of the ideal, hence I give birth to monstrosities, and hence, too, reality does not correspond to my burning desires—and God grant that this may not be the case with my love; for here also a secret dread grips me lest I have mistaken the ideal for a reality. God forbid! Until now at least it is not the case. But this anxiety which makes me so fain to see the future in advance also makes me fear it.

We must understand that the dread and hopelessness he bewails was not due to any doubt about the possibility of winning the lady. 'Such a thought', he says somewhere, 'is beneath my dignity.'[2] In a letter to Boesen just after his own engagement was broken he finds himself obliged to rebuke his friend for the faint-heartedness with which he had resigned himself to the loss of the lady with whom he in his turn was in love.

> If a girl had made so deep an impression upon me as she has upon you, I would have declared war; and then I am in my element, war itself is my enjoyment. The thought has never yet found place in my (if you will) four-cornered or proud head, that a girl might be invincible.[3]

It was in this bold spirit that S. K., soon after his return from Jutland, 'declared war' upon Regina.[4]

> In the summer of 1840 I took the official examination in theology.
>
> Then straightway I made a visit to the house. I took the journey to Jutland, and already perhaps was fishing a little for her—for example, by lending her books in my absence, and by indicating a particular passage she was to read in one of them.
>
> In August I came back. The period from August 9 till into

September may be said in a strict sense to be the period when I approached her. On the 8th of September I started out from home with the resolute intention of deciding the matter. We met on the street just outside her house. She said there was no one at home. I was audacious enough to understand this as an invitation, as just the opportunity I wanted. I went up with her. There we stood alone in the sitting-room. She was a little uneasy. I begged her to play a little for me, as she did at other times. She did so, and that wouldn't satisfy me. Then suddenly I take her music-book, close it not without a certain vehemence, throw it down on the piano and say, Oh, what do I care about music! It is you I want, I have wanted you for two years. She remained silent. For the rest, I had done nothing to beguile her; I had even warned her against myself, against my melancholy. And when she spoke about a relationship to Schlegel I said, So let this relationship be a parenthesis, for anyway I have the first priority. *Marginal note.* N.B. It was, however, on the 10th she talked about Schlegel, for on this occasion she uttered not a word. She was entirely silent. Finally I went away, for I was in fear lest some one might have come and found us two together, and she so disturbed. I went directly up to the Councillor, I know that I was terribly concerned at having made so strong an impression upon her, as well as for the fear that in some way my visit might give occasion to misunderstanding, even to the point of hurting her reputation.

The father said neither yes nor no, but nevertheless he was willing enough, as I could easily understand. I asked for an opportunity to talk with her. I got it for the 10th of September in the afternoon. I said not a single word to beguile her—she said, Yes.

Immediately I took over the relationship to the whole family. My virtuosity was especially directed towards the father, whom by the by I always cared a great deal for.

But inwardly—The next day I saw that I had made a blunder. A penitent as I was, my *vita ante acta*, my melancholy, that was enough.

I suffered indescribably in that period.

Regina's description is not substantially different.[1]

[You remember that] one day when he met you in the street

and would follow you home, and your reply to this was that there was no one at home, you scarcely observed that he ignored your answer and still followed you. On arriving home, you proposed to play for him—that you were wont to do, for he loved music. But soon he shut the music-book in front of you and declared that it was not for this he had come. When thereupon he confessed his love, you became perfectly speechless and without a single word or any explanation, but merely with a sign, you showed him hastily to the door!—Your strange way of taking the thing made Kierkegaard uneasy about you, he therefore immediately sought your father in his office and recounted to him the whole scene.—Your father said nothing to commit you, but two days later when Kierkegaard came again you gave him your consent—but only after you had mentioned that there was a teacher in your schooldays you cared a great deal for, and who, you believed, was also attached to you. This, however, Kierkegaard did not trouble himself about in the least, for he said later, 'You could talk about Fritz Schlegel till doomsday—that wouldn't help you in the least, for I *will* have you.' You were 18 years old.

As a matter of course, Regina was unaware of the 'inward' change in S. K. which followed so swiftly upon this brisk wooing. No one could be more adroit than he in hiding the doubt and despair which began to distract him. And besides, his doubt was not constant; it alternated with hope and exuberant joy. 'I live continually', he said, 'on the border of the happy and the desert Arabia.'[1]

How are we to understand his situation?

His niece Henriette Lund reports:[2]

In the last year of his life, when I met Uncle Søren in the street, he expressed to me his astonishment at my interest in Shakespeare's 'Hamlet', which led me to read it again and again both in the original and in translation, as well as to follow the performance of it with strained attention to the least details. I sought to engage his interest in the matter by asking him whether he was not captivated by this extraordinary drama, whether it did not stir him deeply too. 'Yes, indeed, but for me it is an entirely different thing.' And as I looked at him questioningly he added as a sort of explanation, 'That you cannot understand now—some day perhaps you will understand it.'

It is interesting to learn that S. K. was himself impressed by the similarity of his situation and that of Hamlet, for a student of his life cannot fail to think of the resemblance. We have seen that he had, like Hamlet, a disposition to reflection which checked decisive action, that he was constantly checked by the thought of a parent's guilt which he dared not reveal, and was prompted (we might say) by his father's ghost. And now Ophelia comes upon the scene, and the tragedy of his situation (more particularly the sense of a task he must perform) hinders him from marrying the girl he devoutly loved.

S. K. says in a certain place, 'If you can explain Abraham's collision [in the offering of his son Isaac], you have explained my whole life.' Likewise I would say: If you can explain to me Hamlet, I shall be able to understand S. K.

I cannot get it through my head how a man like the notorious Schrempf can believe that S. K. was not really in love, and how others can chide him for proposing to Regina without due deliberation. For we have seen that he had been weighing this step for more than two years and had weighed it before God. For my part I can easily conceive that new and undreamed-of factors emerged to confound his whole reckoning the moment he held Regina in his arms and realized the joy of possessing her.

There are not many entries in the Journal which we can ascribe to the first months of the engagement, and if any were made during the last period of it, S. K. must have destroyed them. Probably he made none. For he was not only engaged in writing his master's dissertation on *The Concept of Irony*, but at the same time he was writing a considerable part of the second volume of *Either/Or*, the section concerned with 'the aesthetical value of marriage'. Indeed we can hardly suppose that in the distressing conflict of that time he could have set down such reflections in his Journal as he afterwards incorporated in Quidam's Diary and in the conversations and letters of the 'young poet' of the *Stages*.

Quidam's Diary registers the following on the day of his engagement:[1]

The first kiss—what bliss! A girl joyful in mood, happy in youth! And she is mine. What are all gloomy thoughts and imaginations but a mere spider-web, and melancholy only a mist which flees before her reality, a sickness which is healed and is being healed by this abundant health, this health which indeed is mine since it is hers, who is my life and my future. Riches she has not, that I know well enough, it is entirely unnecessary, but she can say as the Apostle said to the lame man: Silver and gold have I none; but what I have, that I give thee: Arise and be strong. . . . Enviable lot, to be capable of being so much to a man.

But the very first entry in the Journal which we can ascribe to the time of the engagement gives us a great deal to think about:[1]

The dreamer raises himself continually to higher and higher 'powers' (to use that word in the mathematical sense). Hence a dream within a dream (whereby the first becomes a sort of reality) is so infinitely more ethereal. With what boundless enthusiasm a youth can read Paul Møller's words in 'The Aged Lover':

To my arm-chair there comes a dream
From my youthful years,
A yearning intense
For thee, thou sun among women!

For the youth, the dream is here raised to the 2nd power; he first dreams himself an old man, in order that thereby, through a whole life-time as a medium, he may absorb the most aromatic instant of his earliest youth.

This is very characteristically Kierkegaardian, but it may not seem significant to the reader until he has devoted some reflection to it. How significant this thought was to Kierkegaard we can judge by the fact that he plays upon it in four of his love-letters to Regina, that he lets the young poet of the *Stages* repeat these verses again and again with melancholy enthusiasm, and that he permits Constantine to analyse ruthlessly the sentiment he distilled from them.

An understanding of this is so vital to a comprehension of S. K.'s situation as a lover that I shall quote his first love-letter[2]—since at least one should be presented as a sample—and I shall also report Constantine's reflections.

My Regina!

Es endet Schmertz
So wie die Schertz
So wie die Nacht
Eh' man 's gedacht.

(Pain ends
As play ends
As night ends
Before we think it.)

You recounted recently, when you were up at my house, that your father had presented you at your confirmation with a bottle of lily of the valley (*extrait double de muguet*). You supposed perhaps that I did not hear it, or you supposed perhaps that it passed my ear by like much else that does not echo within. But far from it! But as this flower hides itself so charmingly within the large leaf, so I also allowed the plan of sending you the accompanying object to hide itself at first in the half-transparent misty veil of forgetfulness, in order that thus, liberated from every even the most remote solicitation, rejuvenated to a new life in comparison with which the first was only an earthly life, it could now spread its perfume which longing and remembrance vie with it to produce ('From my youthful springtime' [P. Møller's poem]). Almost did it prove impossible, however, to procure such an extract in Copenhagen. Yet in this respect also a providence rules, and the *blind* God of love perceives a way. That you receive it at this moment (just before you go out) is because I know that you recognize the infinity of the instant. If only it does not arrive too late. Haste, my messenger. Haste, my thought. And do thou, Regina, stand an instant, just an instant, stock still.

Thine for ever
S. K.

We are prompted first of all to reflect that such a letter as this exacted of Regina very considerable mental agility. All of the love-letters are as subtly expressed. But perhaps S. K. had trained his fiancée to understand them more readily than we do. I did not clearly understand the meaning of all this—and how ominous a symptom it was—until I read in *Repetition* what

Constantine Constantius has to say about it.[1] The young poet, immediately after his engagement, came to Constantine to confide in him the overwhelming experience of his love.

> While he paced up and down the floor he repeated again and again the lines of Paul Møller's poem [the same which we recited above]. His eye filled with a tear, he threw himself down on a chair, he repeated the lines again and again. Upon me this scene made a harrowing impression. Great God! thought I, such a melancholy has never before presented itself in my practice. . . . He was in love, deeply and sincerely, that was clear, and yet right away, on one of the first days, he was capable of recollecting his love. At bottom he was through with the whole relationship. At the very moment of beginning he took such a tremendous stride that he has leapt clear over the whole of life. Though the girl were to die to-morrow, it will not make any essential difference, he will again throw himself down, his eye will again fill with a tear, he will again repeat the poet's words. What a strange dialectic! He longs for the girl, he has to exert violence upon himself not to be staying with her the whole day, and yet at the very first moment he has become an old man so far as regards this relationship. There must be a misunderstanding at the bottom of it. For a long time nothing has moved me so much as this scene. That he must become unhappy is clear enough, that the girl also must be unhappy is no less clear, although it is not possible at once to foresee in what way this will come about. So much, however, is sure, that if any one can discourse about love as a recollection, he can too. Recollection has the great advantage that it begins with the loss, and therefore it is safe, for it has nothing to lose.
>
> . . . .
>
> And yet I hold to the view that his mood was right as an erotic mood; and he who in his love-making has not experienced it precisely at the beginning, has never loved. Only, one must have another mood alongside this. This potentialized recollection is the eternal expression of love in its beginning, it is a token of genuine love. But on the other hand an ironical elasticity is required in order to be able to make use of it. This he lacked, his soul was too soft for it. It must be true that at the

> first moment one's life is over, but there also must be vitality enough to kill this death and transform it into life. In love's first dawn the present and the future are at strife with one another to produce the eternal impression, and this recollection is precisely the counter-current of eternity flowing back into the present—that is to say, in case this recollection is healthy.
>
> We went back to his home. I bade him farewell; but my sympathy was aroused almost too powerfully. I could not get rid of the thought that in a very short time this must lead to a terrible explosion.

That S. K. here describes himself there can be no doubt, but the reader must be alert to observe that he also satirizes himself—very much as Barrie at once describes and satirizes himself in 'Sentimental Tommy'. 'His eye filled with a tear'—just *one*—that is satirical. And we know very well that S. K. would not confess of himself that 'his soul was too soft' to possess 'ironical elasticity'. He possessed something of the hardness of Constantine along with the softness of the young poet. This passage, therefore, does not give us a complete account of the tragedy of S. K.'s love. The reader must observe, moreover, that when he was writing *Repetition* he was indulging the thought of a possibility of a repetition with Regina—'vitality enough to kill this death and transform it into life'.

The passage we have just read apprises us how deeply S. K. was versed in psychology, although he had no inclination to 'lecture' upon it like a professor. We discover too that what he knew he had not learnt out of a book but out of his own experience. And how much he had learnt from Regina, or rather with her!

> How strange! Socrates was always saying that he had learnt from a woman. Ah, I can say that I owe my best to a girl; not precisely that I have learnt from her, but with her.[1]

And we can detect here a certain advantage in S. K.'s method of 'indirect communication', which does not present us with a result to be learnt by rote, but shows *how* it resulted from life and in life—so that if it is to be truly learnt we must literally learn it *by heart*. We have here an example of what S. K. called 'double reflection'. That is to say, the truth is presented, not abstractly, but as it is related to life and reflected from life. Here it is illustrated by the case of a fictitious individual under the observation of a pseudonymous author. The reduplication, however, cannot be counted complete until it is reflected in one's own life. But double reflection is here seen to have its perils. As in the case of a dream within a dream, it may become with every step more remote from reality. We shall see later (p. 256 f.) that just as he was finishing *Repetition* S. K. abruptly completed his 'educatoin in the possibility', and learnt at bitter cost how perilous the ethereal potentializing of reflection may be. He discovered too tardily that, though one can say that it is raised to a 'higher power', it has a minus sign in front of it. This he learnt, and this is one of the important lessons he has to teach. Perhaps the world might have learnt it from him sooner if he had been willing to lecture a little. Now, at all events, the notion that all philosophy and all knowledge, if it is to be of any avail, must be drawn from life and expressed again in life is the starting-point of the newer philosophy in Germany, which acknowledges its debt to him by describing itself as *existential* philosophy, using a word which he had coined in this sense.

It would be interesting to read more of the love-letters, but that would lead us too far. The complaint has been made, justly enough, that they are stilted. But what wonder! Not only was S. K. incapable at that time of direct communication (even of his love to Regina), but, much as he loved her, he was already tormented by the doubt whether he could marry her. S. K., to use his own figure, was like a man walking on artificial legs and anxiously intent that no one should know it—least of all Regina. In such a situation, how carefully and calculatingly a lover must write, if he would give pleasure to his beloved and yet say nothing untrue. And when he signed himself 'Thine for ever' was that not untrue? No, that was only too true—so hotly true that I wonder it did not scorch the page. He knew that he was hers for ever, although she might not be his.

The few entries in the Journal which we can ascribe to this period are more informing than the letters.

> It is well known that there are insects that die in the very instant of fecundation. Thus in general all joy, life's highest and most exuberant instant of enjoyment—is attended by death.[1]

This must not be understood as an expression of despair. It indicates rather an ecstatic will to die. He would have been glad to die, if only he might have possessed Regina—or perhaps rather, I should say, glad to possess Regina, if only at that instant he might die. In 1843 he wrote (with reference to the story of his love which he had thought of putting in *Either/Or* and finally incorporated in the *Stages*):[1] 'His love rendered him indescribably happy in the moment, but when he thought of time he despaired.' We have learnt that the 'aesthetic' life is 'in the moment', and that it suffers shipwreck upon time.

But here is a passage depicting a struggle with doubt which means despair to the verge of madness:[2]

> My doubt is terrible.—Nothing can bring me to a stop—there is a cursed hunger: every argument, every comfort and consolation I am capable of devouring—I run with a speed of 10,000 miles a second, passing every obstacle head over heels.

And here is a bitter reflection:[3]

> I could take pleasure in handling in a romantic manner a man who had to traffic with a jeweller. This must be a Jew. His clinging to these precious possessions (he could sometimes become irresolute whether he must sell them, so dearly did he love them), the prodigious glimpse into the story of prosperity and opulence—this gem belonged to a man who in his time had command of two tons of gold; I do not name him, he still lives and is a respected man, but his money has taken wings. The prodigiously painful scenes when a man like that disposes of such things, the otherwise humble Jew feels that he has the upper hand, the humiliating glimpse into his plight, the mysterious whispers between the Jew's fellow initiates as to how far that man is totally ruined, or only momentarily, &c., &c.

Does it need to be said that the jewel was Regina and the Jew Schlegel—to whom he feared he must relinquish her? At another moment, when he felt that, although the engagement was not yet broken, the loss was inevitable, he described his joy in the past tense:[4]

> . . . and I loved her so much, she was as light as a bird, as audacious as a thought; I let her rise higher and higher, I

stretched out my hand and she perched upon it and beat her wings, and she called down to me, 'Here it is splendid', and she forgot and did not know that it was I that made her light, that I gave her audacity of thought and trust in me which made it possible for her to walk upon the water, and I acclaimed her, and she accepted my acclaim.—At other times she threw herself down before me, wanted only to look up, wanted to forget everything else.

'Several months' after the beginning of the engagement came the brief episode which S. K. characterizes as

The 2nd Period

She makes an attempt at boundless presumption. Instantly my melancholy is practically gone, so far as that case was concerned, and the pangs of conscience are no longer relevant to it. I breathe as freely as ever.

Here lies a fault of mine. I ought to have used the moment to break off, so that it would have been the triumph of her presumption.

But the thing for me was too serious, since it involved the question whether I could realize a marriage, and also there was something childlike in her presumption.

In any case, I took counsel of myself in a way and attacked the situation with some little reference to her. [This is a euphemistic way of saying that he made an angry and masterful rejoinder.]

The 3rd Period

She surrendered and was transformed into the most lovable being. At the same instant my first situation returned again [i.e. his melancholy], and in a higher power by reason of my responsibility which was augmented by her womanly, almost appealing devotion.[1]

This account hardly seems intended to make plain what actually occurred; but unfortunately S. K. has said a great deal more about this episode, recurring to it again and again as an amazing example of how presumptuous a young girl can be, but without disclosing any fact that would make his condemnation of Regina less incredible. We cannot wonder that a beautiful young girl whose lover often sat beside her weeping, or was cold and distant when he encountered her, as Madame Schlegel reports, might have found in this sufficient provocation for the petulant saying which S. K. reports: 'If she believed that it was out of habit I come, she would at once break off', or (as S. K. reports in another passage) that she had accepted him out of pity. It is very clear that S. K. neglected a good opportunity to put an end to the engagement, but it is also clear enough that he was too much in love with her to make so shrewd a calculation.

At this point I am so indignant, so exasperated with S. K., that I can hardly bear to say another word about this episode, not knowing anything that could be said in extenuation of his conduct. I think how intolerable it would have been for Regina if she had been united in marriage to such a man. In fact, S. K. knew that very well too, and this was one of the principal reasons he had for separating from her.

> How great is woman's devotion!—But this is the curse that rests upon me, never to dare to let any person attach himself to me deeply and sincerely. God in heaven knows what I have suffered on the many occasions when with childlike joy I have thought out something that would thoroughly delight her, and I must make it my principle never to carry out anything at the moment of joy, but wait until understanding and prudence had prohibited it for fear of drawing her nearer to me. My relation to her I think can truly be called an unhappy love.[1]

After this episode the worst was yet to come, but in no other instance was S. K. so entirely in the wrong. I have reflected that our hero appears to the greatest disadvantage precisely in those passages which he wrote for the public eye and treasured in the rosewood 'pedestal', for they were written as an apology for his conduct, and they are fiercely apologetic, because the only way he could be apologetic was to be polemical. These are the documents most conspicuously in evidence, and therefore most commonly referred to, but the spontaneous entries in his Journal are far more ingratiating, and if they do not always prove that he was in the right, they show how much he was to be pitied. 'Guilty?' 'Not Guilty?' was the title he gave to the story of the young man in the *Stages*, and this was the query that tormented him all his life long. In only one respect was he perfectly clear about his guilt. Again and again he repeats this accusation against himself: 'My guilt is that I dragged her out with me into the stream.' He ought never to have proposed to her.

This strange engagement had lasted for eleven months and a day, when S. K., on August 11, 1841, made a resolute endeavour to put an end to it.[1]

> Had I not been a penitent, not had my *vita ante acta*, not been melancholy—union with her would have made me happy as I had never dreamed of becoming. But inasmuch as I (because unfortunately I was such as I am) must say that I could be happier in unhappiness without her than with her—she had moved me deeply, and I would gladly, more than gladly, have done everything. But there was a divine veto, as I understood it: the marriage vow. I must conceal prodigiously much from her, base the whole thing upon an untruth.
>
> I wrote to her and sent back her ring. The note is found verbatim in 'The Psychological Experiment'. I have intentionally let it be purely historical, for I have spoken to no one, not a single soul, I who am more silent than the grave. If she should come to see this book, I wished expressly that she might be reminded of it.

He wished her to be reminded of her share of responsibility for the two months of excruciating torment which followed for them both when she refused to let him break the engagement. The note, as printed in Quidam's Diary, reads as follows:[2]

> Not to put often to the test a thing which must be done, and which when once it is done will supply the strength that is needed—so let it be done. Above all, forget him who writes this; forgive a man who, though he may be capable of something, is not capable of making a girl happy.

'What did she do? In womanly desperation she overstepped the limit.'[3] This is his oft repeated expression. In another passage he says, In her desperation she overstepped her limit and would compel me to overstep mine. Then the situation became dreadful.' What actually happened was that Regina regarded this note as a symptom of the melancholy it was her task to cure. Consequently she hastened to his room, and not finding him at home, left for him a note, adjuring him 'in the name of Christ and by the memory of his deceased father' not to desert her. This adjuration made a prodigious impression upon S. K.—'naming the name of Christ to one who has such a tender conscience!' It compelled him to return to her—not, however, with a change of purpose, but with the intention of weaning her from him. It was understood between them that the ultimate decision should be postponed until he had finished his dissertation 'On the Concept of Irony', defended his thesis, and got the book ready for the press. For his own part it was clear that 'there was but one thing to do, to repel her with all my might. It was a frightfully agonizing time—to be obliged to be so cruel, and at the same time to love her as I did. She fought like a lioness. Had I not conceived that I had a divine opposition, she would have conquered.'

I have never been able to understand why this long account of 'My Relationship to "Her"' seemed to S. K. 'something poetical'. It seems to me the least poetical thing he ever wrote. If it had any literary character in the beginning, it has been completely marred by numerous notes in the margin which we do not know well where to place. And it fails to tell us clearly what he wanted the world to know. We have to learn from other entries that to save her reason, if not her very life, and to render her free to marry, he felt compelled to resort to the cruel expedient of making out that he was a mean deceiver, a thorough scoundrel who had no love for her but had been trifling with her affections. He cynically suggested that she should accept Schlegel after all.

S. K.'s point of view is expressed in the following entry:[1]

> But in the case of marriage it does not hold good that everything is understood to be sold in the condition it is in when the hammer falls. Here a little honesty is in place with regard to the earlier period. Here again my chivalry is clear. Had I not honoured her as my future spouse more highly than myself, had I not been prouder of her honour than of mine, I might have kept silence and fulfilled her wish and my own, let myself be married to her—there are so many marriages which hide little stories. That I would not do, she would thus have become my concubine—I would rather have murdered her. But had I explained myself, I must have initiated her into terrible things, my relationship to my father [that is, presumably, solidarity with him in the guilt of blasphemy], his melancholy, the dreadful night which broods in the inmost depths,

my wildness, lusts and excesses, which yet perhaps were not so heinous in the sight of God.

But Regina and her family took an entirely different view and made it as difficult as possible for S. K., as we see from the following:[1]

About 'Her'

So costly this girl had to become to me, or so costly I had to make her for religious reasons.

She herself besought me with tears and adjurations (for Jesus Christ's sake, by the memory of my deceased father) not to forsake her, for the rest I might do anything with her, absolutely anything, she would submit to it unconditionally and thank me all her life long for her relationship to me as for the greatest charity. Her father, who interpreted my behaviour as eccentricity, begged and adjured me not to forsake her, 'she was willing to submit unconditionally to everything'; so far as he was concerned and the rest of the family, he promised me most emphatically, if such was my wish, that neither he nor any of his family would ever set foot across my door-sill; once I was married to her she should be as absolutely in my power as if she had neither kindred nor friends.

Well, so I could have let myself marry her (if there had not been inward difficulties on my part), I could at a cheap price have bound them all to gratitude, and for the rest always played the tyrant, having constantly at my disposition this frightful means of compulsion, that it was a charity I had done her. Truly, if I had done that, I should have been a scoundrel indeed; I should have been meanly taking advantage, with a revolting meanness, of a young girl's moan which led her to say what she never ought to have said or could really have meant. At the same time she was not so far wrong in this, inasmuch as she understood well enough that, if only I once decided to take her, I should certainly do all in my power to make her life worth living. That is to say, she trusted me.

So I got married to her, let us suppose. What then? In the course of half a year, in less than that, she would have worn herself out. About me—and this is at once the good and the bad in me—there is something rather ghostly, which accounts for the fact that no one can put up with me who must see me in everyday intercourse and so come into real relationship with me. Of course, in the light surtout in which I commonly show myself it is different. But at home it will be observed that essentially I live in a spirit-world. I was engaged to her for a year, and still she did not really know me.—So then she would have gone to smash. And she in her turn would presumably have broken me, for I should have been constantly on the point of straining myself by lifting her, for her substance was in a certain sense too light. I was too heavy for her, and she too light for me, but both cases may perfectly well cause a strain. . . .

The case is perfectly simple. My reason told me clearly enough that what I proposed to do was the right thing, the only right thing. But had I not had a conscientious scruple to sustain me, she must have won. I could not have ventured merely at the dictates of my reason to defy her tears, her adjurations, her father's suffering and my own wish—and I must have yielded. But I had to fight the case before a much higher tribunal, and hence my firmness, which was taken for heartlessness.

. . . . . .

After what she has gone through with me, her relation to Schlegel might even become very pretty. There she has got a man, a fine man, whom she was in love with before. Then she will grow womanly, installed in her rights, for her life will have great significance to him, he will gratefully appreciate every day and hour of their life together, all her lovely charm. And if not, he truly would be a beast. Ah, I am now once for all something ghostly, and it would have been a torment to behold all this lovely charm in the attitude of a suppliant wasted upon me, just as if it were not something of infinite worth, just as if the fault lay with her and not with me; but out of this delusion I never should have been able to get her, for she was overwhelmed, and she would have become more frightfully so by living daily with me in my house.—Thus would her relationship to me become beautifully arranged again [i.e. in case a friendly *rapprochement* might be possible]. She did not become a beggar in my house, but the beloved, the only beloved. As such she belongs to history.

I do not especially cling to life but would rather be dead. The day I die her situation is enviable. She is happily married, and her life has such a significance as a woman's rarely has for a man, who indeed is not far from worshipping her—and then my life too gives expression to the fact that she was the only beloved, my whole existence as an author shall lay stress upon her life. And if not before, at least in eternity she will understand me.

Here we must turn back again to the so-called 'poetical' report in order to get a consecutive view of the conclusion of this story:[1]

From time to time I said to her bluntly, 'Yield now, let me go, you can't stand it'. To this she replied passionately that she had rather stand anything than let me go. I tried also to so turn the matter that it was she who broke off the engagement, so as to spare her all mortification. This she would not hear of; she replied that if she had stood the other things, she could stand this too, and not unsocratically she remarked that there was surely no one who in her presence would let her notice an affront, and that what they said in her absence was a matter of indifference.

Then it broke, after about two months. [On October 11, 1841. The thesis had been publicly defended on September 16, and the dissertation was ready for the printer on the 29th.] For the first time in my life I scolded. It was the only thing to do.

I went from her immediately to the theatre, for I wanted to see Emil Boesen. . . . The act was over. As I went up to the second parquet, the Councillor came up from the first and said, May I speak with you? I followed him to his home. She is desperate, he said; this will be the death of her, she is perfectly desperate. I said, I shall still be able to tranquillize her, but the matter is settled. He said, I am a proud man, this is hard, but I beseech you not to break with her. In truth he was proud, he touched me deeply. But I held to my own. I took supper with the family that evening. I talked with her, then I left. Next morning I got a letter from him saying that he had not slept all night, that I must come and see her. I went and talked her round. She asked me, Will you never marry? I replied, Well, in about ten years, when I have sown my wild oats, I must have a pretty young miss to rejuvenate me. She said, Forgive me for what I have done to you. I replied, It is rather I that should pray for your forgiveness. She said, Kiss me. That I did, but without passion. Merciful God!

To get out of the situation as a scoundrel, a scoundrel of the first water if possible, was the only thing there was to be done in order to work her loose and get her under way for a marriage.

So we separated. . . . I wrote a letter to the Councillor which was returned unopened. I passed the night weeping in my bed. But in the day-time I was as usual, more flippant and witty than usual—that was necessary. My brother said to me that he would go to the family and show them that I was not a scoundrel. I said: You do that and I will shoot a bullet through your head—the best proof how deeply the matter [of carrying out the deception] concerned me.

I journeyed to Berlin. I suffered a great deal. I remembered her in my prayer every day. To this date I have absolutely kept to that—to pray for her every day at least once, often twice, besides all the times I thought about her. [She had asked him to remember her sometimes—as he often recalled with a keen sense of the irony of it.]

When the tie was broken my feeling was this: Either you throw yourself into wild diversions or religiousness absolute, of a different sort from that of the parsons.

Where is the 'poetical' in all this? S. K.'s behaviour seems almost inhuman, not only because of the cruel suffering it involved for him and for her, but for its rigid adherence to so strange a plan. And yet I do not presume to think that I know better than S. K. what was necessary in this case. The amazing persistence with which she clung to him makes it seem not improbable that she would have preferred a single life had she conceived that her lover was leaving her for a religious motive—we might say, for the cloister. S. K. gave her credit for enough religiousness to do that, though perhaps her religiousness was not what he meant by 'the decisive categories of Christianity'. 'She lacked a disposition to religion', he affirmed. According to her report, they never had any serious religious conversation, but occasionally he read Mynster's sermons to her and was rather astonished that she was surprised at it. In later years (to quote again Miss Mourier) she resented the imputation that she was not religious:

> You told me about your mother, that she took you when you were still a child to the 'meeting of the Sanctified' [Moravians?] and that like her you had a religious disposition. You found satisfaction in reading *The Imitation of Christ* by Thomas à Kempis, and you found your refuge in God.

Regina proved, indeed, to have more resiliency than S. K. expected, and he was not altogether pleased when after only two years she accepted Schlegel. Yet he was perhaps justified in believing that he had made the marriage.

The scandal in Copenhagen was enormous. Every one regarded him as a mean scoundrel. Regina's elder sister Cordelia was one of the few exceptions. 'I do not understand Magister Kierkegaard', she said, 'but I believe all the same that he is a good man.' S. K. felt deeply the contempt to which he had exposed himself. Nevertheless he thought it necessary for the success of his deception to face brazenly the gossip of Copenhagen for a full fortnight before he escaped to Berlin, nominally for study, and especially to hear Schelling lecture.

At this point the Journal begins again, and for several months it contains hardly any entries which are not concerned with Regina. It is a relief to turn from the too much meditated reflections of a later time to these contemporary and spontaneous records. We might write as a motto over them all the words he wrote in 1844:[1]

She chose the cry, I chose the pain.

Of the entries of this period which have to do with Regina I quote nearly one-third. The first four were written on the steamboat as he voyaged to Germany, the others were all written in Berlin.[2]

> You say, What I have lost or rather deprived myself of—ah, how should you know that or understand it? When this subject is mentioned you would do well to hold your peace. And how should any one know better than I? . . . What have I lost?—the only thing that I loved. What have I lost?—in men's eyes my knightly word. What have I lost?—that which I always have and, in spite of this shock, always shall set my honour upon, my joy, my pride—to be faithful.—Yet my soul is as uneasy as my body at the moment I write this, in a cabin shaken by the double motion of the steamship.

And it is hard for me especially in this case where I am so fain to act, to see myself relegated to the one activity which commonly is left to women and children—to pray.

You say, She was fair. Oh, what do you know about that?—I know it, for this beauty has cost me tears.—I bought flowers to adorn her. I would have hung all the world's ornaments upon her—naturally only in so far as they would serve to enhance her charms.—And when she stood there attired in all her pomp—then I had to go—when her delighted joyful glance met mine—then I had to go—then I went out and wept bitterly.

She did not love my well-formed nose, nor my fine eyes, nor my small feet—nor my high intelligence—she loved only me, and yet she did not understand me.

And you suppose I do not long to give her this proof of my love, this redress for all the humiliation she may have suffered from sympathizing kindred and friends. . . . And in truth, if it were not that I abhorred suicide, if it were not that I felt that all such virtues are splendid vices, I would have returned to her—and with that brought my life to an end, a plan which, alas, was in my mind for only too long a time, and which made the separation from me doubly hard for her, for who indeed loves like a dying man, and as such I have always thought of myself every time I abandoned myself to her—to live with her (in the quiet and confident sense this word has) never occurred to me. Truly this is enough to make a man desperate! To remain with her was my only wish; but from the moment I began to feel that it must turn out amiss (and that, alas, occurred very early) I determined to make her believe that I did not love her. And now here I am, hated by all for my faithlessness, apparently to blame for her unhappiness, and yet I am as faithful to her as ever, and if I could but see her happy with another, painful as that would be to human pride, I should rejoice; but now she consumes herself with sorrow at the thought that I who could have made her happy would not. And truly I could have made her happy, were it not, &c.

And notwithstanding it is imprudent for my peace of mind, I cannot leave off thinking of the indescribable moment when I might return to her. And although I think I am pretty strong for bearing what I regard as God's punishment upon me, yet at times this becomes too hard for me. At the same time it seems to me that I have done her a wrong in not letting her know how much I suffer. And when once in a while I reflect upon my remark that learning would lose in me a votary, then I feel only too keenly how untrue that was, for just in the fact that I do not remain with her, learning has lost what it can lose in me; for only of her do I now think, and I am convinced that she does not suffer so much as I. God grant that from my sufferings there may come some good to her.

Thou art to know that thou dost regard it as thy happiness never to have loved another besides her, that thou dost make it a point of honour never again to love another.

. . . And this terrible restlessness—every moment as though I would persuade myself whether it might not still be possible to return to her—would to God that I might! It is so hard, upon her I had set my last hope in life, and I must deprive myself of it. How strange, I have really never thought of being married, but that the thing might turn out thus and leave so deep a wound, that I have never supposed. I have always ridiculed those who talked of woman's power, that I still do, but a young, beautiful girl, full of animation, who loves with her whole mind and with her whole thought, who surrenders herself entirely, who beseeches—how often have I been on the point of inflaming her like a firebrand, not to sinful love, but I needed only to say that I loved her, and all was set in motion to bring my young life to an end. But then it occurred to me that thereby she would be badly served, that I should be bringing perhaps a storm upon her head, in case she should account herself guilty of my death. I elected to do what I have done. My relationship to her was always kept so vague that it remained in my power to give it what interpretation I would. I gave it the interpretation that I was a deceiver. Humanly speaking, it is the only way to save her, to give her soul resiliency. My sin was that I did not have faith, faith to believe that with God all things are possible. But where is the line between this and tempting God? But my sin has never been that I did not love her. If only she had not abandoned herself so completely, trusted herself to me, ceased to live for herself in order to live for me; then indeed the whole affair would have been as simple as bread and butter. To make game of the whole world, that does not rest heavily upon me—but to deceive a young girl!

Ah, if I might dare to return to her, and she who, even if she did not believe that I was false, yet most surely believed that when once I had become free I would never return. But be tranquil, my soul, I will act resolutely in accordance with the view I think the right one. Also I will watch over my letters. I know my moods. But in a letter I cannot as in conversation instantly dispel the impression when I perceive that it is too strong.

. . . . . .

And yet an apprehension still worries me. Suppose that she becomes sincerely convinced that I am a deceiver, suppose that she becomes engaged to another (which in many ways I naturally must wish)—suppose that then she suddenly gets to know that I really have loved her, that I have done it out of love for her, out of the sincere conviction that it must go amiss, or at all events that with the greatest joy in the world, with thanks unto God, I would share with her my joy, but not my sorrow. Ah, the last may become worse than the first.

Yes indeed—if only it were she that had broken with me, much as I loved her, it would be easy for me to forget her; I should venture to set all sail in order to forget, I could venture to put her into poetry—but now I cannot bring myself to do that. I remind myself of the thing often enough, and often enough memories come without my needing to call them forth. Therewith my soul becomes more solemn—ah, would that it might be for my good!

The matter is now settled, and yet I am never through with it. She does not know what an advocate she has within me. She was clever. In parting she begged me still to remember her once in a while. She knew very well that so soon as I once begin to remember there is the devil to pay. Still, even if she had not begged me to do it, I should have done it.

. . . and it was his eyes' delight and his heart's desire. And he stretched out his hand for it and grasped it, but he could not retain it; it was proffered to him, but he could not possess it—alas, and it was his eyes' delight and his heart's desire. And his soul was near to despair; but he preferred the greater pain of losing it and relinquishing it, to the lesser of possessing it wrongfully—or more rightly expressed (for so we would express ourselves here upon this holy spot), he chose the lesser pain of doing without it, rather than the greater of possessing it with a troubled soul . . . and strangely it proved that it was for his good.

The complete self-revelation of these passages stands in marked contrast with the four letters written from Berlin to Emil Boesen. They are lively and spontaneous letters, which tell us much we want to know, addressed to the one man he called his friend, to the only person to whom he confided the meaning of his behaviour to Regina, whom he enlisted as a reluctant fellow conspirator to carry on the deception in Copenhagen, to spy upon Regina and report how she was bearing up—yet even to him S. K. could not reveal himself completely and confessed that he did not. The letters deal chiefly with the details of his intrigue for deceiving Regina and all the world, but by assuming an air of bravado S. K. also deceives Boesen with respect to his deepest feelings. Space forbids me to quote more from these letters than the few extracts which follow.[1]

In all that you write there is only one thing that seems to me a little suspicious, and this is the fact that she has had Henry, Michael &c. come to her. [That is to say, S.K.'s four nephews and two nieces, who were very dear to him and with whom she had promptly formed a friendship which she ever afterwards maintained.] She is clever, and a year under my auspices has not exactly made her more simple-minded, and she has learnt among other things that I notice the most trivial trivialities.

It is to be understood that the deepest secrecy is to be maintained about this writing of mine, you must not let fall a word about it. [He refers to *Either/Or*, which he was writing at prodigious speed, in spite of the fact that he was attending lectures in the University of Berlin. This occupation saved him from despair. In 1847 he wrote in his Journal,[2] 'When I left her I chose death—just for that reason I have been able to work so enormously.']

Just as much as I feel that I am uncommonly erotic, just so well do I know that I am a poor husband and always shall be.

Her soul by contact with mine must have gained in elasticity, and I can well say that for a young girl it is no joke to battle with me. Either must this elasticity lift her higher than she otherwise would have risen—that will occur if only she can hate me (everything is planned for that)—or it thrusts her down. In that case I am at her disposition, and though I am a poor husband, though my soul is preoccupied with many other things, yet she will be well enough off with me. I do not thereby under-estimate myself, but my intellectual life and my significance as a husband are two incommensurable quantities.

Everything is arranged so that she can see in me a deceiver: if that can succeed, then she is helped, then she is again afloat; if she cannot do that, then I always have a vessel in commission whose captain knows what he has to do.

I have been ill (that is to say, I have had a great deal of gout in my head), often have not slept at night. I could have called a physician, perhaps something could have been done for it. If I called a physician, all the Danes here would know it in a minute. Perhaps it might occur to one of them to write home, that might get to her ears, that might unsettle her—*ergo* I call no physician, and it is better that way because I am true to my principle, and a physician would perhaps, despite all his skill, do me harm because I should come into conflict with my principle.

And I who could not endure to have her stand by my side, because it seemed to me humiliating to her, because in a certain way she was lost to sight alongside my oddity.

In the last letter he refers to the news that Regina was ill and makes known his purpose to return at once to Copenhagen, instructing Boesen to disguise the fact that he was moved by anxiety for her in returning after only half a year's absence when he had planned to be away a year and a half. He was to explain that Schelling's lectures would soon be over. In fact he had had enough of Schelling, and he needed to be at home to put *Either/Or* through the press. Regina reports (in Mourier's words):

Some time after the engagement was broken you were ill, it was feared that your lungs were affected. The tension and sorrow you had gone through at your tender age were too great and hard for you.

When we have finished this chapter we have by no means done with Regina. She was not an episode in S. K.'s life. He had the whole of his life in mind when he said: 'I owe everything that I am to the wisdom of an old man and the simplicity of a young girl.' If I should attempt to crowd into this chapter all that needs to be said about S. K.'s relation to Regina, the story of his later life would be deprived of a major interest. The chapter which immediately follows this, though it has not Regina as its subject, may be said to have her as its substance.

I desire to conclude this chapter with a quotation from the last passage (it is at least the last dated passage) S. K. ever wrote. I take it from an article entitled 'My Task' in that tenth number of *The Instant* which lay on his desk ready for the printer when he died. The article is dated September 1, 1855. The part that I quote might be entitled 'What it Cost'. I introduce it here with the hope of conciliating the reader who may be indignant with S. K. It will at least inspire a great pity.[1]

> Yet it is as I say: in the 1800 years of Christendom there is nothing corresponding to my task, nothing analogous to it; it exists in 'Christendom' for the first time.
>
> That I know, and I know also what it has cost, what I have suffered, which can be expressed, however, in a single word: I was never like others. Oh, in the days of youth, of all torments the most horrible, the most excruciating—not to be like others, never to live a single day without being painfully reminded that one is not like others, never to be able to run with the crowd, the pleasure and joy of youth, never able to abandon oneself freely, always, so soon as one would venture upon that, to be reminded of the chains, the isolation of separateness, which with a pain close to despair divides one from all that is called human life and cheerfulness and joy. One can, it is true, by the most frightful efforts, endeavour to conceal what one at that age regards as his disgrace, that he is not like others; this may perhaps succeed up to a certain point; but nevertheless the torment is in the heart, and the success is assured only up to a certain point, so that a single inadvertence revenges itself frightfully.
>
> With the years, certainly, this pain disappears more and more; for in the measure that one becomes more and more spirit, it is no longer painful not to be like others. Spirit is just this—not to be like others.
>
> And so perhaps there comes at length the moment when the Power which for a time has almost maltreated one—so indeed

it seems sometimes—explains himself and says: 'Hast thou anything to complain of? Doth it seem to thee that in comparison with what is done for others I have treated thee badly? Although—out of love—I had to embitter thy childhood, both thy earlier and thy latter youth, doth it seem to thee that with what thou hast received instead I have duped thee?' and to this the only reply can be: 'Nay, nay, thou infinite Love!'—while yet the mass of men will certainly beg to be excused from becoming what I have become in such an agonizing way.

Indeed, it is by such torments as mine that a man is educated to endure to be a sacrifice; and the infinite grace which was shown unto me and still is shown consists in being selected as a sacrifice—selected for this end, yes, and then still further developed to the point where one can maintain that this is the highest degree of grace that the God of love can show to any man, hence only to His beloved.

This is what is described to-day as the Sublimation of Eros.

II. AWAY FROM THE AESTHETICAL!

1841–4

KIERKEGAARD describes one stage of his education in Christianity as 'Away from speculation!' It is important to recognize that his philosophic reflections and the books in which he registered them have this tendency. He was seeking reality; and although, in attacking the speculative system of Hegel, he was obliged to use a technical language which makes it difficult for the plain man to follow, his aim was to make the truth accessible to the simple. It is equally important to recognize that the 'aesthetic works', with which we first have to deal, are not an exaltation of the aesthetic stage but a movement away from it, a fond farewell, and represent the first decisive step in his education in Christianity. If a reader should carelessly fail to observe that *Either/Or* presents an either/or—*either* the aesthetic/*or* the ethical life—and should happen to be unaware that the author had already chosen decisively the second alternative, he might regard the book as a sample of Romanticism, and under this misapprehension his praise of the book or his condemnation would be alike futile. S. K. is like a policeman facing a mob: he cries, 'Back! Away from the aesthetical!' The danger of misapprehension is greater with respect to the philosophical writings, for the either/or is not so definitely expressed, and one might regard these writings as egregious examples of speculative philosophy, if one does not hear the warning, 'Away from speculation!' In both instances I ensure that this warning shall be heard, for I inscribe it as the title of the two chapters which deal with the aesthetic and the philosophic works. And yet I must admit that the two movements thus described are not entirely separate: we must be prepared to discover in the 'aesthetic works' (*Either/Or*, *Repetition*, *Fear and Trembling*, and *Stages on Life's Road*) signs of the movement away from speculation. All of these books except the last were written for Regina; and here we have another criterion for classification, which also I have indicated in the titles. Between the aesthetic and the philosophic works (the *Scraps* and the *Postscript*) we have *The Concept of Dread*, which is expressly described as 'psychological'. It thus indicates the direction of the flight from speculation: it is a movement *back to reality*.

§ 1. BOOKS WRITTEN FOR REGINA, 1843

A. *EITHER/OR*

On October 25, 1841, S. K. took boat for Stralsund on his way to Berlin. The motive of this journey was not merely a desire to escape the general hostility aroused by his treatment of Regina, for he had other reasons for desiring to visit the city, which was then the intellectual capital of Europe, where Marheineke enjoyed short-lived renown as a theologian and where Schelling was engaged in demolishing the Hegelian system, to the applause of the court as well as of the university. He had planned to remain there a year and a half, and although actually he stayed only four and a half months, he accomplished in that time a prodigious amount of work, as we learn from a letter to Boesen written not long before his departure:[1]

> This winter in Berlin will always have great significance for me. I have got a great deal accomplished. When you consider that I have heard from three to four lectures daily, have a language lesson daily, and that I have got so much written [of *Either/Or*] (and this in spite of the fact that at first I had to spend so much time writing out Schelling's lectures, which I did in a fair copy), got a great deal read—so that one cannot complain. And on top of that, all my pains and all my monologues. I have not long to live (I have a feeling) and I have never expected to, but I live for a brief term and so much the more intensively.

We have seen in the entries and letters which were quoted in the last chapter how acute were the 'pains' he suffered in his separation from Regina, and how endless his 'monologues'—for this reason, among others, that they never concluded with the clear verdict that she was for ever lost to him. He was candid enough to write to Boesen, 'I regard the relationship as dissolved only in a certain sense.' At this time, as throughout the remainder of his life, intense intellectual labour was his only defence against melancholy. In Berlin he lived entirely alone, avoiding other young Danes for fear some news of him might reach Regina, and making no intimate contacts with Germans because he was shy about using their language. Instead of living like a student, he took a room in a hotel and had his meals there alone.

Having followed this young man in his ardent quest for truth, and seen how he had revolted from the dominant philosophy of Hegel, we can well understand the enthusiasm with which he listened to Schelling's first lectures:[1]

> I am so glad to have heard Schelling's second lecture—indescribable! Long enough have I groaned and my thoughts groaned within me; when he uttered the word 'reality', referring to philosophy's relationship to reality, then the babe of thought leapt within me for gladness, as the babe leapt in Elizabeth. I remember almost every word he uttered from that moment on. Here perhaps there may come clarity. This one single word recalls to me all my philosophic sufferings and torments.—And if only she could participate in my gladness—how willingly I would return to her, how willingly I would fool myself into believing that it was the right thing! Ah, if only I could do that!—Now I have set all my hope on Schelling—but yet if I only were sure I could make her happy, I would start off on the journey this evening. It is indeed hard to have made a person unhappy, and hard that to have made her unhappy is almost the only hope I have of making her happy.

If you note how strangely philosophy and love are here mingled, you will feel no surprise at discovering that these two factors are predominant in the book S. K. was then writing.

Alas, the hope he had set on Schelling was soon to be disappointed. He expressed his bitter disillusion in one of the *Diapsalmata* in *Either/Or*:[2]

> The fact that philosophers talk about reality is often just as deceptive as when a man reads on a sign-board in front of a shop, 'Ironing done here'. If he should come with his linen to get it ironed, he would be making a fool of himself, for the sign-board was there only for sale.

He doubtless remembered the words for which he had once thanked Lichtenberg:[3] 'It is almost like reading out of a cookbook to a man who is hungry.' In one place in the Journal he says of Hegel that 'if he had written his *Logic* without the pretence that it had anything to do with reality and declared in the preface that it was merely a thought-experiment, he would have been the greatest thinker that ever lived—now he is comical'. S. K.'s final conclusion was (as he expresses it in the title to one of the sections of the *Postscript*): 'A logical system is possible; but a system of existence is impossible.' His last letter to Boesen, with the postmark of February 29 (only a week before he left Berlin), begins with the damning declaration, 'Schelling drivels inordinately, both in an extensive and an intensive sense'.[1] He had written the same thing to his brother Peter two days earlier, suggesting an odious comparison with the most consummate twaddlers of their acquaintance.[2] Already by the middle of January he had practically done with Schelling, and wrote to Boesen, 'Schelling's later lectures have unfortunately little importance';[3] and on February 6 he reports,[4] 'I have given up Schelling entirely, I merely hear his lectures, writing nothing down either on the spot or at home.' How unfortunate that he did not turn to Trendelenburg, who was lecturing in Berlin at this very time!

S. K. learnt through Boesen that Regina was unwell. This sufficed to bring him back in haste to Copenhagen, but it was a motive he could not avow without belying his whole scheme of deception. He could explain to Boesen that he needed to be back in Copenhagen to finish his book and prepare for its publication, but as he laid great stress upon the importance of issuing this book anonymously, he could explain to the general public his unexpected return only by alleging that he was disappointed in Schelling. He confessed to Boesen that he did owe Schelling something, for the visit to Berlin had given him a taste for foreign travel. It is strange that, having the means to travel, and having acquired the taste, he never again went farther than Berlin, where he made four short visits. He often proposed to travel: 'I must travel,' he said, 'for I am a poet'—but he never did. In fact he was no more inclined to travel than Socrates.

We cannot count it strange that the philosophers of Berlin could do nothing to heal a broken heart—not even the theologians could do that. Neither the philosophers nor the theologians were really dealing with reality, with human existence in its concrete terms. S. K. for his part would deal with nothing else. He laid great stress upon the last words of *Either/Or*: 'Only the truth that edifies is truth for thee.' Referring to this in the Journal[5] he says that in the Greek philosophy there was much discussion about the criterion of truth. 'It would be interesting to follow the matter further, but I doubt very much if one will find a more concrete expression for it.' Unfortunately, he says, there are only a few who will perceive the philosophic meaning in it. 'The words are not even printed in italics—Good Lord, so there is presumably no importance to be attached to them.'

We have seen that half of the Second Part of *Either/Or* (the first letter of the Judge) was written in Copenhagen before S. K. had definitely broken his engagement. In the first draft he entitled it 'An Attempt to Rescue Marriage Aesthetically'. There is much pathos in the reflection that he depicted the beauty of the married state so well—so tantalizingly—just at the moment when he felt obliged to renounce it. The second part of this volume (from which so much has been quoted here concerning the solemnity of choice and the relation of the exception to the universal) and presumably a great deal of the first part was written in Berlin; and in November (seven months after his return to Copenhagen) the book was finished. S. K. boasted that all of it was written in eleven months.[1] On February 20, 1843, it was published, in two volumes.

S. K.'s passion for intrigue was at this moment manifested in an extraordinary way:[2]

> A whole book could be written if I should relate how inventive I have been in hoaxing people about my mode of existence.
>
> At the time I read the proofs of *Either/Or* and was writing the *Edifying Discourses* I had almost no time at all to walk in the street. Then I employed another means [of making people believe I was an idler]. Every evening when I left home completely fagged out and had dined at Mimi's I was for ten minutes at the theatre—not a minute more. Being so generally known as I was, I reckoned that there would be several talebearers at the theatre who would report: 'Every night he is at the theatre, he doesn't do anything else.' Oh, you dear gossips, how I thank you! Without you I would not have attained my purpose. In fact it was for the sake of my former fiancée I did this. It was my melancholy wish to be as much derided as possible, merely to serve her, merely in order that she might be able to put up a resistance.

The attempt to give one who has never read it a conception of the content and character of *Either/Or* would be not only presumptuous but silly. For there is nothing remotely analogous to it in the literature of any people. Some idea of the themes that are dealt with may be got by perusing the table of contents in Appendix IV. However, it must be said about these titles (as about most of the titles S. K. used, until he launched his pamphleteering attack against the Established Church) that they were formulated with a view to philosophic precision rather than with poetical taste, or with the aim of making a pungent appeal to the reader. I have not felt free to make them more elegant or attractive, although it must be confessed that as they stand they are not apt to suggest to the reader how much poetry the text contains, how much humour, and how much that belongs to 'the category of the interesting'.

One who reads to-day the three pseudonymous works written for Regina cannot fail to find them interesting, but whether one will understand them is another question. Unless one has a closer acquaintance with S. K. than his contemporaries had, one will not be able to understand these works better than they did. *Either/Or* established S. K.'s fame as a writer. According to a saying which he quotes, 'it was much read and more talked about'. And yet no one understood it. No one but Regina guessed that it was written for her or had any reference to her, and presumably she was unaware that it had a philosophic significance. The great Heiberg, the undisputed arbiter of literary elegance in Denmark, was ready enough to praise the book in a review, but he was struck first of all by the fact that 'the book is so big that one could make money by displaying it', and he cheered the author with the prospect that 'a reader might some day come along who would read both parts, both the Either and the Or'.[1] This furnishes a scale for measuring the competence of S. K.'s contemporaries in his provincial 'market town' to understand the books he poured out for them in rapid succession.

In our day, with S. K.'s whole life before us and his collected works, we are in a better position to understand what he wrote. Johannes Climacus discusses the other pseudonyms and elucidates them;[2] *The Point of View for my Work as an Author* (which was not published in his lifetime) gives more ample orientation, and, of course, the seventeen volumes of the Journals (with more to come) furnish the most essential aid to the understanding of S. K.'s purpose.

The very advantageous position we enjoy may seem, however, a rather dubious advantage when we discover that S. K. alleges so many and such different reasons for writing *Either/Or*: the book was written for Regina; from beginning to end it enunciates a metaphysical position; it is a poetical evacuation, a necessary expectoration; it was a shrewdly planned 'deceit' to entrap men into the truth. Which of these reasons is the true one, or can they all of them be true at the same time? Unless we can answer this last question in the affirmative our confidence in S. K. must be profoundly shaken.

Either/Or was written for Regina.

> When I am not *reus voti* [bound by a vow] nothing succeeds with me. Thus it was I passed my theological examination, thus it was I wrote my dissertation, thus it was that in 11 months I had *Either/Or* entirely finished. If any one should come to know the real motive. . . . Good Lord! One would think that such a big book must have a very deep reason . . . and yet it has to do entirely with my private life—and the purpose—indeed, if one should come to know that, I should be declared stark mad. If it were thought that I myself regarded it as an interesting occupation, I should perhaps be forgiven; but that I considered it a good deed, that this is what most concerns me in the whole affair. . . .[1]

S. K. was probably thinking of the *Two Edifying Discourses* as well as of *Either/Or*, and of the whole intrigue designed to help Regina, when he set down in his journal this curious entry:

> My love-affair is of a very peculiar sort. It is the common tactic of young clergymen to begin by being the teachers of the lady of their choice, exercising in a way the function of spiritual adviser, and to end by becoming lovers and husbands. I began by being a lover and ended by being spiritual adviser.

In the year 1849, reviewing the situation from a remote distance, he wrote:[2]

> It is true that as an author I had from the first a 'religious purpose', but there is another way of looking at the thing. *Either/Or*, and especially 'The Seducer's Diary', I wrote for

her sake, to clarify her out of the relationship.... When I used the expression 'that single individual' (*hiin Enkelte*) in the preface to the *Two Edifying Discourses*, I had that in mind especially—'*my* reader'—for the book contained a little hint to her, and at that particular time especially it was prodigiously true of me that I sought a single reader. Gradually this thought was assimilated [i.e. the individual as a category, contrasted with 'the public']. But here again the part of divine governance is so endless.

What S. K. wanted to say to Regina he was incapable of saying except by way of indirect communication. In 1850 he wrote in his Journal,[1] 'As a matter of fact it was she, my relationship to her, which taught me indirect communication.' I have no doubt about S. K.'s intention of performing a 'good deed' for Regina, a work of charity, believing that if she could be thoroughly convinced he was a scoundrel, she would be 'set afloat' and be able to console herself with another marriage. When he says especially of 'The Seducer's Diary' that 'it was written to repel her', I can readily believe it. This picture of 'a reflective seducer, whose interest was not so much how many he seduced as how he did it', gave him more trouble in the writing than any other part of the book, and caused him many pangs of conscience. He expected that it would repel the public and convince everybody that he was a scoundrel. He was disgusted to find that the public admired it —and this, he said, confirmed him in his contempt of the public. And perhaps it did not have the effect of repelling Regina. At all events, I cannot think that the picture he paints of the young man who had exhausted the possibilities of the aesthetical life and found himself facing the blank wall of despair, would repel anybody. It would be apt rather to arouse the sympathy of the natural heart of man—and especially of woman. We have seen that S. K. does not spare himself when he describes the aesthetic 'A'. The picture of 'A' is a travesty of himself inasmuch as it depicts only the aesthetic side of his character and suppresses the ethical and religious features. And yet he did not succeed in depicting an altogether unlovely personality. In the Preface, Victor Eremita makes it plain enough that 'A' was not the Seducer. The Judge shows a deep affection for his young friend, and even in criticizing him he betrays admiration for his talents.

But even if the first part of the book might be supposed to repel Regina, the second part, which presents the ethical view of life, and of marriage in particular, must have had quite the opposite effect. Victor Eremita, the pseudonymous editor of the papers, suggests the possibility that 'A' and 'B' may have been one and the same person. In an earlier chapter we have seen that 'A' and 'B' do in fact represent two sides of S. K.'s character, and although Victor Eremita remarks that there is nothing in these documents to indicate whether 'B' succeeded in converting 'A', or whether perhaps the exuberant description of the aesthetic life may have had the effect of seducing the moralist, nevertheless the name of Victor was meant to suggest that the better side of S. K.'s soul prevailed—at the cost of loneliness and of separation from the world (Eremita). S. K. did in fact present to Regina an either/or: he may have intended more expressly to repel her, but he loved her too much to be able to play faultlessly the part of the scoundrel, and he could not bear to exclude the possibility that she might support the test triumphantly and prove herself worthy of the name of Victor. In his reflections about the title chosen for this book and the choice of an appropriate name for the editor, S. K. remarks:[1]

> He who says the book is *called* Either/Or really says nothing at all, he on the other hand who says that the book *is* an either/or produces the title himself. This of course every individual reader can do quite as well as the Editor. For this reason accordingly the Preface left it to the reader whether he would so name the work or not. . . . When the reader has independently produced the title 'Either/Or', then would come an instant perhaps when he would be inclined to characterize himself as *Eremita*, for serious contemplation always makes one feel solitary. Perhaps there would come a next instant when he would call himself *Victor*, however he may be disposed to understand this victory more particularly.
>
> Some suppose that *Either/Or* is a collection of stray papers which I had lying in my desk. Bravo!—It is precisely the opposite. The only thing the work lacks [to make it symmetrically complete] is a narrative which I began but left out, just as Aladdin left the window unfinished. It should have been called 'Unhappy Love'. It would have served as a com-

> plement to the Seducer. The hero of it made precisely the same motions as the Seducer, but the reason for it was melancholy. He was not unhappy because he could not get what he loved. Heroes of that kind are beneath my dignity. He had powers like the Seducer, he was confident of captivating her. He won her. So long as the contest lasted he did not observe any difficulty—then she surrendered, he was loved with a young girl's whole enthusiasm—then he became unhappy, then his melancholy was awakened, then he drew back, he could combat the whole world, but not himself. His love made him indescribably happy in the moment, as soon as he thought of time he despaired.[1]

This is of course S. K.'s own story, which he found the courage to write some years later, for it is incorporated in the *Stages* under the title 'Guilty?'/ 'Not Guilty?', which is a way of indicating that this too presents an either/or. And in a certain way this question also was put to Regina, though it was then too late to make much difference how she responded to it, for already she was engaged to Schlegel. Why he could not write such a story earlier he makes clear enough when he writes in his Journal:

> I cannot get rid of this relationship; for I cannot poetize it, the instant I essay to do so there comes over me an anxious dread and an impatience to act.

He remarks in his Journal[2] that 'a real love-affair could not find place in Part I, because that always grips a person so profoundly that he is brought into the ethical sphere'. Of course this story of unhappy love as the counterpart of the Seducer must have been intended for the conclusion of Part II. If this window had been finished the whole work would have had a greater symmetry, and it would have been more evident that an either/or was addressed to Regina. But even as the work now stands, concluding with a sermon, Regina could easily enough detect that this dilemma was proposed to her. 'To leave her in uncertainty', S. K. said to Boesen,[3] 'was never my purpose.' I have no doubt he spoke truly, for he did not conceive that the answer to this either/or must be an uncertain one. And in fact Regina's conclusion was not an uncertain one—in spite of S. K.'s ingenious efforts to make her believe he was a scoundrel. I feel sure that this book contributed to annul the effect of the part he played with so much histrionic talent. I suspect that, without meaning to do so, he practised the shrewd counsel we find in *Hudibras*:

He that will win his dame must do
As Love does, when he bends his bow;
With one hand thrust the lady from,
And with the other pull her home.

For Regina's sake he felt bound to repel her, for his own sake he was fain to attract her.

Yet the fact that this big book addressed slyly a question to Regina in particular does not in the least exclude a wider reference, nor belie S. K.'s assertion that it presented to his contemporaries a philosophic view of life and a definite metaphysical thesis. Such was evidently the purpose of the *Stages on Life's Road*, which contains so many traits which were meant particularly for Regina's eye. But this book is only a very much revised edition of the earlier work, corresponding to S. K.'s maturer reflection upon the stages of life, and advancing beyond the ethical to the religious stage. Therefore we must trust the assertion that the same broad purpose which prompted the later book concurred with other motives to prompt the writing of *Either/Or*. Yet this is a truth we might not have known unless S. K. had revealed it to us—and he did not reveal it to his contemporaries.[1]

> The fact that there is a plan in *Either/Or* which stretches right from the first word to the last, likely never occurred to anybody, since the Preface treats the thing jestingly and utters never a word about speculation.
>
> What I am essentially concerned about with regard to *Either/Or* as a whole is that the metaphysical significance which is at the bottom of it all may become duly evident, the fact, namely, that everything brings one up squarely against the dilemma.[2]

The dilemma is of course perfectly evident in the book as a whole: either the aesthetic life/or the ethical. The first volume presents the 'either'; the second, the 'or'. We have seen also, in several long quotations from the second volume, that the phrase 'either/or' is used emphatically by the Judge as an expression for the solemn importance of choice. But we might not have guessed, unless S. K. had told us, that he understands this phrase as the counterpart of the Hegelian 'mediation'—of which he says, 'Give that up, and there is no speculation; if you admit it, there is no absolute choice, no either/or.'[1]

But this same phrase is used lightly by the author of the aesthetic papers and by the 'young friend' in the second part, who is rebuked by the Judge for taking this word in vain. We can sympathize with the exasperation of the Judge, for his young friend uses this phrase precisely in the sense of the Hegelian mediation, exactly inverting its meaning—with a certain air of plausibility which S. K. owed to Socrates. This sophistry is developed at considerable length in the *Diapsalm* entitled 'Either/Or—An Ecstatical Address',[2] which begins as follows: 'Marry, you will regret it; Do not marry, you will regret that also; marry or do not marry, you will regret both; either you marry or you do not marry, you regret both.' The rest is a satire upon the philosophies he most detested, including the phrase *eterno modo* of Spinoza. The following *Diapsalm* is found in the Journal[3] but was not included in *Either/Or*:

> This word either/or is a double-edged little dagger I always carry with me and with which I can assassinate the whole world of reality. For I say: Either it is this or it is that; but since nothing in the world is either this or that, therefore it *is* not at all. I have seen jugglers do their tricks, heard them say the explanatory word, seen the crowd amazed, but yet I have performed things much more astonishing with my magic formula. One can argue everything away—indeed one can help oneself out with it capitally; for the fact is, one constantly lives in such a way that he has in him some factors of everything, so that the devil himself is not cunning enough to find the goods on him: either he is a deceiver (there is something that suggests it), or he is not (there is something that bears witness to this)—ergo he *is* not at all,—that is to say, let us leave him stay, as the peasant said about the round tower.

This magic formula assassinates the whole of existence by proving the truth of the motto which stands before the *Diapsalmata*:

> *Grandeur, savoir, renommée,*
> *Amitié, plaisir et bien,*
> *Tout n'est que vent, que fumée:*
> *Pour mieux dire, tout n'est rien.*

S. K. points out that the same significance is to be discovered in 'the little philosophical article on "Tautology as the Highest Principle of Thought" ', which is found among the *Diapsalmata*.[1]

> That is to say (ah! how many will understand it?), in case the principle of contradiction is true (and that is expressed in either/or), this principle of tautology is the most accurate expression for mediation, and it is the only unity into which all can be resolved and by which the System becomes possible. It would not be aesthetically right to include in this work a treatise upon the principle of contradiction—no, it is evidenced personally [i.e. in the situation of the dramatis personae]—but the same principle viewed from a speculative standpoint (if one would not 'go farther') is the deification of tautology.[2]

The philosophic character of the book is sometimes plainly enough hinted at in the text. For example, it is incidentally revealed to us that the Judge's earnest injunction, 'Choose thyself', corresponds to the oracular advice of which Socrates made so much: 'Know thyself.'[3]

> The ethical individual knows himself, but this knowledge of his is not mere contemplation, for in this the individual is envisaged as determined by necessity [he is what he is]; it is rather a reflection upon oneself which is at the same time an act [to become what one is], and hence I have deliberately used the expression 'to choose oneself', instead of 'to know oneself'. The individual has not done with the affair in the fact that he knows himself; on the contrary, this knowledge is fruitful in the highest degree, and out of this knowledge issues the true individual.

Not altogether unconnected with this is the assertion of the Judge that 'without courage I see absolutely nothing eternal, and also nothing at all of the beautiful'. We begin here to get an inkling of the fact that S. K.'s philosophy is tending towards some form of voluntarism, at the farthest remove from rationalism. If we read attentively, and have some knowledge of the philosophy of Hegel, we cannot fail to detect innumerable passages which are formulated in strident opposition to the System. The first words of the Preface were placed in a prominent position to make the reader attentive to the philosophical theme of the book.

> It has perhaps from time to time occurred to you, dear reader, to doubt a little the justice of the well-known philosophical maxim that the outward is the inward, and the inward the outward.

This in fact was the point where S. K.'s doubt about the System was first awakened. He had learnt in particular that his father's 'outward' did not at all correspond to his 'inward'; and in his own relation to Regina he knew very well that the exterior appearance of a deceiver contrasted stridently with the faithfulness of his heart. If this first word was a hint to Regina, it certainly was not calculated to repel. There is no evidence that any one seriously heeded this warning to 'stop, look, and listen' for intimations of a profound philosophy. They were merely intimations, and therefore they could be overlooked. For S. K. would not lecture, and he insisted upon using indirect communication. Imitating the reserve of Socrates, he proposed to teach merely by 'making people *take notice*'—of the existence of God, or other prime factors of existence, and especially of the fact of their own existence. To accomplish this end he had amazing talents at his disposal: irony, humour, imagination, the invention of striking phrases, the tactic of surprise, skill at 'wounding from behind'—and yet in his own day hardly any one took notice. In the course of his travels Gulliver discovered a land inhabited only by philosophers, who were so absent-minded that every man must strike his companion over the head with a bladder filled with beans to call attention to what was said. In my boyhood I thought this tale extravagant—and yet I see that S. K. used in vain a more potent method.

We should hardly guess unless we were informed of it how carefully everything was planned, even to the minutest details.[1]

> The first *Diapsalm* [following the title-page] is really the theme of the whole work—which is resolved only in the last word of the Sermon. . . . The last *Diapsalm* [p. 106] gives us to understand how a life like this has found its satisfying expression in laughter.

Another *Diapsalm*[2] gives us to understand how personal to S. K. was his description of the pitiable position of the poet:

> *In vain I strive against it. My foot slips, my life becomes a poet-existence nevertheless.* Can anything more unhappy be thought

of? I am a marked man, fate derides me when suddenly it discloses to me *how everything I do to resist it becomes a factor in such an existence.*

It is the more evident that this is personal because the lines here printed in italics are underscored with pencil in S. K.'s own copy. And yet when he wrote this he did not know how true it was. At a later period of his life the struggle 'away from the poetical' became acute and resulted at last in victory.

But I have no space—and perhaps no talent—for following further the philosophic implications of *Either/Or*. I turn now to the consideration that, over and above all this conscious planning, the aesthetic works were a spontaneous outpouring, a product of genius. From this I am unable to separate sharply the consideration of S. K.'s claim that the whole thing was, in a way, 'a deceit'.

The Journal contains a very Kierkegaardian entry entitled 'My Verdict upon *Either/Or*':[1]

> There was a young man, as richly gifted as an Alcibiades. He went astray in the world. In his need he looked about for a Socrates, but among his contemporaries he found him not. Then he begged the gods to transform him into one. And behold: he who had been so proud of being an Alcibiades became so shamefaced and humbled at the grace of the gods, that when he had received just what might properly have made him proud, he felt himself inferior to all.

In the aesthetic writings it is much more evident that S. K. still retained the genius of an Alcibiades than that he had become a Socrates. Much later (in 1849) he wrote in the Journal:[2]

> *To such a degree I am a genius that I cannot assume directly personal credit for the whole without encroaching upon divine governance.* Every genius is predominantly immediacy and immanence, knows no wherefore, and hence it is my genius again which permits me to see—now, looking backward—the endless wherefore in the whole. *On the other hand, I am not to such a degree the religious character that* [like a prophet] *I can ascribe it all directly to God.*

The same year that S. K. made this entry he published (as one of the *Two Minor Ethico-Religious Treatises*) his reflections upon

'The Difference Between a Genius and an Apostle'. This little essay is more significant than appears on the face of it, for it is the only item he published of all the lucubrations which were prompted by 'the case of Adler', in which he was deeply engrossed for the space of two years (1846-7). Adler was a pastor deposed on account of the fantastic claim that his writings were the product of divine inspiration, indeed that they were dictated by Jesus Christ. This was a phenomenon of great interest to S. K., because he felt the necessity of coming to a clear understanding about his own case, in view of the spontaneity of genius which he possessed and the insistent sense he had of a call to do a particular work for God. He sturdily resisted the temptation to confound genius with religious inspiration, and he recognized that his mind was far too reflective to serve as a *channel* of divine communication to men. For this reason he so frequently asserted that he had 'no direct relationship to God' and therefore emphatically protested that he was 'without authority'. Hence the truth he sought to impart, chiefly by indirect communication, was submitted to the independent judgement of the individual reader, who could appropriate it only as he himself performed the same motions of thought and applied the criterion S. K. proposed: 'Only the truth that edifies is truth for thee.' This represents the rational side of S. K., the opponent of mysticism. But on the other hand he approached mysticism almost as closely as one could without becoming a mystic. For when he looked back upon the work his genius had performed he was struck with awe at the apprehension that all as in a piece of art is toil co-operant to an end, and that this was an end he had not consciously before him when he wrote. In this he detected the hand of God, divine providence; but he spoke of it significantly as Governance (*Styrelsen*). I do not feel free to translate this word by 'guidance', for that would imply the mystical immediacy which he repudiated. He indicates a divine intervention which did *not* co-operate with his conscious intelligence, but ruled and overruled it. Looking back, he perceived that the aesthetical works were important and necessary in relation to his production as a whole, and that they came at precisely the right place, namely, at the beginning. It is perfectly true that they were a spontaneous outpouring, but viewed in relation to the whole plan they were a 'deceit'; there was a 'duplicity' from the very beginning, which he was inclined to magnify rather than to explain away; but he was deeply concerned to show that it was present from the very beginning. He was not an aesthetical writer who with advancing age had become religious; for he could point to the fact that every one of the aesthetic works was punctually accompanied by a volume of 'Edifying Discourses', and that his own name was attached only to these religious works, whereas the aesthetic works, because they were not directly exponents of his attitude at the time of writing, were attributed to pseudonyms.

This is a digression we are compelled to make here (anticipating prematurely a later stage in S. K.'s life) because we must transport ourselves to the year 1849 in order to understand the passage last quoted and the two short quotations now to follow, which are taken from *The Point of View for my Work as an Author*, written that same year, but not published in his life-time because it was so intimate a revelation of himself.[1]

> Regarded integrally in its relation to the work as a whole, the aesthetical production is a deceit, and herein lies the deeper significance of the 'pseudonyms'. A deceit, however, is rather an ugly thing. To this I will respond: Be not deceived by the word 'deceit'! One can deceive a person about the truth, and one can (remembering old Socrates) deceive a person into the truth. Indeed when a person is under an illusion, it is only by deceiving him that he can be brought into the truth.

In this same book he develops the proposition that the true art of teaching consists in finding where a person is and beginning there. It can be assumed that most men are in the aesthetic stage, hence it is there one must begin, with the interests which really engross the man, and then lead him adroitly to a higher conception. He acknowledges that in the stricter sense his aesthetical production was not a deceit, inasmuch as it was not in the first instance accompanied by a clear consciousness of aim, but was a spontaneous, instinctive, and necessary evacuation of the poetical. He says of Goethe's choice of the name 'Poetry and Truth' as the title of his autobiography, 'When a man has really experienced something, it will be impossible for him not to reproduce it.'[2] We have seen that his own vivid experiences constituted the substance of his aesthetic works—to such a degree that by quoting them we have been able to make this biography an autobiography.

We can understand, therefore, how it was possible for him to pour out these works so rapidly and so copiously.[1]

> Yes, the poetical had to be evacuated—anything else was an impossibility for me. But the whole of this aesthetical production was laid claim to by the religious; the religious assented to this evacuation, but it lay in wait for it, as though it would say, 'Are you not nearly finished with this now?' While the poetical production was being brought forth the author was living in decisive religious categories.

We have already passed beyond *Either/Or* and have been considering the significance of the aesthetic works as a whole. I am aware that this first book has not been adequately described. But what is one to do? Another volume would be necessary if I were to give it its deserts. The reader can refer here to several long quotations from Part II (pp. 79 ff.). But not so much has been quoted from Part I, which is vastly the more interesting. S. K. makes somewhere the remark that the ethical as such is naturally 'uninteresting'. Before we leave this book I am fain to quote a passage from the 'Nugatory Introduction' to the section entitled 'The Unreflective Erotic or the Musical Erotic', illustrated by the Page in *Figaro*, by Papageno in *The Magic Flute*, and by Don Juan.

As preliminary to this I would remark that S. K.'s adulation of Mozart is so extravagant that the reader may be tempted to suspect it of not being genuine. The following passage, I think, disposes of this base suspicion—especially in view of the words here printed in italics, which S. K. in his own copy of the book underscored in pencil:[2]

> Immortal Mozart! Thou to whom I owe all, to whom I owe it *that I lost my reason*, that my soul was in amaze, that I was dismayed in my inmost being. Thou to whom I owe it that I did not go through life without anything occurring that was capable of perturbing me deeply. Thou to whom I give thanks that I did not die without having loved, even though my love was an unhappy one.

The passage I am about to quote is printed in one long paragraph by S. K.—as though to obscure the fact that the central portion, in marked contrast to the affectedly scientific character of the first part, is a poetic and exquisitely personal panegyric upon Eros. It was S. K.'s fond farewell to 'erotic immediacy', which, as soon as it is made the object of rational reflection, proves unable to endure the test of 'the many questions'. Eros was never so beautifully described—except in Greek marble. And yet the reader will notice that it is not personified here. It is indicated by the neuter pronoun 'what', with somewhat the same effect of mystery as is suggested by the so-called 'deep psychology' of our day, which refers to this mighty force as 'it'.

I have here divided the one long paragraph into three, in order to distinguish from the eulogy of Mozart the ecstatical farewell to Eros.[1]

> What these investigations expressly aim at is to show the significance of the musical-erotic, and with this in view to indicate the various stages, which, having all of them in common the quality of erotic immediacy, accord also in the fact that they are all essentially musical. What I am able to say on this subject I owe exclusively to Mozart. Hence if one or another should assent to what I have the honour to set forth, and yet may be a little dubious whether it is actually contained in Mozart's music, or whether it is not rather I that import it therein, I can assure him that, not only is the little I am able to set forth actually contained in Mozart's music, but infinitely more; indeed I can assure him that it is just this thought that encourages me to make bold to undertake the explanation of individual traits in Mozart's music.
>
> What one has loved with youthful fervency, what one has marvelled at with youthful enthusiasm, what in one's inmost soul one has maintained a secret, enigmatical commerce with—that one always approaches with a certain shyness, with mingled feelings, when he knows that the aim is to will to understand it. What one has learnt to know bit by bit, as a bird culls every little straw, one by one, more joyful over every little part than over all the rest of the world; what the loving ear has absorbed in solitude, solitary in the great crowd, unnoticed in its secret hiding-place; what the greedy ear, never satiated, has picked up, the avaricious ear has jealously treasured, never feeling secure, whose softest resonance never has eluded the watchful ear's sleepless attention; what one has lived in by day, what one has lived through again at night, what has

chased sleep away and rendered it restless, what one has dreamed of in sleep, what one has wakened to, only to dream of it again when one is awake, for the sake of which one sprang up in the middle of the night for fear of forgetting it; what has appeared before one in the moment of highest enthusiasm, what one has always had in hand like a woman's occupation; what has followed one in the bright moonlit nights, in solitary forests by the sea-coast, in dark streets, in the middle of the night, at break of day, what has sat beside one on horseback, what has been company in the carriage, what the home has been saturated with, what the chamber has been witness to, what the ear has echoed to, what has resounded in the soul, what the soul has spun into its finest tissue—that appears now before thought; just as those enigmatical creatures in tales of olden time ascend up from the bottom of the ocean clothed in seaweed, so does it rise up out of the sea of recollection woven in remembrance. The soul becomes sorrowful and the heart tender; for it is as if one were saying farewell to it, as if one were parting, never to meet thus again either in time or eternity. It seems as if one were unfaithful to it, as if one had broken one's vow, one feels that one is not any longer the same, not so young, not so childlike; one is fearful on one's own account lest that should be lost which made one joyful and happy and rich; one is fearful on account of the thing one loves, lest by this transformation it may suffer, may appear perhaps less perfect, that possibly it may not be able to make answer to the many questions—alas, and then all is lost, the enchantment vanishes, and never more can it be produced.

So far as Mozart's music is concerned, my soul knows no fear, my confidence has no limit. On the one hand, what I have until now understood is only a very little, and there always remains sufficient over, which hides in the shadow of presentiment; on the other hand, I am convinced that if in any wise Mozart should become wholly comprehensible to me, then indeed he would be to me completely incomprehensible.

Immediately after this passage there follows a development of the risky thesis that 'Christianity brought Sensuality into the world', from which I have already made a long quotation on p. 131.

B. *THE REPETITION* AND *FEAR AND TREMBLING*

On Easter Sunday at evensong in the Church of Our Lady (during Mynster's sermon) she nodded to me—I could not tell whether it signified entreaty or forgiveness, but in any case it was so friendly. I had seated myself in a retired place, but she discovered it! Would to God she had not done it! Now the sufferings of a year and a half are wasted, all my prodigious efforts—she still does not believe that I was a deceiver, she believes in me. What trials now await her! The next one will be the notion that I am a hypocrite. The higher up we get the more terrible it is: to think that a man with my sincerity, my religiousness, could so behave! And yet I cannot any longer live only for her, cannot continue to expose myself to men's contempt and lose my honour, as indeed I have done. I will not be mad enough to go and become a scoundrel merely to get her to believe it. And what help would that be—she still will think that I was not a scoundrel before!

Every Monday between 9 and 10 in the morning she has encountered me in the street [i.e. during a period preceding Easter]. I have not taken a single step to bring it about. She knows what way I am accustomed to take, and I know what way she [Here a page has been torn from the Journal].[1]

Six years later S. K. registered in his Journal a more precise account of this disturbing occurrence:[2]

Shortly before her engagement to Schlegel she espied me in church. I let her catch my eye. She nodded twice. I shook my head. That meant, you must give me up. Then she nodded again, and I nodded as kindly as possible—that meant, you retain my love.

In the preliminary draft of 'Guilty?'/'Not Guilty?'[3] it is said that Quidam was doubtful, in view of the distance, whether he apprehended aright—whether she actually did nod, or whether perhaps she was nodding to somebody else. At all events it might have been 'only for his eye that it had this immense significance'. Certainly this nod had immense significance for S. K. In 1843 Easter fell on April 16. Not till May 6 were the *Two Edifying Discourses* ready for the printer, and on the 8th S. K. left for Berlin, prompted to flee again from Copenhagen by the new train of thought and feeling which was started by Regina's nod. The first entry dated from Berlin (on May 10) begins as follows:[1]

> The day after my arrival I was very bad, my knees ready to sink under me. At Stralsund I almost went mad at hearing a young girl playing over and over on the piano Weber's last waltz, among other pieces.

Of course this new experience prompted him again to write. Or rather it prompted him to drop the philosophic work he was engaged with at that moment (*Johannes Climacus or De Omnibus Dubitandum Est*) and to write two more books for Regina, presenting her again with an either/or, though it was couched in very different terms. In an entry of May 17 he says:[2]

> I have begun a new story entitled, Guilty/Not Guilty; naturally it will contain things which could astonish the world, for in a year and a half I experience in myself more poetry than is in all romances put together.

Presumably this was substantially the story he had thought of including in *Either/Or* (Aladdin's unfinished window), and the same reason which prevented him from printing it there still inhibited him from including it in the two books he was now writing for Regina—the fact, namely, that he could not yet bring himself to poetize her. The entry quoted just now proceeds to divulge the reason why he can get no further with such a story:

> But I cannot and will not—my relationship to her shall not be evaporated into poetry, it has an entirely different sort of reality, she has not become a stage-princess, if possible she shall become my wife. Good Lord, that was my only wish, and yet I had to renounce it. [This entry begins:] If I had had faith, I should have remained with Regina. Praise and thanks be to God that I have now perceived it. [The following short entry reads:][3] Faith has hope also for this life—but (let it be noted) in virtue of the absurd, not in virtue of the human understanding—otherwise it is only worldly wisdom, not faith.

This story, 'Guilty?'/'Not Guilty?', was eventually written and was included in the *Stages*—after Regina was definitely lost to him. But in the first book he wrote in Berlin at this time the same theme is evident enough in the anxious inquiry of the young poet of *Repetition*.[4]

It is strange that the entries made in Berlin refer hardly at all to the themes of the books he was actually writing at that time, but very frequently to plots which were to emerge two years later in the *Stages*—including 'The Two Lepers', 'The Ladies' Tailor', 'Nebuchadnezzar' and 'The Mad Accountant'.[1] While he was engaged in writing his two books in an incredibly brief space of time, all of these superfluous plans were surging in his mind.

In a letter to his friend Boesen, with the Berlin postmark of May 25, 1843, he says:[2]

> Again a little while and ye shall see me. I have finished one work which I regard as important, and I am in full swing with a new one, and my library is necessary as well as the printing-press. In the beginning I was ill, now I am well, so to say—that is, my mind expands and presumably is killing my body. I have never worked so hard as now. During the morning I go out a little while. Then I come home and sit in my room uninterruptedly until about three o'clock. I can scarcely see out of my eyes. Thereupon I shuffle with the aid of my cane to the restaurant, but am so weak, I believe that if any one were to call out my name aloud, I should fall over dead. Thereupon I go home and begin again. During the past months [in Copenhagen] I have been indolently pumping up a veritable shower-bath, now I have pulled the cord, and the ideas stream down upon me—healthy, happy, plump, merry, blessed children, easily brought to birth, and yet all of them bearing the birth-marks of my personality.

The two books he was then writing were *The Repetition* and *Fear and Trembling*. They are universally mentioned in the inverse order; but seeing that they were published together on the same day (Oct. 16, 1843), there is no external criterion to determine which was written first—which it was he referred to as the 'one' already finished on May 25 (only 15 days after he reached Berlin!), and which was the 'new one' he had already commenced at that date. The manuscript of *The Repetition* is dated: 'Berlin in May 1843'. This does not absolutely determine the sequence. But there are reasons which seem to me conclusive for putting *The Repetition* first. It is incredible enough that either book could have been written in a fortnight, but the difficulty is in some degree diminished if we suppose it was the shorter one, which also was one of the most personal and the least reflective of all his works, recalling vividly his late experience, and attaching itself closely to the hope and fear prompted by Regina's nod, so that we can imagine him pouring it out rapidly. It is a significant fact that 'repetition' is the theme of the last pages of the philosophical work he laid aside in obedience to Regina's nod, and 'Guilty'/'Not Guilty' (a note so fundamental in the young man's letters) was the theme he was engaged with seven days after his arrival in Berlin.

Of course it was only the first draft which was finished in two weeks. As a matter of fact, *The Repetition* is the only book of S. K.'s which did not undergo a second and a third revision before it was sent to the printer. This first draft must have been finished before he heard of Regina's engagement, which reduced the purpose of the book to an absurdity and discouraged the poor author from the task of making a fair copy, when he could dispose of a subject that had become painful to him by noting a few changes in the margin and rewriting the conclusion.

Even if there were not such strong objective reasons for putting *The Repetition* first, I should be inclined to place it in this position because it evidently is the 'either' corresponding to the 'or' presented by the other work. It was not the same 'either' that was proposed to her earlier in the year (in *Either/Or*). At this time she had triumphantly overcome the temptation to believe him a voluptuary and a deceiver, yet she might succumb to the suggestion he now proposes, that, like 'the young poet here described', he was too soft and sentimental and melancholy to resist the suggestions of his evil genius Constantine Constantius, living only on the verge of religiousness, and fundamentally incapable of 'casting out the incommensurable and becoming commensurable', i.e. of preparing himself effectively for the married life. The other book presents him in a much more advantageous light. Although repetition is not expressly the theme of this book, it is exemplified here as a reality—a possible impossibility—especially in the sublime case of Abraham who recovers Isaac after he had performed the motions of infinite resignation. S. K. (in the person of the pseudonym, Johannes de silentio) appears here as 'the knight of infinite resignation', living in expectation of attaining a higher order of chivalry, becoming a 'knight of faith' —of the faith that with God all things are possible.

That these two books were meant as a mysterious communication to Regina is indicated first of all by the name of the pseudonym, *de silentio*, and by the motto of *Fear and Trembling* (in German, quoted from Hamann): 'What Tarquinius Superbus in his garden spake by means of the poppies was understood by the son, but not by the messenger.' Moreover, Constantine's letter to the reader remarks[1] that 'Clemens Alexandrinus did very well to write his book in such a way that the heretics could not understand it'. The motto first chosen for this book was copied from a passage by Herder, but with the suppression of its optimistic conclusion:[2] 'Write!'—'For whom?'—'Write for the dead, for them thou lovest in a time that is past.'—'Will they read me?'—'Nay!' The motto of *Repetition* is: 'On wild trees the flowers are odorous, on tame ones the fruit.' (From Flavius Philostratus the Elder.)

These books, being among the most poetic that S. K. ever wrote, have an interest for every one, yet the specific question put to Regina no one but she was in a position to understand. Even she must have been amazed at discovering in *Fear and Trembling* that S. K. conceived of himself as a second Abraham—and that she was Isaac! Isaac, who was sacrificed and regained! The story of Agnes and the Merman (in S. K.'s version of it) more obviously depicted the relationship between her and her lover; but (as though to ensure that the heretics would not understand) this passage was obscured by its inconspicuous position.

Perhaps not even Regina would have been able to perceive that S. K. cherished the hope that union with her might be possible as a consequence of repentance and by means of faith in virtue of the absurd. At all events, the suggestion was proposed too late. After only three weeks in Berlin (where his later visits were even shorter) S. K. was back in Copenhagen, and both books were finished by July.[3] But in the meantime something had happened in June—Regina became engaged to Fritz Schlegel. Owing to his absence, S. K. had no inkling of what was going on, as we learn from an entry of 1849:[4]

When she had become engaged to Schlegel she met me on the street and greeted me in as friendly a way and as ingratiatingly as possible. I didn't understand her, for at that time I knew nothing of the engagement. I merely looked at her questioningly and shook my head. Undoubtedly she supposed that I knew it and was seeking my approval.

The day that became delight for her [her wedding] I sat in the Church of the Saviour [where Regina was married on Nov. 3, 1847].

This engagement, though it was ostensibly the purpose S. K. sought to accomplish by his elaborate scheme of deception, was nevertheless a stunning blow to him when it became a reality. Some years had to elapse before he was able to do justice to Regina. The pages hastily added to *The Repetition* express plainly enough the contempt he felt for her light-mindedness—though not so brutally as in certain phrases he wrote in the first draft, with the candour one might use in a diary, and then had the grace to suppress. I do not condemn him for this, and I cannot wonder at it, when I reflect that the news of Regina's engagement suddenly revealed to him that the hope which inspired the two works just then finished with prodigious effort was a comical delusion, that his first great work was addressed to her under a misapprehension, and that the deception which had cost him so much agony was presumably superfluous.

To meet this emergency, the first of the two books had to be altered drastically. Originally it had been called, in the sub-title, 'A Fruitless Attempt'. It was necessarily fruitless on the part of Constantine Constantius:[1]

'Repetition' is and remains a religious category. Hence Constantine Constantius cannot get further. He is shrewd, ironical, devoted to the pursuit of the interesting, but does not perceive that he is mired there. The first form of the interesting is change, the second is the will to repetition, but in self-sufficiency, without admixture of pain—therefore Constantine fails to attain the aim which he himself envisaged, and the young man gets further.

The young man got further, because he was hovering on the border of religiousness, yet for him also the attempt to obtain a repetition was fruitless; there was nothing left for him to do but to shoot himself dead when the lady pressed him too hard (by a nod in church?) and he realized that he was unable to make himself commensurable. Constantine's judgement is:[2]

If he had had a deeper religious background, he would not

have become a poet. Then everything would have had religious significance for him. The occurrence in which he was entangled would indeed have had significance for him, but then the shock would have come from a higher source, he then would have possessed an authority of an entirely different sort, though it were purchased by a suffering still more painful; he then would have acted with an iron consistency and firmness, he would then have acquired a factor of consciousness he could steadily cling to, which never became ambiguous to him, but was pure earnestness, inasmuch as it was posited in him by virtue of his relationship to God.

We do not know precisely how the story originally ended, for at least ten pages were torn from the manuscript (after the letter of Feb. 17), to give place to the present conclusion. But it is evident that, though Constantine's attempt was fruitless and comical, the young man's was fruitless and tragical. In the version that was published, the young man attained the repetition, but in a comical way—and so the whole work became comic. Therefore Vigilius Haufniensis, in *The Concept of Dread*,[1] can describe it as 'a droll book'. In his letter of March 31 the young man exclaims:

> She is married, . . . I am again myself, . . . here I have the repetition. . . . Is not this then a repetition? Did I not receive again everything double? Did I not recover myself again, precisely in such a way that I must feel doubly the significance of it?

The other book, *Fear and Trembling*, was not rendered nugatory by Regina's engagement.[2] Indeed it must have been written in great part after the announcement of that event. The profound reflections upon faith as illustrated by Abraham, and upon repentance as experienced by the Merman, were not rendered vain by the failure of a repetition *in time*—in case Abraham did not literally receive Isaac back, nor the Merman win Agnes. S. K.'s faith became only more expressly eschatological—though his was an eschatology without the least trace of apocalyptic. In *The Concept of Dread* Vigilius Haufniensis points out that even Constantine was capable of perceiving that 'repetition indicates the serious side of life' (in contrast to variety and change in which the personality is dissipated), and that 'eternity is the true repetition.'[3]

But it is clear that S. K. attained a deeper apprehension of the meaning of 'repetition' *after* he had written his book about it. Inasmuch as he wrote obscurely, in order that the heretics might not understand, his indignation at Heiberg's misunderstanding was not altogether reasonable. 'The Rector Magnificus of Literature' included an appreciative comment upon it in a pretty gilt-edged 'gift-book', appropriate for the New Year's sale, from which S. K. deduced that he had read only the comical part, and had failed to notice that a second title-page introduced the serious consideration of 'repetition'. Heiberg's solemn judgement was:[1]

> Repetition has an essentially different significance in the natural and in the spiritual sphere. The author has presumably had in view the natural categories [natural law, according to which repetition is always occurring], and, perhaps without knowing it, has stretched the application of the concept beyond its proper limits.[2]

This must of course have been exceedingly exasperating to S. K., and to us it serves as a measure of the incapacity of his contemporaries to understand him. For it was precisely in the spiritual sphere that S. K. discovered the significance of repetition —not as a law of nature, but as an acquist of freedom:[3]

> That repetition is not merely an object of contemplation, but is the task of freedom, is freedom itself (which is consciousness raised to the 2nd power); that it is the special '*interest*' of metaphysics, and at the same time the interest upon which metaphysics founders, that it is the solution of every ethical point of view, the *conditio sine qua non* of every dogmatic problem, that the true repetition is eternity, although it is true that when it is followed so far that it vanishes from the eye of psychological research as a transcendental fact, as a religious movement in virtue of the absurd, which occurs when one reaches the bounds of the miraculous—although repetition, I say, so soon as the problem is expressed dogmatically will come to signify atonement, which cannot, any more than a religious movement that is dialectical only with reference to fate and providence, be defined by mediation fetched from immanence —all this, my dear reader, is a misunderstanding which only could occur to one who is unacquainted with the exposition

of repetition which we owe to Professor Heiberg and which is quite as profound as it is original.

I do not wonder that Professor Heiberg failed to discover in the book all that is implied in this tremendous sentence, which I have not tried to make any easier than it is. In the book it seems as if 'the young man' were attracted by the story of Job principally because Job actually got everything double, but subsequently S. K. reveals to us that the principal consideration was that Job was in the right, that he was vindicated.[1]

The passage just quoted hints at the relation of 'repetition' to transcendency, and so sets it in opposition to immanence and mediation. Repetition is the aim of freedom in its highest form, for it ensures continuity (personal identity) in the midst of change. Repetition and change are thus correlative opposites. Not from the book called by this name, but from Journal entries of a subsequent date and from a subsequent book, *The Concept of Dread*,[2] do we learn that 'repetition is the decisive expression for that which corresponds to remembrance as conceived by the Greeks . . . the same movement, but in the opposite direction, . . . by which one comes into eternity forwards'—instead of remembering oneself backwards into eternity, which was the way Socrates realized his immortality. From this standpoint we can see how the category of repetition is related to S. K.'s category of 'the instant', and to the whole problem of time to which he has recalled the attention of the modern world.[3] All of these notions emerge again in the next following works—*Philosophical Scraps* and *The Concept of Dread*—where they are further developed.

It is evident enough that something had happened to deepen S. K.'s apprehension of the significance of 'repetition'. Knowing that this something was the news of Regina's engagement, the cause may seem disproportionate to such an immense effect, and in order to understand how this cause affected him so prodigiously we must consider what he meant when he said that he was 'educated by the possibility'. His bitter disillusion was promptly expressed in the Journal:[4]

> The most dreadful thing that can happen to a man is to become ridiculous in his own eyes in a matter of essential importance, to discover, for example, that the sum and substance of his sentiment is rubbish. A person can easily incur this danger

in his relationship to another person—by believing, for example, in cries and screams. Here is a case where one needs to be stoutly built.

S. K. was anything but stoutly built, and yet he possessed a resiliency which enabled him to support this crushing experience and receive education from it. It seems clear to me that in the last chapter of *The Concept of Dread*, which he entitled, 'Dread as a Means of Salvation in Conjunction with Faith', S. K. described his own experience at this moment, and regarded it as a crucial experience of conversion.[1]

Educated by the Possibility

It is told of an Indian hermit who lived two years solely upon dew, that he went one day to the city, tasted wine, and thereupon became a drunkard. This story, like every other of the sort, can be understood in many ways: one can make it comic, one can make it tragic; but the man who is educated by the possibility has more than enough to occupy him in such a story. Instantly he is absolutely identified with that unfortunate man, he knows no finite evasion by which he might escape. Now the dread of the possibility holds him as a prey, until it can deliver him saved into the hands of faith. In no other place does he find repose, for every other point of rest is mere nonsense, even though in men's eyes it is shrewdness. This is the reason why the possibility is so absolutely educative. No man has ever become so unfortunate in reality that there was not some little residue left to him, and, as common sense observes quite truly, if one is ingenious he will find a way. But he who went through the curriculum of misfortune offered by possibility lost everything—absolutely everything, in a way that no one has lost it in reality. If in this situation he did not behave falsely towards the possibility, if he did not attempt to beguile the anguish which was intent to save him, then he received everything back again, as in reality no one ever did, even when he received everything double; for the pupil of the possibility received infinity, whereas the soul of the other expired in the finite. No one ever sank so deep in reality that he could not sink deeper and that there might not be one or another deeper sunk than he. But he who sank in the possibility has an eye too dizzy to see the measuring-rod that Tom,

Dick, and Harry held out as a straw to the drowning man, his ear is closed so that he cannot hear what the market price for men is in his day, cannot hear that he was just as good as the most of them. He sank absolutely, but then again he floated up from the depth of the abyss, lighter than all that is oppressive and dreadful in life. Only I do not deny that he who is educated by the possibility is exposed—not like those who are educated by the finite, to the danger of bad company and dissoluteness of various sorts, but—to one danger of downfall, and that is self-slaughter. If in beginning his education he misunderstands anguish and dread, so that they do not lead him to faith but away from faith, then he is lost. On the other hand he who is educated by the possibility stays with the dread, does not allow himself to be deceived by its countless falsifications, he recalls the past with precision; then in the end the attack of dread becomes fearful indeed, yet not such as to cause him to flee from it. Dread becomes for him a serviceable spirit which against its will leads him whither he would go. Then when it announces itself, when it craftily insinuates that it has now discovered an entirely new instrument of torture, far more terrible than anything used before, then he does not recoil, still less does he attempt to hold it off with clamour and noise, but he bids it welcome, he hails it solemnly, as Socrates solemnly flourished the poisoned goblet, he shuts himself up with it, he says, as a patient says to the surgeon when a painful operation is about to begin: Now I am ready. Then dread enters into his soul and searches it thoroughly, constraining out of him all the finite and the petty, and leading him hence whither he would go.

The spiritual experience of rising up out of the deep is described here in terms of a natural analogy, the experience of learning to swim. A man is able to swim when he acquires the confidence that he is lighter than water:[1]

> The religious experience is essentially an expression of the confidence that man by God's assistance is lighter than the whole world, the same sort of faith which makes it possible for a man to swim.

With evident reference to this experience of the swimmer, S. K. in subsequent works frequently spoke of faith as 'floating over 70,000 fathoms'. From the passage here quoted it is clear that he regarded this definite experience of education by the possibility as a decisive religious experience, a real conversion. And this accords with the fact that in *The Point of View* he does not refer his decisive conversion to the experience of an 'unspeakable joy' antecedent to his father's death, which we recognized as his first conversion (pp. 170 ff.), but to the result of his experience with Regina. He speaks of this reticently as 'a fact':[1]

> Antecedent to the very beginning of my serious literary activity there lies an occurrence, or it would be better to say, a fact. For presumably an occurrence would not have been enough, it was a fact, I had to take an active part myself. About that fact, wherein it consisted, how terribly dialectical it was in its combination (although in another sense it was entirely simple), wherein the collision properly consisted—all this I cannot elucidate more particularly, but can only beg the reader not to think of revelations or anything of the sort, for with me everything is dialectical. On the other hand, I shall give an account of the consequences of the fact, in so far as that may serve to throw light upon my authorship. It was a duplex fact. Humanly speaking, I had leapt over childhood and youth —however much I have experienced it in another sense. Presumably this loss had to be compensated for (such was the opinion of divine governance)—instead of having been young I became a poet, which is a second youth. I became a poet; but with my qualifications for religion, indeed with my very decided religiousness, this very fact was at the same time a religious awakening, so that in the most decisive sense I got an understanding of myself in the matter of religion, in the matter of religiousness, which hitherto I had treated as a possibility. The fact made me a poet. If I had not been what I was, the occurrence also what it was, and if I had not dealt with it as I did, it would not have come to anything more—I should have become a poet, and then perhaps after the lapse of many years come into relation with the religious. But precisely because I was so religiously developed as I was, the fact struck far deeper, and in a certain sense demolished with religious impatience what I had become: the poet. It demolished it, or at any rate I found myself commencing at the same time at two different points, but in such a way that this thing of being

a poet was something essentially irrelevant to me, was what I had become by means of another, while on the other hand the religious awakening, though it was certainly not what I had become by myself, was what I became in accordance with myself, that is to say, I did not in the deepest sense recognize myself in this thing of becoming a poet, but in the religious awakening.

The crisis here described, though it deepened S. K.'s conception of 'repetition', did not so obviously exalt his conception of faith as this is exhibited in *Fear and Trembling*. This book is concerned principally with Abraham in his relation to Isaac—first as the expression of the paradox of faith, faith in the incredible or 'by virtue of the absurd' (that he would receive Isaac back), and second as a prerogative instance of an exception to the universal (in the fact that he was prepared to kill Isaac at God's command). S. K., as we have seen, began already in *Either/Or* to wrestle seriously with this theme. Now it takes the form of the query, 'Is there such a thing as a teleological suspension of the ethical?' —that is, can the universal maxims of morality be suspended by the pursuit of a particular end indicated directly by God?[1] In answer to this query his assertion is:[2]

> The paradox of faith is this, that the individual is higher than the universal, that the individual determines his relation to the universal by his relation to the absolute, not his relation to the absolute by his relation to the universal.

S. K. had perceived very early that the conception of faith which the philosophers shared with the ordinary man was entirely inadequate:[3]

> What Schleiermacher calls 'religion' and the Hegelian dogmatists call 'faith' is at bottom nothing else but the first immediacy, the requisite for everything—the vital fluid—the atmosphere we breathe in a spiritual sense—and which therefore cannot rightly be indicated by these words.
>
> In that way faith comes into rather simple company with feeling, mood, idiosyncrasy, &c.[4]

But though faith is not 'the first immediacy', he early recognized that it is 'a second immediacy'.[5] Perhaps he did not get the experience of this, however, until a later conversion in 1848, when he said:[6] 'Now I have reached to faith in the deepest sense.

Faith is immediacy after reflection.' I can say no more here about this important subject. But one thing ought to be noticed: that at this time the paradox of faith ('faith by virtue of the absurd'), though it evidently is not a faith founded upon reasonings, does not yet seem to be regarded as against reason:[1]

> The absurd has nothing to do with the differences which lie within the proper compass of the understanding. It is not identical with the improbable, the unexpected, the unlikely.

Some light is thrown upon S. K.'s conception of faith when we consider what he has to say about doubt. He has a great deal to say about it—especially, of course, in the unfinished treatise, *De Omnibus Dubitandum Est*. There it is the philosophers' doubt he is scornful of—the pretence of the *followers* of Descartes that they begin by doubting everything. . . . 'One hour each term—these scientific doubters!'[2] But honest doubt he did not despise, and he had to wrestle with it in his own life. We must note that he did not think of it as the precise opposite of faith, for faith has relation to the whole personality, including the will, whereas doubt (as he conceived at this time) has to do only with thought and is therefore necessitated. Judge William says, discriminating between doubt and despair:[3] 'Doubt is thought's despair, despair is personality's doubt.' And though he asserts that no one can despair without 'choosing to despair', he recognizes that doubt may be a sheer necessity of thought. S. K. experienced this necessity. The *Scraps* and the *Postscript* (the philosophical works which he attributed to the pseudonym Johannes Climacus) may seem like a dogmatic defence of the specific doctrines of Christianity; but S. K. remarks that 'defence and attack resemble one another to a hair', and in the same passage (written in 1849)[4] he reveals the fact that as late as 1844–5 he shared to some extent the scepticism he attributed to Climacus:

> 'Johannes Climacus' was really a deliberation, for when I wrote it there lay yet in my soul a possibility that I might not let myself be won entirely over to Christianity, although it was my honest determination to devote my life with daily diligence to the cause of Christianity.

A little later we find also these two passages in the Journal:[5]

> At the same time I concealed within me a deep doubt, so

deep as hardly any of my contemporaries here [had experience of]. My thought was to hide it, to see for myself if in all quietness I might not clear it up, but never to communicate what I must perceive could only be misleading, alarming, disturbing.

It must always be remembered that to communicate doubt (a sickness) when one possesses no cure is a responsibility. According to my theory, one should never begin to communicate doubt before he has the cure, and never more doubt than he can check.

Even Regina may have had difficulty in recognizing S. K.'s own personal trial in the trial of Abraham, though he gave her this one hint:[1] 'Every closer definition of what is to be understood by Isaac, the individual reader must supply.' In the Journal we find the statement:[2] 'The point of the whole story is that Abraham really was sure that he loved Isaac better than himself.' The situation would have been plainer if S. K. had not discarded 'a plan' he mentions in the Journal, where he reflects upon one of the possible ways of conceiving of Abraham's treatment of Isaac, namely, a resort to the pretence that he had gone crazy, so that Isaac's trust in God might not be destroyed by the knowledge that his father was acting in obedience to a divine command. It is in this connexion that S. K. appeals to the analogy of the mother who blackens her breast when she must wean her babe.[3] And in this same passage he exclaims: 'He who has explained this riddle has explained my life.'

Abraham's first position, his first attainment, was that of 'endless resignation'. Johannes de silentio declares that this is the last position anterior to faith, without which no real faith is possible; although he himself has reached that position, he despairs of attaining the higher position of faith, and frequently exclaims that he cannot understand Abraham. While he was perfectly well able to understand the sort of faith Abraham had, and was able also to expound it very clearly, he was not able to understand how any man could attain it.

He says in *Fear and Trembling*:

Infinite resignation is the last stage before faith, so that one who has not performed this movement does not possess faith; for it is only in infinite resignation that I become clear in my own mind with respect to my infinite worth, and only then can there be any question of taking possession of existence by virtue of the absurd. . . . The absurd is not to be ranked with the distinctions which fall within the proper compass of the understanding. It is not identical with the improbable, the unexpected, the unforeseen. The instant the knight made the act of renunciation he convinced himself of the impossibility. Humanly speaking, this was the very result the understanding came to, and he had sufficient vigour to think it. On the other hand, it was possible in the sense of the infinite—that is, taken in conjunction with the act of renunciation; but such possession as this is at the same time abandonment.

There can be no doubt that when S. K. wrote *Fear and Trembling* he thought of himself as a knight of infinite resignation, but he was not yet a knight of faith. At that moment he almost believed, 'by virtue of the absurd', that he would get Regina back. But this was merely faith in a repetition *in time*. He was to attain a sublimer faith . . . after he had made the discovery that 'infinite' resignation can become still more infinite. The description Johannes de silentio gives of the knight of faith is adequate, as he thinks, to the highest attainment. The reader may find this description merely whimsical, but to me (though I smile at it) the passage seems essentially serious, because it depicts the 'saint' as the Protestant has preferred to conceive him. S. K. here represents that the 'saint' has absolutely no external marks by which he can be identified. But it looks as if he had already begun to suspect that 'the religion of hidden inwardness', which he was then inclined to extol, might really be non-existent. He confesses here that he had 'never yet found such a type'. At a later period this ideal became his pet aversion.

I crave the indulgence of the reader while I gratify my own predilection by quoting a description of the knight of faith. He is distinguished here from the knight of infinite resignation, and in this book both of these chevaliers are contrasted with the hero of classical tragedy:[1]

The knights of infinite resignation are easily recognized: their gait is gliding and assured. On the other hand, they who carry in their bosom the treasure of faith can easily delude one, because their exterior is strikingly similar to the figure which infinite resignation as well as faith so deeply despises—the philistine. I candidly admit that in my practice I have not found a reliable instance, though I am not disposed for this reason to deny that every second man I meet with may be such. At any rate, in the course of many years I have sought for it in vain. Generally one travels the world around to see rivers and mountains, new stars, birds of bright plumage, strange fishes, queer races of men, yielding to the brutish stupor which gapes at existence and thinks it has seen something. This does not concern me in the least. On the other hand, if I knew where there lived such a knight of faith, I should make a pilgrimage on foot to see him; for this prodigy concerns me absolutely. I should not let him out of my sight for an instant, every moment I should be attentive to see how he performed his movements; I should consider that I had a job for life and should divide my time between watching him and repeating the exercises myself, so that my whole time would be employed in admiring him. I have said that I have never yet found such a type. Nevertheless I can well imagine him. Here he is. The moment my eyes first fall upon him I instantly cast him from me and take a leap backward, clapping my hands in amazement and saying half aloud, 'Good Lord! Is this the man? Is it really he? He looks to me like a tax-collector.' Nevertheless it is he. I attach myself to him more closely, watching the least movement to see whether there might not be apparent some slightest trace of enigmatical telegraphy from the infinite, a glance, a look, a gesture, a sadness, a smile which betrayed the presence of the infinite in its heterogeneity with the finite. No! I examine his figure from top to toe to see whether there might not be a fissure through which the infinite peers out. No! He is solid through and through. His tread?—It is firm, belonging completely to the finite; no smartly dressed bourgeois who walks out to Fresberg on Sunday afternoons treads the ground more solidly, he belongs completely to this world, no philistine can belong to it more thoroughly. There is no trace of that aloof and superior nature by which one recognizes the knight of infinity. He is delighted with everything, takes part in everything, and every interest that engages him he pursues with a persistence which denotes the earthly man whose soul is absorbed in such things. He is attentive to his business. When one sees him at that, one might think him a quill-driver who had lost his soul to the Italian book-keeping system, so punctual he is about it. He keeps Sunday. He goes to Church. No heavenly glance, no sign of the incommensurable betrays him; if one did not know him, it would be impossible to distinguish him from the rest of the crowd; for his healthy, hearty hymn-singing proves at the most that he has good lungs. In the afternoon he goes out to the forest. He rejoices at everything he sees, at the human swarm, the new omnibuses, the water of the Sound—when one encounters him walking on the beach one might suppose that he was a mercenary drudge taking his fling—he lets himself go just like that. For he is not a poet, and I have sought in vain to detect in him the poetical incommensurability. Towards evening he goes home, with a gait as tireless as a postman's. On the way he reflects that his wife doubtless has an extra little warm dish waiting for him when he gets home—roast calf's-head, for example, garnished with vegetables. If he encountered an acquaintance of similar tastes he could continue to discourse about that dish as far as the East Gate, with a passion which would be appropriate in a restaurant-keeper. As it happens he has not so much as four shillings to his name, and yet he believes confidently that his wife has that appetizing dish ready for him. If she has it, the sight might well arouse the envy of superior people and the enthusiasm of common folks, for his appetite is greater than Esau's. His wife has no such thing ready—strangely enough, it is all the same to him. . . . He leans out of the open window and watches the square on which he lives—everything that goes on there, how a rat creeps under the curb of the gutter, how the children play—as tranquilly occupied with it all as if he were a girl of 16 years. And yet he is not a genius; for I have sought in vain to detect in him the incommensurability of genius. He smokes his pipe in the late afternoon, and seeing him then one might swear that over there lay a huckster vegetating in the twilight. He lets five count as an even number as nonchalantly as if he were a light-minded good-for-nothing; and yet he buys up at the highest price every instant he lives, the acceptable time; for he does not do the least thing except by virtue of the absurd. And yet, and yet, I could be furious about it—if for no other reason, than for envy, because this person has performed and every instant continues to perform the movements of infinity. In infinite resignation he drains the deep sadness of existence, he knows the blessedness of infinity, has experienced the pain of renouncing all, even the dearest thing he has in the world, and yet to him the finite tastes fully as good as to one who has never known anything higher, for his continuance in the finite bears no trace of a cowed and anxious discipline, and his enjoyment of the finite has a quality of assurance, as if it were the most certain thing of all. And yet, and yet, the whole earthly form he produces is really a new creation by virtue of the absurd. He resigned everything infinitely, and then grasped it again by virtue of the absurd. He constantly makes the movements of infinity, but he does it with such correctness and security that he constantly gets the finite as a result, and there is not a second when one is prompted to surmise anything higher. It must be a difficult thing for a dancer to attain a definite attitude with a leap, in such wise that there is not a second when he is groping after it, but with the leap itself he comes into that posture. Perhaps no dancer can do this. This knight can. Multitudes of men live forlorn in earthly sorrow or joy—these are they that 'sit out' and never get into the dance. The knights of infinity are dancers and possess style. They perform the upward movements and come down again. This is a diversion which has its own blessedness, and it is not an unlovely sight to behold. But every time they come down they are unable to assume the attitude at once, they waver an instant, and that wavering shows that they are strangers in the world. This is more or less obvious according to the skill they possess, yet even the best trained of these dancers cannot entirely hide this wavering. It is not in the air one ought to watch them, but only at the moment they touch or have touched the ground—and then one recognizes them. But to be able so to come down that in the same second it looks as if they were standing or walking, to be able to transform life's leap into a walk, to be able to express absolutely the sublime in the pedestrian—this is a thing which only that knight [of faith] can do—and this is the one thing miraculous about him.

But the religious theme has already been followed so far that I must press on to speak of S. K. as the author of the 'edifying discourses'. We ought not to postpone the consideration of his religious works, seeing that he himself so much insists upon the fact that he was a religious writer from the beginning, and that from the beginning the Discourses accompanied the pseudonymous works. He observed plaintively that he had offered his aesthetical works with his left hand and his religious works with the right, but his contemporaries had stretched out the right hand to take what he held in his left.

§ 2. THE EDIFYING DISCOURSES, 1843

Either/Or, *The Repetition*, *Fear and Trembling*, and the *Stages* are commonly described as 'the aesthetical writings of Søren Kierkegaard'. If I had used that title for the heading of this chapter, I must have gone on at once from this point to speak of the *Stages* and stopped with that. For the *Edifying Discourses* are certainly not aesthetical writings, and neither is *The Concept of Dread*. Both of them, however, represent the movement 'away from the aesthetical', and therefore we are free to proceed here in the chronological order, which in this case is also the psychological order.

Before S. K. invented the title 'Edifying Discourses' he did not scruple to publish a 'sermon'. He put it at the conclusion of *Either/Or*, as a hint that aesthetical/ethical is not the last alternative. I quote the conclusion of this sermon because it is characteristic of S. K. that he does not attempt to compel belief, but would elicit it out of the reader's own heart—even when the theme is so unusual as 'the edification of the thought that before God we are always in the wrong'.[1]

Could you wish?

> As against God we are always in the wrong—this thought checks doubt and assuages its distress, it animates and incites to action.
>
> Your thought has now followed the course of this exposition—swiftly, perhaps, when it was along familiar paths it led you; slowly, perhaps reluctantly, when the path was strange to you—but this you must concede, that the case really is as it was represented, and your thought has nothing to object against it. As we are about to separate, one more question, my hearer: Did you wish? could you wish that it might be otherwise? Could you wish that you should be in the right? Could you wish that the beautiful law which in the course of

thousands of years has upheld the human race through life, and every generation of the race, that beautiful law, more glorious than the law which upholds the stars in their courses above the vault of heaven, could you wish that this law might be broken, with results more dreadful than if that law of nature were broken and all were resolved into horrid chaos? Could you wish it? I have no word of wrath to affright you with, your wish shall not issue from dread at the presumption of the thought of willing to be in the right against God; I only ask you, do you wish that it might be otherwise? Perhaps my voice does not possess sufficient power and sincerity, so that my cry cannot pierce to your inmost thought—O, but ask yourself, ask yourself with the solemn uncertainty with which you would address a man who was, as you knew, in a position to decide the happiness of your life, ask still more solemnly, for it is verily a question of salvation. Check not your soul's flight, do not make sorrowful the better side of you, quench not the Spirit with half-wishes and half-thoughts. Ask yourself, and keep on asking until you find the answer. For one can have known a thing many times, accepted it; one can have willed a thing many times, attempted it; and yet only the deep inward movement, only the heart's indescribable emotion, only that assures you that what you have known belongs to you and that no power can take it from you; for only the truth that edifies is truth for you.

The best text to start with as we essay to study the author of the *Edifying Discourses* is the preface S. K. wrote for the little volume which contained the first two of them, and which he repeated, with minor variations, every time he published a small group of them (2, 3, or 4 at a time), until in the course of hardly more than a year eighteen had appeared and were then republished in one volume. The *Edifying Discourses* have also this in common, that they were all of them dedicated to his father, in the simple and touching terms we have already quoted (p. 26). These, and all the other expressly religious writings, except the two attributed to Anti-Climacus, bore the author's own name.

Preface

In spite of the fact that this little book (which is called 'discourses', not sermons, because the author has no authority

to **preach**; 'edifying discourses', not discourses for edification, because the speaker makes no claim whatever to be a **teacher**) wishes only to be what it is, a superfluity, and desires only to remain in retirement, as it was in concealment it had its origin, yet I have not taken leave of it without an almost romantic hope. In so far as its publication implies that in a metaphorical sense it is about to start as it were upon a journey, I allowed my eye to follow it a little while. I saw then how it made its way along solitary paths, or went solitary on the highways. After one and another misunderstanding, due to its being deceived by a casual resemblance, it encountered finally that single individual (*hiin Enkelte*) whom it sought, that individual whom I with joy and gratitude call **my** reader, that individual whom it seeks, towards whom as it were it stretches out its arms, that individual who is willing enough to let himself be found, willing enough to receive it, whether at the moment of encounter it finds him joyous and confident or weary and pensive.—In so far as its publication implies in a more literal sense that it stands stock still without moving from the spot, I let my eye rest upon it for a little while. So it stood there like an insignificant little flower in the cover of a great forest, not sought after either for its splendour, or for its sweet scent, or for its nourishing properties. But I saw then also, or fancied that I saw, how a bird which I call **my** reader suddenly cast an eye upon it, swooped down in its flight, plucked it and carried it off. And when I had seen this, I saw no more.
Copenhagen, May 5 [his birthday], 1843.

S. K.

About the fate of this preface S. K. relates in his Journal this singular story:[1]

It is a singular thing. That little preface to the 'two sermons' I had determined to alter because it seemed to me to contain a certain element of the spiritual erotic, and because I found it so exceedingly hard to surrender myself so peaceably that the polemical contradiction fails to be clearly expressed. I hasten to the press. What happens? The type-setter intercedes for this preface. I laughed at him a little, to be sure; but, on the other hand, in my heart I thought, 'So it might in fact be he that is the single individual.' In my delight at this I at first was minded to have two copies printed and inscribe one of them to the type-setter. It was really very pretty to see how much moved he was. A type-setter, who must be as tired of the book, one might suppose, as the author is.

At this point the reader should recall the passage quoted on page 239, wherein S. K. reveals that when he first used the expression 'that individual' he had in mind especially Regina. In Danish the reflexive pronoun leaves the sex of the reader undetermined. I have had to translate by 'himself'. When the same preface was repeated with succeeding issues of the Discourses this word had no longer a personal reference to her. He clung to it as an apt expression of his highly characteristic theory of individualism, which is compendiously expressed in the 'two notes', entitled *The Individual*, published posthumously along with *The Point of View*.

A great deal can be learnt from this preface about S. K.'s characteristic attitudes of thought, but one must interpret it with caution. His preference for the word 'discourses' to describe his sermons is significant, yet they *are* sermons nevertheless. In the passage last quoted he himself expressly refers to them as such, it was a 'sermon' which concluded *Either/Or*, and the first draft[1] of the preface to the *Two Edifying Discourses* (which was entirely different from the form eventually used) also regarded them as 'sermons'. The Journal shows that S. K. was not diffident of his capacity to write sermons:[2]

The prime requisite of the sermon is not to soothe, not to attain a metaphysical standpoint, but to clear for action. That is what I can do at any time.

An entry of 1847 is entitled:[3] Distinction between the Christian Discourse and the Sermon'.

The Christian discourse deals in a certain measure with doubt—the sermon functions absolutely, solely and only, by means of authority, that of the Scriptures and of the Apostles of Christ. It is therefore absolute heresy to deal in a sermon with doubt, even if one knows never so well how to handle it. . . . The sermon implies the priest (ordination); the Christian discourse can be [delivered by] the ordinary man.

This definition recalls the criterion of 'authority' which S. K.

emphasized in the preface. But this is a point where we must be very cautious, for it seems almost as if he used this word with the intent of leading us astray. He himself, as a candidate in theology, was given legal authority to preach, and five or six times he actually did so in one church or another, especially at the Friday celebration of the Holy Communion. In the preface to one of his collections of 'discourses' he calls attention to the fact that some of them had actually been delivered and therefore, in distinction from the rest, had obviously the character of 'spoken discourses'. It is true that most of his discourses were of a sort that the ear could not readily follow. They were too deeply reflective. But this is only a formal distinction. The question is whether S. K. really was of the opinion that the 'priests'—'especially in Protestantism, and more especially in Denmark'—by reason of their ordination enjoyed an authority which morally exacted assent. Certainly not, I would say. He complained that they did not exercise the authority which belonged to them as priests because they did not themselves believe in it, and he concluded that they had forfeited it. S. K. remarked that from childhood up he had been 'educated by Mynster's sermons', both in their spoken and printed form. He was until the end of his life a diligent attendant at church and therefore a constant hearer of sermons, but his Journals reveal that he was an exceedingly critical hearer, and indignation against the 'priests' and their sermons had long been smouldering in his heart before it blazed out in the open attack. He died without receiving the Sacrament because he was not willing to receive it from the hands of a parson, but only from a layman.

I suspect S. K. of irony—at least a little bit of it—when he spoke of the priests' authority to preach. But whatever he may have meant by the word 'authority' in the Preface, he meant something deeper than we are likely at first to perceive by the declaration he so commonly made: 'I am without authority.' We are to think rather of the sense in which the word 'authority' is used in the Gospels when it is said that Christ taught with authority and not as the scribes, and that with authority he cast out devils. S. K. did not *expressly* deal with the question, 'Where is the seat of authority in religion?' but he wrestled long and earnestly with a still more personal question, 'What religious authority as a teacher do I, Søren Kierkegaard, possess?' It is significant that he did not seek to settle that question by having himself ordained.

In his constantly recurring reflections about seeking a pastorate this aspect of the question never emerged. But it was the problem of personal authority which prompted him to ponder so long upon the case of Adler, who claimed some sort of inspiration. It is a testimony to the essential sobriety of S. K.'s mind that he resisted the temptation his extraordinary natural gifts suggested, and declared stoutly to himself and to others, 'I have no supernatural gifts—I am without authority.' His reflections on this theme were the more poignant because the time was manifestly out of joint and urgently needed a prophet. He became convinced, therefore, that a prophet must come; but when he asked himself (for no one else asked such a question), 'Art thou that Prophet?' he answered, 'No.' 'What art thou then?' He answered at first, in deep self-disparagement, 'I am only a poet.' Subsequently he found a more satisfactory answer: 'I am a poet and thinker.' But though he stuck to it that he was only a reflective thinker, he ventured to query within himself whether he might rise to the utmost height attainable to such a character and become in a decisive sense 'a witness for the truth'—even in the most decisive sense of being a martyr. This thought engrossed him during his last years, and he was sublimely comforted in his death by the conviction that he had dared to be a martyr, and that such a death, though it did not stamp his teaching with infallible authority, must avail to further the one end he had always in mind, 'make people take notice' of the truth.

Behold how far we are carried when we follow the apparently trivial clue furnished by the word 'authority' in the Preface to the first Discourses! For S. K. himself was carried thus far by following passionately this line of thought, and the eighty sermons which he modestly called discourses accurately register his spiritual progress in the course of this arduous ascent. Not only do these register his religious progress, but also, in the order in which they appear, the expressly religious works, *The Sickness unto Death* and *Exercises in Christianity* (which only for a scruple of spiritual modesty he attributed to Anti-Climacus), and of course the last books which were named *For Self-Examination* and *Judge for Yourself*, and contain very serious sermons. The newspaper and pamphleteering explosion of the last period cannot be justly understood except as the culmination of the spiritual ascent. At this point the reader should study attentively the synopsis of S. K.'s works in

Appendix IV. The titles and texts suffice in a measure to indicate the progress S. K. was making, and to show that it was marked not only by an increase in boldness and vehemence, but by a real growth in spiritual apprehension—this in spite of the fact that the text of his first sermon was also the text of his last. S. K. said of his works, 'They were my own education in Christianity.' We can perceive that (with the exception of the two books attributed to Anti-Climacus) the pseudonymous works register a stage the author had recently passed. For this reason among others he was insistent that the utterances of the pseudonyms should not be supposed to represent his deliberate judgement. The reader is following the flight of a bird and can determine its successive positions only after they have been passed and left long behind. We can understand that each position he relinquished was more decisively transcended the moment he had poetized it and put it in writing. His religious works indicate his successive positions in a very different way, for they register with scrupulous honesty the position he occupied at the moment of writing—just that and no more. This is a singular distinction among writers of edifying discourses. For how many are there who have not yielded to the temptation of uttering more spiritual truth than they have actually appropriated, either in thought or in terms of 'existence'?

S. K. was not unaware that he was employing a repellent word when he described his Discourses as 'edifying':[1]

> It is singular what hatred Hegel had for the edifying, as is prominent everywhere in his writings. But the edifying is not an opiate which lulls to sleep, it is the Amen of the infinite Spirit, and it is an aspect of cognition which ought not to be overlooked.

He expressly declined, however, to describe them as intended 'for edification', because this phrase implies the spiritual arrogance of the teacher who presumes to be in a position to make other people better than they are. Only God can do that. Because S. K. with Socratic modesty refrained from infringing upon this divine prerogative, he was able to be so honest.

Georg Brandes remarks:

> Judge William says in *Either/Or*, 'I have an idiosyncracy against edifying works and printed sermons.' But even if one shares this feeling in general, one reads Kierkegaard's Edifying

Discourses with respect. A noble spirit of moderation prevails in them. It makes a profound impression to hear this same man who is able to make himself the interpreter of the wildest passions speaking here to his fellow men so simply, so composedly, so solicitously, and offering them the best comfort he knows how to give for their pilgrimage through life.

It may be that this free-thinking Jew was thinking here only or chiefly of the *Eighteen Edifying Discourses*, for the 'spirit of moderation' is not so evident in the later discourses. It is significant of the deep religious impression made upon S. K. by the last phase of his 'education by the possibility' that for more than a year after he learnt of Regina's engagement he published nothing but a succession of religious discourses. They were edifying to their author, at all events, and he expressed himself as content if they should prove edifying to him alone. He himself is responsible in part for the misunderstanding, which one writer repeats after the other, that the discourses in general represent a standpoint not distinctively Christian. It is true of the earlier Discourses that they do not deal with what S. K. understood as 'the specifically Christian', with the 'Paradox'; they belong to the sphere which in the *Stages* he distinguishes as 'religion A', i.e. 'religion within the sphere of imminence'; but if this may be said in disparagement of them, the reader must not suppose that they sound less distinctively Christian than the great majority of sermons that are now heard even from orthodox pulpits.[1] We can note in the later discourses a constant advance in the direction of the specifically Christian, which corresponds *pari passu* with S. K.'s own advance. In 1847 the sermons which he published under the title *The Works of Love* bore the sub-title 'Christian Reflections in the Form of Discourses'; the following year he ventured to give the title of *Christian Discourses* to a series of twenty-eight sermons. The third section of this series being expressly polemical, he is only in apparent contradiction with his principle when he uses the title: 'Thoughts which Wound from Behind—for Edification.' In 1849 he called his three sermons on *The Lilies of the Field*, &c., 'Godly Discourses'.

At this point I have anticipated the development of S. K.'s history and surveyed roughly the whole field of the religious discourses which accompanied the pseudonymous writings from the beginning to the end. It would be futile to say more about them to one who has not read them. My regret is that I have no space to make adequate quotations. But I will quote from the *Stages* what Frater Taciturnus has to say about a real sermon, which is evidently an expression of S. K.'s ideal and is a fair description of his own religious discourses:[1]

> It is quite different in the case of the religious man. When he talks it is merely a monologue. Though he is concerned solely with himself, he speaks aloud—and that is what is called preaching. If there is some one who hears him, he ignores all relationship to such a person, and particularly all claim to gratitude, since what he is bent upon accomplishing is to save himself. Such a solemn monologue, which bears Christian witness in a Christian way, is called a sermon when it is so moving that it moves the speaker, the witness-bearer, because he is speaking about himself. World-historical perspectives, systematic results, gesticulation and wiping the sweat from the brow, power of voice and nervous force, and the employment of all such means to *accomplish* something, are aesthetic reminiscences, which do not even know how to accentuate rightly the passions of fear and pity in the Aristotelian sense. For world-historical perspectives are no more apt to arouse fear than are systematic results, whereas beating the pulpit and wiping away the sweat arouse at the most a genuine pity for the sweater. . . .
>
> The religious speaker who by means of fear and pity purifies these passions does not perform the amazing exploit of rending asunder the clouds so as to show the heavens opened, the judgement-day at hand, with hell in the background, himself and the elect triumphing—he performs the commoner, the simpler, the more humble feat, which ought to be so very easy: he lets the heavens stay closed, recognizing with fear and trembling that he himself is not 'ready', and he bows his head while the discourse pronounces judgement upon the thoughts of his heart. He does not perform the amazing exploit that would ensure his being hailed with acclamation upon his next appearance, he does not thunder so that the congregation may be kept awake and be saved by *his* discourse—he performs the commoner, the simpler, the more humble feat, which ought in

this case to be so very easy: he lets God keep the thunder and the might and the honour; he talks in such a way that though all were to go amiss, he can yet be assured that there was one hearer who was seriously moved—the speaker himself; that though all were to go amiss, there was yet one hearer who went home strengthened—the speaker himself; that though all were to go amiss and all the people were to stay away, there was yet one who in life's difficult complications craved the discourse's edifying instant—the speaker himself. He is not lavish in dispensing the abundance of the mouth and of learning, but is niggardly of the revenues of edification, seeing to it economically that the admonitions bind him before they pass on to somebody else, and that the comfort and truth do not depart from him . . . as a way of communicating them more prodigally. Hence if you should see him (says the religious man) seated apart in a solitary place, forsaken of all and convinced that he is accomplishing nothing by speaking, if you saw him there, you would find him just as much moved as ever he was; if you should hear his discourse, you would find it as powerful as ever, without deceit, without calculation, without straining after effect, and you would apprehend that there was one who must be edified—the speaker himself. He will not become tired of talking; for the lawyers and public speakers who have a worldly aim, or a worldly conceit with respect to an eternal aim, become tired when they cannot reckon on their fingers what they are accomplishing, when existence does not cunningly deceive them with an optical illusion that they are accomplishing something; but the religious speaker always has his principal aim—the speaker himself.

Thus it is (as I have convinced myself by experimentation) that the religious man by means of fear and pity works for the purification of these passions. Every other way of going about it produces confusion by putting forward half-aesthetical categories—by making the speaker aesthetically important and helping the hearers to lose themselves dizzily in something generic.[1]

§ 3. BOOKS WRITTEN IN 1844

The Repetition and *Fear and Trembling*, though they were finished in July 1843, were not published until October 16—and then perhaps reluctantly, seeing that their definite purpose had been rendered vain by Regina's engagement. Until June of the following year S. K. published nothing but edifying discourses. By that date there were fourteen of them, and the four which appeared in August brought the number to eighteen, which were soon afterwards republished in a single volume.

Nevertheless, during the year 1844 he was engaged in the composition of a great variety of other works. Most of them were published in June: *Three Edifying Discourses* on the 8th; *Philosophical Scraps*, by Johannes Climacus, on the 13th; *The Concept of Dread* and *Prefaces*, both of them on the 17th. His big work entitled *Stages on Life's Road* was almost completely written during this year, although it was not published until April of the year following.

In this section I say nothing more, of course, about the Discourses, and I must also leave the *Scraps* to another chapter, where we listen to his warning, 'Away from Speculation!'

It is an embarrassment to the biographer that the logical order does not correspond at all points with the chronological and biographical. But psychologically we can understand at this point that it was natural for S. K. to revert now to the philosophic reflections he had put aside when Regina nodded. The same character, Johannes Climacus, reappears, and yet the *Scraps* is philosophic more in appearance than in reality. It deals with the Christian Paradox, though only as a 'thought-experiment'.

Prefaces, by Nicholas Notabene (one of the few pseudonyms which has no obvious significance), is rightly described in the title as 'light reading'. It deals in a sarcastic but entertaining fashion with authors, publishers, and reviewers. Why such a book had to come out at this time we learn from the Journal, where the substance of it is found in the form of open letters to Professor Heiberg, voicing S. K.'s indignant but amusing protest against this great man's review of *The Repetition*. This voice was not meant to be heard beyond S. K.'s study, but the gist of his protest against professional writers he had to 'get out of his system', as they say, by expressing it in a public document.

On the other hand, *The Concept of Dread* is a profoundly serious book, entirely in keeping with the serious religious experience of this period. S. K. rightly describes it as 'a deliberation on psychological lines', but he also says truly in the title that it is 'in the direction of the dogmatic problem of original sin', and in conclusion, when psychology has said its last word, the case is handed over to the theologian. Here the name of the pseudonym is an indication of the serious intention of the book. Vigilius Haufniensis, being translated, means the Watchman of Copenhagen. S. K. had never until now published a book so completely serious, even in form, that he could venture to dedicate it, as he does this, to the memory of his revered teacher Paul Martin Møller (see pp. 143 ff.). A passage from the end of this book, which was quoted in the preceding section, is enough to show how serious this book is, and the reader has been made acquainted with other quotations from it which I used in earlier chapters to illuminate S. K.'s own experiences as a youth.

I am only a biographer. It is in this sense I have understood my task. It would hardly be possible for me to be at the same time a critic or an expounder of S. K.'s many and great thoughts—even if my mind were capacious enough to hold so much. But we have seen that S. K.'s works contain an immense amount of biographical material, and in utilizing that I have already made the reader acquainted in a measure with the works which I name in this chapter, and which I can hardly do more than name. It is a matter of course that the biographical application of these works is to a period anterior, and often far anterior, to the year in which they were written or published, for they were written to register experiences that were past and a stage that had been left behind.

This is obviously true of the *Stages on Life's Road*, which registers two stages S. K. had definitely left behind him: the aesthetic, represented by the speakers at the banquet of 'In Vino Veritas', and the merely ethical, represented by Judge William's defence of marriage. *Either/Or*, as S. K. himself said of it, 'went no farther than the ethical'; but here the religious stage has due recognition, although it is exemplified only in the person of the young man, 'the *quidam* of the experiment', who is depicted in the initial throes of a religious experience, while Frater Taciturnus, who comments upon this case, confesses that his profound knowledge of religion is due not to personal experience but merely to observation. As an observer he is not *concerned* about religion but greatly interested in it 'as a phenomenon'.

Many of the themes which were introduced in the earlier books emerge again in the *Stages*. S. K. was exceedingly tenacious of the ideas which principally concerned him, and his growth in the apprehension of them we can clearly trace from book to book. We meet here also the same characters. The new pseudonym, Hilarius Bookbinder, had no part to play beside collecting the documents and preparing them for the press; but among the speakers and writers we find Constantine Constantius, Victor Eremita, John the Seducer, and our old friend Judge William, who previously had the title of 'Assessor' (which I did not use) but was now advanced to the rank of Judge and grown decidedly more dogmatic. The young man (here referred to as *quidam*) who is the subject of the psychological experiment of Frater Taciturnus is the same and yet not quite the same as the 'young man' who was the object of Constantine's observation. Another young man (who may be the same young man at an earlier stage) figures among the speakers at the banquet, along with the Ladies' Tailor; but the Frater is the only new character of importance. This work therefore was a sort of 'repetition'—and a risky one, as S. K. himself reflected with some trepidation.[1] It is a marvel that it succeeded—in being the same and yet different. 'That is art!' exclaims S. K. He could not have been ambitious of higher praise than Brandes gives when he says of the Banquet, which is described in 'In Vino Veritas' and which obviously was suggested by Plato's *Symposium*, that 'it does not suffer even in comparison with this masterpiece'.

The *Stages*, regarded as a repetition of *Either/Or*, supplies the defect which S. K. likened to the uncompleted window in Aladdin's palace, that is, the story of his own unhappy love. We have seen that he was at work upon that before he got fairly started with *The Repetition*, and that he was at that time unable to write it because he could not yet poetize his relation to Regina. Now that she was definitely lost to him he could do it, and it is amazing how thoroughly he did it. Two-thirds of the *Stages* consists of this story, under the title 'Guilty?'/'Not Guilty?' In this book we have been scrupulous to tell the story of S. K.'s unhappy love chiefly in the words of his Journal; but it is exactly the same story that is told here, completely and with the most exhaustive analysis, in a document which he made public in his lifetime. How amazing that a man so secretive and self-contained could bring himself to do such a thing! We are impelled at first to judge that such a precise account of his own love-affair agrees badly with the canon of good taste which he himself enunciated (p. 200). For the facts are here set down without any essential alteration—although the whole document is ascribed to a pseudonym, and Frater Taciturnus, after beguiling the reader with a fantastic story of fishing up Quidam's Diary from the bottom of a lake, refers to it subsequently as his own incredible invention. But we cannot say that S. K. offended against his own canon when we note that none of his contemporaries guessed that he was telling his own story in every detail—none, that is to say, except Regina, and to her, after she was engaged to another, he evidently wanted to make himself understood. He recognizes unequivocally his own guilt in beginning the affair; but he protests that for the fearful way in which it ended he was not guilty, or not alone guilty, and he would have 'her' recognize where she had been at fault.

In this most personal account of his love affair he introduces the six symbolical stories ('Solomon's Dream', &c.) which we have quoted to illustrate his childhood and youth, and so this whole section is exquisitely autobiographical. The Quidam of the experiment is simply S. K. himself—neither more nor less—and I am inclined to believe that the 'young man' who spoke at the Banquet was not an entirely different person, but represents S. K.'s innocent ignorance of women before he encountered Regina. The high estimation of marriage which the Judge maintains must be taken to represent S. K.'s own opinion at that time, and is therefore a measure of his renunciation.

In our day, when love is so prominent a theme in literature, and on the stage, and on the silver screen, and when marriage is so much attacked and so much defended, it seems to me that S. K.'s works are just 'what the age demands'; for there is no other author but Dante that has so much to say about love (from the aesthetic, the ethical, and the religious points of view), and no other has so ably defended the monogamous ideal of marriage, which is not only a Christian ideal but the custom of the Germanic peoples.

The title originally chosen for the *Stages* was 'Right hand and Left'. This clearly enough indicates the purpose of presenting sharply contrasted positions. S. K. himself remarks[1] that there are 'three stages and yet an either/or'. That in fact is what we find here. Judge William's 'Remarks about marriage in reply to objections' are placed immediately after the speeches at the Banquet, in which marriage was scouted and (as S. K. said in his Journal) 'woman is described essentially but falsely'.[1] The opposition here is between the aesthetic and the ethical, which is sharply expressed, though it is not here, as in the earlier works, expressed in the form of a dilemma or put as a question. Then follows Quidam's Diary, in clear enough opposition to the self-assured position of the Judge, who argues from his own experience of a happy marriage, but shows by his dogmatism that there are things in heaven and earth not dreamt of in his philosophy. He makes grudging allowance for the exceptional individual, but is quite unable to conceive of a religious collision such as that which made Quidam incommensurable for marriage. 'I could whisper a little secret in his ear', said Frater Taciturnus.

But it is far from my purpose to give a description of the *Stages*.[2] I have said enough to orient the reader who may be inclined to adventure himself upon this new ocean of thought. If I were to attempt a résumé of such a book, I could only succeed in making it dull—and I can think of no worse offence against S. K. Fortunately, the reader has in the course of this book been made acquainted already with many passages translated from the *Stages*. (See Appendix II.)

In conclusion I would quote from the *Stages* a short passage which, to my mind, suggests that, in one respect at least, Constantine's account of man's relation to woman is not so manifestly false as it is 'essential':[3]

> So it is perfectly true in a sense that 'ideality came into human life through woman. What would a man be without her?' Through a maiden, many a man has become a genius; through a maiden, many a man has become a hero; through a maiden, many a man has become a poet; through a maiden, many a man has become a saint—but he didn't become a genius through the girl he got, for with her he became merely state-councillor; he didn't become a hero through the girl he got, for through her he became merely a general; he didn't become a poet through the girl he got, for through her he became merely a father; he didn't become a saint through the girl he got, for he got none at all and would only have the one he didn't get—just as each of the others became

genius, became hero, became poet by the help of the girl he didn't get.

§4. ABOUT THE PSEUDONYMS

At this point I begin to reap the fruits of the labour I expended in earlier parts of this book to illustrate S. K.'s childhood and youth by quotations from the works of his maturity. Now when I have reached the period when these great works were produced, I can describe them compendiously without fear of scanting so great a subject. And brevity has now become a necessity, seeing I have reached a point where I must reflect that some time this book must be brought to a close.

Even the complicated question of the pseudonyms I can treat briefly, because incidentally so much light has been thrown on this subject in the course of the story, and also because it does not seem to me quite so difficult a problem as many writers are inclined to think. Although we have not yet quite done with the pseudonymous writings, we have already become acquainted with all of the pseudonyms—except Anti-Climacus, who is not strictly a pseudonym, or at all events belongs to a class by himself. It is high time, therefore, that we face the question, Why? Why did S. K. resort to pseudonyms at all? and why did he employ so many? and in what relation does he himself stand to the persons and speeches of his pseudonyms and to the fictitious characters they create?

The one public document in which S. K. professes to account for his use of pseudonyms is 'The First and Last Explanation', which he appended to *The Concluding Unscientific Postscript* to make formal acknowledgement of his authorship of the pseudonymous works. In my estimation this 'explanation' explains both too much and too little. I quote the essential passage:[1]

> My pseudonymity, or rather polynymity, did not have an accidental reason in my *personal* situation (certainly not the fear of punishment at the hand of the law, in which respect I am not conscious of any infraction, and, moreover, the printer as well as the censor, a civil functionary, has always been officially informed who the author was coincidently with the publication of the book), but it had an *essential* reason due to the character of the production, which, for the sake of the psychologically diverse individualities of the characters and their spoken

> parts, required a sheer abandonment in the direction of good and evil, of contrition and exuberance, of despair and presumption, of suffering and exultation, &c., limited only ideally by psychological consistency, and which no actually existing persons under the ethical limitations of reality would dare to permit himself or would desire to. . . . My relationship is even more external than that of a poet who *poetically creates* personalities and yet appears himself in the preface as the *author*. In the present case I am impersonal, or personal only in the third person, a stage-prompter, for I have poetically produced *authors*, the preface being their own production, and even their names too. So in the pseudonymous books there is not a single word of mine. I have no opinion about them except as a third person, no knowledge of their meaning except as a reader, not the remotest private relationship to them—which indeed it would be impossible to have with respect to a double-reflected communication. . . . The juridical and literary responsibility is mine.

I am not at all inclined to reject this statement—as Schrempf and some others do, with the intent of proving that S. K.'s use of pseudonyms was only an imitation of the fashion of the German Romanticists, and that therefore all that they write can be regarded without more ado as an expression of S. K.'s own thought at the time the book was written. Certainly this was a common practice of the Romanticists, yet on the other hand it was a trait very natural to S. K.'s 'intriguing pate'. He took a boyish delight in the reflection that he had made the whole thing as complicated as a Chinese puzzle, 'box within box'. This, however, is a more superficial explanation than he himself gives. And it seems to me that he says too much when he claims that pseudonymous *authors* were necessary for the aim he had in view, where fictitious *characters* would evidently suffice. This whole 'Explanation' was really superfluous when everybody knew that he was the author of the works he then for the first time enumerated and acknowledged. His last two works bore his own name on the title-page as editor. Although he announced to Boesen that anonymity was of the utmost importance in the case of the works addressed to Regina, and although he sought to mystify the public before the publication of *Either/Or* by letters addressed to a daily paper complaining that several works had been attributed to him for which he was not responsible—and with which, in fact, no one had ever dreamt of connecting him—notwithstanding all this, it is evident enough that he neither expected nor desired to maintain his incognito long. He was playing a game of hide and seek, expecting to be found. He knew very well, and was proud to proclaim it, that his style was peculiarly his own, 'like a water-mark' on every page, so that even imitators could readily be recognized as plagiarists. Certainly he had never desired to avoid personal responsibility for his works. No one ever inveighed more indignantly against the evil of irresponsible anonymity than he did after he had tasted the bitterness of it in the attack of the 'Corsair'. And he protests too much—at least he may be taken to imply too much—when he affirms that 'in the pseudonymous books there is not a single word of mine', &c. I regard this as a wholesome admonition, and accordingly I am disposed to use the utmost caution in searching these pseudonymous scriptures for reliable information about S. K.'s life and thought. I grant that neither the reputed authors of the books, nor the characters they produce, are any of them the whole Søren Kierkegaard, and that we cannot assume with respect to any utterances they make that S. K. in his own proper person would have expressed the same judgement in the same way at the time he was writing the book. And yet his voluminous journals show conclusively that many passages in his books were the expression of his most intimate personal thought. The reader will note that this book has been written on the assumption that much is to be learnt about S. K. from his pseudonymous works by the exercise of due diligence and discretion.

On the other hand, S. K. says too little in this passage, and likewise in another to the same effect in his Journal:[1]

> I stand in a purely poetical relationship to my works, hence it is that I am pseudonymous.

But speaking of his literary work as a whole, he says something more illuminating in the little pamphlet, *About my Work as an Author*, which was written at about the same time as the 'Explanation', but not published until 1851:[2]

> It began **maieutically** with aesthetical productions, and the whole aesthetical production is such a *maieutic*. Hence that

production was pseudonymous, whereas the direct religious writings bear my own name.

But an entry in the Journal gives a far more adequate explanation of his use of pseudonyms—perhaps more profoundly true than he himself suspected:[1]

> Through many years my melancholy was the cause that in the deepest sense I could not attain to the point of saying Thou to myself. Between my melancholy and my Thou there lay a whole world of imagination. It is this that I have in part emptied out in the pseudonyms. Just as he who has no happy home fares forth as much as possible and fain would be away from his home, so has my melancholy kept me outside myself, while in exploration and poetical experience I have travelled through a whole world of imagination. Like one who has been put in possession of a great landed estate and cannot get through becoming acquainted with it—so by reason of melancholy I have comported myself towards the possibility.

A passage in *The Repetition*[2] is evidently not less personal than this:

> The individual has manifold shadows, all of which resemble him and from time to time have an equal claim to be the man himself.

From time to time we have seen reason to believe that some of the pseudonyms and the characters they produce represent fractions of S. K.'s personality. Such a use of the pseudonyms suggests the suspicion that S. K. suffered from a divided personality. I do not say 'a double personality', for that would be saying both too much and too little. A double personality is in some respects a more sinister symptom than that of the man who could say, 'I am legion.' And I do not say a split personality, for I think of him rather as a splintered personality. Many as there were of him in the possibility, he succeeded in holding them together by the force of his religious character and his pre-eminent power of honest reflection. In 1847, when he wrote the entry quoted above, he had not yet attained to a religious regeneration, the true 'repetition', or 'immediacy after reflection', which would integrate his personality on a higher plane. He envisaged it only and longed after it. It meant to him the coming of the Holy Ghost the Comforter. It came. He attained the 'purity of heart' which consists in 'willing one thing'. And as a unified personality S. K. had no longer any use for pseudonyms. His discovery of Anti-Climacus meant something quite different. It meant spiritual modesty.

HARPER TORCHBOOKS / The Bollingen Library

Rachel Bespaloff — ON THE ILIAD. Introduction by Hermann Broch TB/2006

Elliott Coleman, *ed.* — LECTURES IN CRITICISM: *By R. P. Blackmur, B. Croce, Henri Peyre, John Crowe Ransom, Herbert Read, and Allen Tate* TB/2003

C. G. Jung — PSYCHOLOGICAL REFLECTIONS. Edited by Jolande Jacobi TB/2001

Erich Neumann — THE ORIGINS AND HISTORY OF CONSCIOUSNESS. *Vol. I,* TB/2007; *Vol. II,* TB/2008

St.-John Perse — SEAMARKS. Translated by Wallace Fowlie TB/2002

Jean Seznec — THE SURVIVAL OF THE PAGAN GODS: *The Mythological Tradition and Its Place in Renaissance Humanism and Art.* Illustrated TB/2004

Heinrich Zimmer — MYTHS AND SYMBOLS IN INDIAN ART AND CIVILIZATION TB/2005

HARPER TORCHBOOKS / The Academy Library

James Baird — ISHMAEL: *A Study of the Symbolic Mode in Primitivism* TB/1023

Herschel Baker — THE IMAGE OF MAN: *A Study of the Idea of Human Dignity in Classical Antiquity, the Middle Ages, and the Renaissance* TB/1047

Jacques Barzun — THE HOUSE OF INTELLECT TB/1051

W. J. Bate — FROM CLASSIC TO ROMANTIC: *Premises of Taste in Eighteenth Century England* TB/1036

Henri Bergson — TIME AND FREE WILL: *An Essay on the Immediate Data of Consciousness* TB/1021

H. J. Blackham — SIX EXISTENTIALIST THINKERS: *Kierkegaard, Jaspers, Nietzsche, Marcel, Heidegger, Sartre* TB/1002

Walter Bromberg — THE MIND OF MAN: *A History of Psychotherapy and Psychoanalysis* TB/1003

Abraham Cahan — THE RISE OF DAVID LEVINSKY. A novel. Introduction by John Higham TB/1028

Helen Cam — ENGLAND BEFORE ELIZABETH TB/1026

Joseph Charles — THE ORIGINS OF THE AMERICAN PARTY SYSTEM TB/1049

T. C. Cochran & William Miller — THE AGE OF ENTERPRISE: *A Social History of Industrial America* TB/1054

Norman Cohn — THE PURSUIT OF THE MILLENNIUM: *Revolutionary Messianism in Medieval and Reformation Europe and its Bearing on Modern Totalitarian Movements* TB/1037

G. G. Coulton — MEDIEVAL VILLAGE, MANOR, AND MONASTERY TB/1022

Wilfrid Desan — THE TRAGIC FINALE: *An Essay on the Philosophy of Jean-Paul Sartre* TB/1030

Cora Du Bois — THE PEOPLE OF ALOR: *A Social-Psychological Study of an East Indian Island. Vol. I,* 85 illus., TB/1042; *Vol. II,* TB/1043

George Eliot — DANIEL DERONDA. A novel. Introduction by F. R. Leavis TB/1039

John N. Figgis — POLITICAL THOUGHT FROM GERSON TO GROTIUS: 1414-1625: *Seven Studies.* Introduction by Garrett Mattingly TB/1032

Editors of *Fortune* — AMERICA IN THE SIXTIES: *The Economy and the Society* TB/1015

F. L. Ganshof — FEUDALISM TB/1058

G. P. Gooch — ENGLISH DEMOCRATIC IDEAS IN THE SEVENTEENTH CENTURY TB/1006

Francis J. Grund — ARISTOCRACY IN AMERICA: *A Study of Jacksonian Democracy* TB/1001

W. K. C. Guthrie — THE GREEK PHILOSOPHERS: *From Thales to Aristotle* TB/1008

Marcus Lee Hansen — THE ATLANTIC MIGRATION: 1607-1860 TB/1052

Alfred Harbage — AS THEY LIKED IT: *A Study of Shakespeare's Moral Artistry* TB/1035

J. M. Hussey — THE BYZANTINE WORLD TB/1057

Henry James — THE PRINCESS CASAMASSIMA. A novel. Intro. by Clinton Oliver. TB/1005

Henry James — RODERICK HUDSON. A novel. Introduction by Leon Edel TB/1016

Henry James — THE TRAGIC MUSE. A novel. Introduction by Leon Edel TB/1017

William James — PSYCHOLOGY: *The Briefer Course.* Edited with an Introduction by Gordon Allport TB/1034

Arnold Kettle — AN INTRODUCTION TO THE ENGLISH NOVEL. *Vol. I, Defoe to George Eliot,* TB/1011; *Vol. II, Henry James to the Present,* TB/1012

Samuel Noah Kramer — SUMERIAN MYTHOLOGY: *A Study of Spiritual and Literary Achievement in the Third Millennium B.C.* Illustrated TB/1055

Paul Oskar Kristeller — RENAISSANCE THOUGHT: *The Classic, Scholastic, and Humanist Strains* TB/1048

L. S. B. Leakey — ADAM'S ANCESTORS: *The Evolution of Man and His Culture.* Illustrated TB/1019

Bernard Lewis — THE ARABS IN HISTORY TB/1029

Ferdinand Lot — THE END OF THE ANCIENT WORLD AND THE BEGINNINGS OF THE MIDDLE AGES TB/1044

Arthur O. Lovejoy	THE GREAT CHAIN OF BEING: *A Study of the History of an Idea* TB/1009
Robert Lowie	PRIMITIVE SOCIETY. Introduction by Fred Eggan TB/1058
Niccolo Machiavelli	HISTORY OF FLORENCE AND OF THE AFFAIRS OF ITALY: *From the Earliest Times to the Death of Lorenzo the Magnificent.* Introduction by Felix Gilbert TB/1027
J. P. Mayer	ALEXIS DE TOCQUEVILLE: *A Biographical Study in Political Science* TB/1014
John U. Nef	CULTURAL FOUNDATIONS OF INDUSTRIAL CIVILIZATION TB/1024
Jose Oretga y Gasset	THE MODERN THEME. Introduction by Jose Ferrater Mora TB/1038
J. H. Parry	THE ESTABLISHMENT OF THE EUROPEAN HEGEMONY: 1415-1715: *Trade and Exploration in the Age of the Renaissance* TB/1045
Robert Payne	HUBRIS: *A Study of Pride.* Foreword by Herbert Read TB/1031
Samuel Pepys	THE DIARY OF SAMUEL PEPYS: Selections, edited by O. F. Morshead; illustrated by Ernest H. Shepard TB/1007
Paul E. Pfeutze	SELF, SOCIETY, EXISTENCE: *Human Nature and Dialogue in the Thought of George Herbert Mead and Martin Buber* TB/1059
Georges Poulet	STUDIES IN HUMAN TIME: *Montaigne, Molière, Baudelaire, Proust, et al.* TB/1004
George E. Probst, *Ed.*	THE HAPPY REPUBLIC: *A Reader in Tocqueville's America* TB/1060
Priscilla Robertson	REVOLUTIONS OF 1848: *A Social History* TB/1025
Ferdinand Schevill	THE MEDICI. Illustrated TB/1010
Bruno Snell	THE DISCOVERY OF THE MIND: *The Greek Origins of European Thought* TB/1018
C. P. Snow	TIME OF HOPE. A novel TB/1040
Perrin Stryker	THE CHARACTER OF THE EXECUTIVE: *Eleven Studies in Managerial Qualities* TB/1041
Percy Sykes	A HISTORY OF EXPLORATION. Introduction by John K. Wright TB/1046
Dorothy Van Ghent	THE ENGLISH NOVEL: *Form and Function* TB/1050
W. H. Walsh	PHILOSOPHY OF HISTORY: *An Introduction* TB/1020
W. Lloyd Warner	SOCIAL CLASS IN AMERICA: *The Evaluation of Status* TB/1013
Alfred N. Whitehead	PROCESS AND REALITY: *An Essay in Cosmology* TB/1033
Louis B. Wright	CULTURE ON THE MOVING FRONTIER TB/1053

HARPER TORCHBOOKS / The Science Library

Angus d'A. Bellairs	REPTILES: *Life History, Evolution, and Structure.* Illustrated TB/520
L. von Bertalanffy	PROBLEMS OF LIFE: *An Evaluation of Modern Biological and Scientific Thought* TB/521
David Bohm	CAUSALITY AND CHANCE IN MODERN PHYSICS. Foreword by Louis de Broglie TB/536
R. B. Braithwaite	SCIENTIFIC EXPLANATION TB/515
P. W. Bridgman	THE NATURE OF THERMODYNAMICS TB/537
Louis de Broglie	PHYSICS AND MICROPHYSICS. Foreword by Albert Einstein TB/514
J. Bronowski	SCIENCE AND HUMAN VALUES TB/505
A. J. Cain	ANIMAL SPECIES AND THEIR EVOLUTION. Illustrated TB/519
R. E. Coker	THIS GREAT AND WIDE SEA: *An Introduction to Oceanography and Marine Biology*. Illustrated TB/551
T. G. Cowling	MOLECULES IN MOTION: *An Introduction to the Kinetic Theory of Gases.* Illustrated TB/516
A. C. Crombie, *Ed.*	TURNING POINTS IN PHYSICS TB/535
W. C. Dampier, *Ed.*	READINGS IN THE LITERATURE OF SCIENCE. Illustrated TB/512
H. Davenport	THE HIGHER ARITHMETIC: *An Introduction to the Theory of Numbers* TB/526
W. H. Dowdeswell	ANIMAL ECOLOGY. Illustrated TB/543
W. H. Dowdeswell	THE MECHANISM OF EVOLUTION TB/527
C. V. Durell	READABLE RELATIVITY TB/530
Arthur Eddington	SPACE, TIME AND GRAVITATION: *An Outline of the General Relativity Theory* TB/510
Alexander Findlay	CHEMISTRY IN THE SERVICE OF MAN. Illustrated TB/524
H. G. Forder	GEOMETRY: *An Introduction.* Illus. TB/548
Gottlob Frege	THE FOUNDATIONS OF ARITHMETIC TB/534
R. W. Gerard	UNRESTING CELLS. Illustrated TB/541
Werner Heisenberg	PHYSICS AND PHILOSOPHY: *The Revolution in Modern Science* TB/549
C. Judson Herrick	THE EVOLUTION OF HUMAN NATURE TB/545
Max Jammer	CONCEPTS OF SPACE TB/533
Max Jammer	CONCEPTS OF FORCE TB/550
S. Korner	THE PHILOSOPHY OF MATHEMATICS: *An Introduction* TB/547
David Lack	DARWIN'S FINCHES: *The General Biological Theory of Evolution.* Illustrated TB/544

D. E. Littlewood — THE SKELETON KEY OF MATHEMATICS: *A Simple Account of Complex Algebraic Theories* TB/525

J. E. Morton — MOLLUSCS: *An Introduction to Their Form and Function.* Illustrated TB/529

O. Neugebauer — THE EXACT SCIENCES IN ANTIQUITY TB/552

J. R. Partington — A SHORT HISTORY OF CHEMISTRY. Illustrated TB/522

H. T. Pledge — SCIENCE SINCE 1500: *A Short History of Mathematics, Physics, Chemistry, and Biology.* Illustrated TB/506

John Read — A DIRECT ENTRY TO ORGANIC CHEMISTRY. Illustrated TB/523

O. W. Richards — THE SOCIAL INSECTS. Illustrated TB/542

George Sarton — ANCIENT SCIENCE AND MODERN CIVILIZATION TB/501

Paul A. Schilpp, *Ed.* — ALBERT EINSTEIN: *Philosopher-Scientist. Vol. I,* TB/502; *Vol. II,* TB/503

P. M. Sheppard — NATURAL SELECTION AND HEREDITY. Illustrated TB/528

Edmund W. Sinnott — CELL AND PSYCHE: *The Biology of Purpose* TB/546

L. S. Stebbing — A MODERN INTRODUCTION TO LOGIC TB/538

O. G. Sutton — MATHEMATICS IN ACTION. Foreword by James R. Newman. Illustrated TB/518

Stephen Toulmin — THE PHILOSOPHY OF SCIENCE: *An Introduction* TB/513

A. G. Van Melsen — FROM ATOMOS TO ATOM: *The History of the Concept* Atom TB/517

Friedrich Waismann — INTRODUCTION TO MATHEMATICAL THINKING. Foreword by Karl Menger TB/511

W. H. Watson — ON UNDERSTANDING PHYSICS: *An Analysis of the Philosophy of Physics.* Introduction by Ernest Nagel TB/507

G. J. Whitrow — THE STRUCTURE AND EVOLUTION OF THE UNIVERSE: *An Introduction to Cosmology.* Illustrated TB/504

Edmund Whittaker — HISTORY OF THE THEORIES OF AETHER AND ELECTRICITY. *Vol. I, The Classical Theories,* TB/531; *Vol. II, The Modern Theories,* TB/532

A. Wolf — A HISTORY OF SCIENCE, TECHNOLOGY, AND PHILOSOPHY IN THE SIXTEENTH AND SEVENTEENTH CENTURIES. Illustrated. *Vol. I,* TB/508; *Vol. II,* TB/509

A. Wolf — A HISTORY OF SCIENCE, TECHNOLOGY, AND PHILOSOPHY IN THE EIGHTEENTH CENTURY. *Vol. I,* TB/539; *Vol. II,* TB/540

HARPER TORCHBOOKS / The Cloister Library

Tor Andrae — MOHAMMED: *The Man and His Faith* TB/62

Augustine/Przywara — AN AUGUSTINE SYNTHESIS TB/35

Roland H. Bainton — THE TRAVAIL OF RELIGIOUS LIBERTY TB/30

C. K. Barrett, *Ed.* — THE NEW TESTAMENT BACKGROUND: *Selected Documents* TB/86

Karl Barth — DOGMATICS IN OUTLINE TB/56

Karl Barth — THE WORD OF GOD AND THE WORD OF MAN TB/13

Nicolas Berdyaev — THE BEGINNING AND THE END TB/14

Nicolas Berdyaev — THE DESTINY OF MAN TB/61

Anton T. Boisen — THE EXPLORATION OF THE INNER WORLD: *A Study of Mental Disorder and Religious Experience* TB/87

J. H. Breasted — DEVELOPMENT OF RELIGION AND THOUGHT IN ANCIENT EGYPT TB/57

Martin Buber — ECLIPSE OF GOD: *Studies in the Relation Between Religion and Philosophy* TB/12

Martin Buber — MOSES: *The Revelation and the Covenant* TB/27

Martin Buber — THE PROPHETIC FAITH TB/73

Martin Buber — TWO TYPES OF FAITH: *The interpenetration of Judaism and Christianity* TB/75

R. Bultmann, et al. — KERYGMA AND MYTH: *A Theological Debate.* Ed. by H. W. Bartsch TB/80

Jacob Burckhardt — THE CIVILIZATION OF THE RENAISSANCE IN ITALY. Illustrated Edition. Introduction by Benjamin Nelson and Charles Trinkaus. *Vol. I,* TB/40; *Vol. II,* TB/41

Emile Cailliet — PASCAL: *The Emergence of Genius* TB/82

Edward Conze — BUDDHISM: *Its Essence and Development* TB/58

Frederick Copleston — MEDIEVAL PHILOSOPHY TB/76

F. M. Cornford — FROM RELIGION TO PHILOSOPHY: *A Study in the Origins of Western Speculation* TB/20

G. G. Coulton — MEDIEVAL FAITH AND SYMBOLISM [Part I of "Art and the Reformation"]. Illustrated TB/25

G. G. Coulton — THE FATE OF MEDIEVAL ART IN THE RENAISSANCE AND REFORMATION [Part II of "Art and the Reformation"]. Illustrated TB/26

H. G. Creel — CONFUCIUS AND THE CHINESE WAY TB/63

Adolf Deissmann — PAUL: *A Study in Social and Religious History* TB/15

C. H. Dodd — THE AUTHORITY OF THE BIBLE TB/43

Johannes Eckhart — MEISTER ECKHART: A Modern Translation TB/8

Mircea Eliade — COSMOS AND HISTORY: *The Myth of the Eternal Return* TB/50

Mircea Eliade	THE SACRED AND THE PROFANE: *The Significance of Religious Myth, Symbolism, and Ritual Within Life and Culture* TB/81
Morton S. Enslin	CHRISTIAN BEGINNINGS TB/5
Morton S. Enslin	THE LITERATURE OF THE CHRISTIAN MOVEMENT TB/6
G. P. Fedotov	THE RUSSIAN RELIGIOUS MIND: *Kievan Christianity, the 10th to the 13th Centuries* TB/70
Ludwig Feuerbach	THE ESSENCE OF CHRISTIANITY. Introduction by Karl Barth TB/11
Harry E. Fosdick	A GUIDE TO UNDERSTANDING THE BIBLE TB/2
Henri Frankfort	ANCIENT EGYPTIAN RELIGION: *An Interpretation* TB/77
Sigmund Freud	ON CREATIVITY AND THE UNCONSCIOUS: *Papers on the Psychology of Art, Literature, Love, Religion.* Edited by Benjamin Nelson TB/45
Maurice Friedman	MARTIN BUBER: *The Life of Dialogue* TB/64
O. B. Frothingham	TRANSCENDENTALISM IN NEW ENGLAND: *A History* TB/59
Edward Gibbon	THE TRIUMPH OF CHRISTENDOM IN THE ROMAN EMPIRE [J. B. Bury Edition, illus., Chapters 15-20 of "The Decline and Fall"] TB/46
C. C. Gillispie	GENESIS AND GEOLOGY: *A Study in the Relations of Scientific Thought, Natural Theology, and Social Opinion in Great Britain, 1790-1850* TB/51
Maurice Goguel	JESUS AND THE ORIGINS OF CHRISTIANITY I: *Prolegomena to the Life of Jesus* TB/65
Maurice Goguel	JESUS AND THE ORIGINS OF CHRISTIANITY II: *The Life of Jesus* TB/66
Edgar J. Goodspeed	A LIFE OF JESUS TB/1
H. J. C. Grierson	CROSS-CURRENTS IN 17TH CENTURY ENGLISH LITERATURE: *The World, the Flesh, the Spirit* TB/47
William Haller	THE RISE OF PURITANISM TB/22
Adolf Harnack	WHAT IS CHRISTIANITY? Introduction by Rudolf Bultmann TB/17
R. K. Harrison	THE DEAD SEA SCROLLS: *An Introduction* TB/84
Edwin Hatch	THE INFLUENCE OF GREEK IDEAS ON CHRISTIANITY TB/18
Friedrich Hegel	ON CHRISTIANITY: *Early Theological Writings* TB/79
Karl Heim	CHRISTIAN FAITH AND NATURAL SCIENCE TB/16
F. H. Heinemann	EXISTENTIALISM AND THE MODERN PREDICAMENT TB/28
S. R. Hopper, *Ed.*	SPIRITUAL PROBLEMS IN CONTEMPORARY LITERATURE TB/21
Johan Huizinga	ERASMUS AND THE AGE OF REFORMATION. Illustrated TB/19
Aldous Huxley	THE DEVILS OF LOUDUN: *A Study in the Psychology of Power Politics and Mystical Religion in the France of Cardinal Richelieu* TB/60
Flavius Josephus	THE GREAT ROMAN-JEWISH WAR, with *The Life of Josephus.* TB/74
Immanuel Kant	RELIGION WITHIN THE LIMITS OF REASON ALONE. TB/67
Soren Kierkegaard	EDIFYING DISCOURSES: A Selection TB/32
Soren Kierkegaard	THE JOURNALS OF KIERKEGAARD: A Selection. Edited by A. Dru TB/52
Soren Kierkegaard	PURITY OF HEART TB/4
Soren Kierkegaard	THE POINT OF VIEW FOR MY WORK AS AN AUTHOR: *A Report to History* TB/88
Alexandre Koyré	FROM THE CLOSED WORLD TO THE INFINITE UNIVERSE TB/31
Walter Lowrie	KIERKEGAARD. *Vol I,* TB/89; *Vol. II,* TB/90
Emile Mâle	THE GOTHIC IMAGE: *Religious Art in France of the 13th Century.* Illustrated TB/44
T. J. Meek	HEBREW ORIGINS TB/69
H. Richard Niebuhr	CHRIST AND CULTURE TB/3
H. Richard Niebuhr	THE KINGDOM OF GOD IN AMERICA TB/49
Martin P. Nilsson	GREEK FOLK RELIGION TB/78
H. J. Rose	RELIGION IN GREECE AND ROME TB/55
Josiah Royce	THE RELIGIOUS ASPECT OF PHILOSOPHY: *A Critique of the Bases of Conduct and Faith* TB/29
George Santayana	INTERPRETATIONS OF POETRY AND RELIGION TB/9
George Santayana	WINDS OF DOCTRINE *and* PLATONISM AND THE SPIRITUAL LIFE TB/24
F. Schleiermacher	ON RELIGION: *Speeches to Its Cultured Despisers* TB/36
H. O. Taylor	THE EMERGENCE OF CHRISTIAN CULTURE IN THE WEST: *The Classical Heritage of the Middle Ages* TB/48
P. Teilhard de Chardin	THE PHENOMENON OF MAN TB/83
D. W. Thomas, *Ed.*	DOCUMENTS FROM OLD TESTAMENT TIMES TB/85
Paul Tillich	DYNAMICS OF FAITH TB/42
Ernst Troeltsch	THE SOCIAL TEACHING OF THE CHRISTIAN CHURCHES. Introduction by H. Richard Niebuhr. *Vol. I,* TB/71; *Vol. II,* TB/72
E. B. Tylor	THE ORIGINS OF CULTURE [Part I of "Primitive Culture"]. Introduction by Paul Radin TB/33
E. B. Tylor	RELIGION IN PRIMITIVE CULTURE [Part II of "Primitive Culture"]. Introduction by Paul Radin TB/34
Evelyn Underhill	WORSHIP TB/10
Johannes Weiss	EARLIEST CHRISTIANITY: *A History of the Period* A.D. *30-150.* Introduction by F. C. Grant. *Vol. I,* TB/53; *Vol. II,* TB/54
Wilhelm Windelband	A HISTORY OF PHILOSOPHY I: *Greek, Roman, Medieval* TB/38
Wilhelm Windelband	A HISTORY OF PHILOSOPHY II: *Renaissance, Enlightenment, Modern* TB/39